ONE
PERFECT
OP

An Insider's Account
of the Navy SEAL
Special Warfare Teams

WILLIAM MORROW
An Imprint of HarperCollins*Publishers*

ONE
PERFECT
OP

**BY COMMAND MASTER CHIEF
DENNIS CHALKER, USN (RET.)**

WITH KEVIN DOCKERY

HarperCollins books may be purchased for educational, business, or sales promotional use. For information please write: Special Markets Department, HarperCollins Publishers Inc., 10 East 53rd Street, New York, NY 10022.

FIRST EDITION

Designed by Renato Stanisic

Printed on acid-free paper

Library of Congress Cataloging-in-Publication Data
Chalker, Dennis C.
  One perfect op : an insider's account of the Navy SEAL
  Special Warfare teams / by Dennis Chalker with
  Kevin Dockery.—1st ed.
      p.   cm.
    ISBN 0-380-97804-0
    1. Chalker, Dennis C.   2. United States. Navy. SEALs—
History.   3. United States. Navy—Petty officers—Biography.
I. Dockery, Kevin.   II. Title.
  V63.C37 .A3   2002
  359.9'84'0973—dc21
  [B]   2001030837

02   03   04   05   06   RRD   10   9   8   7   6   5   4   3   2

I would first like to dedicate this book to my parents, for getting me to where I am now; to Kitty, who gave me two wonderful girls; and especially to my daughters, Kacy and Tess, who had to grow up with a father who was gone for much of their young lives. They paid the largest price.

And I would like to say a special word about one of my partners and close friends during my career and after—Foster Green (Pooster the Rooster). His career path followed mine, and we worked side by side for years.

Foster passed away in the spring of 2000. He was highly respected by those in the SEAL community and professionals elsewhere. He will be missed by all—especially me.

CONTENTS

ACKNOWLEDGMENTS

No person, ever, has been able to finish BUD/S alone. From the first days in the Teams, you learn to depend on your Teammates as much as they can depend on you. Life might be a little easier on all of us if we learned just how much we need other people to get the job done sometimes.

First of all, I would like to thank Master Chief Tommy Hatchet for giving me my first motivation for getting through BUD/S. And my thanks to all my Sea Daddies, especially Master Chief Gary "Chambo" Chamberlin, Master Chief T. K. "The Old Gummer" Davis, Master Chief Johnny Johnson—whom we all still miss today—and Master Chief Tim Prusak; and to my former COs: Commander Richard Marcinko, Captain Robert Gormly, Captain Richard Woolard, Captain Ronald Yeaw, Captain Parks, and Captain Joe Yarborough; and to my former Team leaders: Commander Duke Leonard, Lieutenant Commander John Koenig, Lieutenant Commander Steven

Fitzgerald, and Lieutenant Commander Brian Losey; and to my other officers from Kilo Platoon, including Lieutenant Steinbaugh and Lieutenant (j.g.) Bunce; and to all the comrades I started out with, including Kurt Feichtinger, Foster Green, Mike Purdy, Francis Fay, Mitch Croft, Kevin Banker, Doc Luben, Clay Sherman; and to all my other partners throughout my career in the Teams whose names I will never forget but cannot list here. They know who they are.

INTRODUCTION:

SNAKE,
AKA
DENNIS CHALKER

You've met Snake in the Rogue Warrior series of books and got a closer look at him in *Real Team*. Now you get the chance to meet him up close, down and dirty—see the world through his eyes, sense the drive and excitement that make him accomplish the mission at all costs, find out what makes him tick and why I was always comfortable when I turned him loose to do the dirty deed. When you get through with this read, it will be your turn to get off your ass and attack life.

As I've said before, Dennis (Snake) is one of those Adonis-looking guys—broad shoulders, good chest, small waist, and an ass so small he has to keep a hard-on just to hold his pants up. He runs like a gazelle, climbs like a spider (drunk or sober), and can drink like a fish. But he's always focused and on target. He felt obligated to serve his country. That obligation became a career after he got through BUD/S (the Basic Underwater

Demolition/SEAL training course), and turned into a "magnificent obsession" when he got to SEAL Team SIX. Follow his growth from a totally dedicated operator and shooter to a slithering, sneaky, deadly warrior with no limits to keep him from accomplishing his goals. Watch his pride and sense of accomplishment bubble over to those around him and help them absorb his infectious spirit and energy. He never hesitated to advise me on operational options, training challenges, or tactical diversity. That's why he will always be the Snake.

Snake says it the way he saw it—often a little different from the way I did—but we got the job done, and we had fun doing it too. Life in the Teams with Dennis "Snake" Chalker was like living and loving the life of the old-style Mafia. We all worked hard; we all played hard; and when the going got harder, we really started enjoying each other's talents as we overcame the challenges thrown at us from both friends and foes. If we didn't work within the rules, we were at least on the fringes. After all, we were told we would not fail. Winning does count. If it doesn't, why the hell do we waste our time keeping score?

Turning Snake loose was like letting the genie out of the bottle; once out, you ain't getting him back in. He just charged on to the next level of expertise and challenges. He never lacked self-generated motivation.

Snake felt that sense of fraternal obligation, that need to give back to the source that gave so much to each one of us. His biggest and final effort (on active duty) was as command master chief at BUD/S. As the senior enlisted man, he had the mission of instilling pride and dedication in the instructors, guiding the policies generated by the officers, and being the supreme example to all the "fledgling tadpoles" looking to make it to the Teams. It was my extreme honor and privilege to be the guest speaker at his retirement ceremony, where I was able to thank him for his dedication and welcome him to the "retired" world where we can share our experiences and spirit with all of you. Through Dennis "Snake" Chalker, Inc., his infectious spirit flows on. Start your induction into the world of the Snake with this read. Enjoy it, or I'll send a bunch of new Snakes your way!

—RICHARD MARCINKO

ONE
PERFECT
OP

CHAPTER 1

ONE PERFECT OP

Spring 1992

Speeding across a dark ocean, rain squalls coming and going and the wind in our faces, I had no way of knowing that I was now on my last combat operation, but if I had known, I couldn't have chosen a better crew to be with than the Teammates I had trained alongside for years.

The mission was to rescue an American citizen—an eighteen-month old baby—and her family from an unfriendly shore. Two black rubber boats were speeding away from a darkened U.S. Navy warship, each boat full of SEALs (Sea, Air, Land) determined to see the operation through.

We had 55-horsepower outboard engines on our Zodiac F-470 boats. With the weight and space factor tight, we had to consider limiting our extras, so we had only two 35-horsepower outboards as spares. A full crew was on each of the boats, and we had to save room for the cargo we were on our way to pick up.

Each SEAL going in with the landing party was armed with a full loadout. I was geared up for a water op, just like everyone else. Wearing my "Farmer John's" wet suit would give me some additional buoyancy. Around my neck I had an inflatable UDT (Underwater Demolitions Team) buoyance vest in case I needed a little extra flotation. And I wasn't running too light in case it came to a fight. My M4 carbine was loaded with twenty-eight rounds in its magazine, each third round a tracer. The last five rounds in the magazine were all tracers, to warn me that it was time to reload. The nine other magazines I had in three pouches at my waist were all loaded the same way. That gave me 280 rounds of 5.56mm killers to depend on.

If I had to dump the M4 and switch to my secondary weapon, I would be well served by my SIG P226 loaded with a full fifteen-round magazine of hot copper-jacketed serrated 9mm hollowpoints. The other four P226 magazines I carried in two separate pouches gave me seventy-five rounds for my pistol alone. Finally, I had my Glock knife at my right hip with a Mark 13 day /night signal flare taped to its scabbard. Hanging around my neck on a line was a set of Cyclops night vision goggles, a binocular NVG with a single tube that would magnify the available starlight 50,000 times. The goggles would make all of the dark surrounding area visible in a green-tinted light.

But it was across my chest that I carried my most important piece of equipment: the black-painted, fully padded baby carrier that I had carried my own baby daughter in. Tied to the carrier, sterilized and sealed in a plastic bag, was a baby's pacifier, an incongruous item among all my lethal hardware.

The boat's crew were all SEALs who had trained for hours to navigate their craft across a dark sea just like the one we were traveling on now. Vectoring in on calculated points, the coxswains for the craft were steering us over ten miles of open water to our target, a small chunk of beach in a big ocean. On that beach would be the target family and some friendlies. Those friendlies would be the only allies that family would have immediately at hand. Other than that, the area was full of armed people who did not want to see that family escape.

We had a very tight timeline. If we were late or missed the target, at best the operation would be scrubbed, at worst the people we were going in to get would be caught and imprisoned. About three hours had been planned for transit to the beach and locating our target. A three-hour tour, only there wasn't any Gilligan on this boat ride, and Mary Ann and Ginger weren't waiting for us at the other end.

That was a lot to think about, but dwelling on the could-bes would take my mind away from the task at hand. Even while bouncing across the waves, licking the salt spray from my lips, I had to concentrate on what was ahead.

It was a warm moonless night and the sky was overcast. The clouds would help to conceal us. When a small storm came up, the little bit of rain that came down would also help reduce the chance of any idle late-night strollers on our target beach. If we were really lucky, the rain might also hold down any local patrols. Continuing on, we rode the high tide along our plotted course line.

The smells in the air were mostly of the ocean, and just starting to come up was the smell of civilization. Our target was only some five miles away from a built-up area, not much more than hooches and huts along with a lot of vegetation. We knew we were headed in the right direction when the sky shine of a small town was visible in our NVGs, along with the outline of hills in the distance.

We hit our first vector point on schedule and turned to aim for the next one: a buoy inside a harbor that was anything but friendly. From that buoy, we would make a straight shot to the target beach. So with everything riding on our tight schedule, it was time for Mr. Murphy to show up and humble us a bit with one of his laws: If anything can go wrong, it will, and at the worst possible time.

Our boat's outboard decided it had been working hard enough. The slight phosphorescent bow wave the boat had been pushing up sagged and faded as our engine sputtered and died. Our coxswain and the rest of the boat crew immediately set to work to repair the engine and get it restarted. They operated as the well-trained and coordinated team they were, in spite of the complete darkness.

Fast whispered conversation between the assault group leader, myself, and the boat crew centered around either taking the time to get the faster 55-horsepower engine going or deep-sixing the damned thing and putting the slower 35-horsepower motor in its place. Of course, that would leave us short a spare engine for the outbound leg of our mission. Although I pushed for dumping the stopped engine, the boat crew continued their laboring in the dark, and with a muffled roar the outboard finally started up.

We were back on our way, but we had fallen critically behind schedule. As we sped toward the last vector point, the horizon was just becoming visible. Looking through the NVGs, I saw a flash of a light beaming up into the sky and pointed it out to the assault group leader. As the officer in charge, he decided to order a change of course, and the boat heeled over as we turned toward the signal. We would save time by going directly toward the signal rather than completing the last leg in from the vector point. We were back on schedule; we still had a chance of pulling this op off.

Now only the coxswains wore their NVGs. To get our eyes used to the darkness, all of us going in to the beach took our goggles off. Despite the darkness, we could soon make out the beach and the tree line beyond.

Just as we'd planned, we came up to the target beach. The

wind was blowing out to sea, so that was in our favor. A slight sound from us would hardly make it to shore. Depending on the situation we found on our arrival, we were prepared to take the boats all the way in to shore. If things were questionable, the landing party would swim in. Radio communications showed up on schedule, and the identifications and authentications were correct. Cutting the outboards to minimize noise, we picked up paddles and brought the boats silently in to shore.

The two security crew boats went out to either flank while the two pickup boats went right up the center. The rubber bows of the boats crunched softly into the sand as we made landfall. There were only some fifteen feet of sand beach before the vegetation began. Our targets were waiting for us somewhere in the vegetation.

Once we were on shore, we pushed the boats back out to sea, and the coxswains took them out about a hundred yards to wait for us. We were in an unfriendly area. If the shit hit the fan, we would grab our people and hit the water, heading back to where the boats were waiting. In that situation, we would be putting out all the firepower we had, and the 470s had some hardware aboard to help us all they could.

Our security detail bristled with weapons, covering the beach area on all sides. With our flanks securely covered, our assault group leader went up to where the light had come from and met the small group of people who were waiting for us. As I came up to the gathering, I could see the mother and baby. I reached out, and the mother put her baby, a not so little girl, into my arms. And then Mr. Murphy showed up again.

This was an eighteen-month-old baby? Damn, this was a big kid. With my weapon slung, I tried to slip the kid's legs through the holes in the bottom of the baby carrier, but they were too fat. There was no way they were going through the holes. Handing the kid back to the mother, I pulled my knife and cut the leg holes larger. The baby carrier was pretty much a total loss as far as taking it back to my wife, Kitty, and using it for our baby, Tess. A little more damage wasn't going to make my explaining it to Kitty any easier once I got home.

Finally I had the kid in the baby carrier, wrapped in the little blanket the mother had given me, and was ready to go. But things still weren't going to run smoothly. Now that the baby was away from her mother and in the hands of a big stranger wearing a rubber suit and with a blacked-out face, she felt it was time to let her feelings be known.

As the baby started to cry, one of the locals began to come a little unglued. The tension for those people had to be severe, and they had been operating under the strain for a lot longer than the few hours we had been on the mission. But with some slight sounds in the distance indicating activity up the beach, now was not the time to lose control.

As the guy started to tell me to shut the baby up, I reached out in the darkness and grabbed him by the throat. "Shut up!" I growled quietly.

Maybe I was feeling the tension a bit myself. Or I was just very concerned with the precious cargo I had taken on board. But my officer was right there, prying at my fingers as they locked around the man's throat. "Denny," he whispered, "leave him alone. Let go now, we have to move. Go, go, go!"

We had only been on shore for about fifteen minutes, but the plan called for us to keep our time on land to an absolute minimum. There were patrols around, and we didn't want to meet any of them.

Immediately I released my grip on the man, and air wheezed into his lungs. Funny, I didn't think I had been holding him that tight. But now wasn't the time for thinking about anything but getting off that beach. I started backing toward the water as our security detail closed in, their weapons still at the ready.

As soon as I slipped into that warm salt water, the kid

stopped crying. The blanket was quickly soaked, but the water was so warm the baby didn't care. This was a SEAL's element. In a combat zone, once in the water we feel safer than in any other place. Each of us was on his own to get to the boats. Our security element remained behind on the beach briefly to ensure our safety. The only thing between us and our way out was a short stretch of water.

As I kicked and stroked out to sea on my back, the baby just lay there on my chest, her head level with my neck. The mother was in good hands with one of my Teammates looking after her. Each of the people we had been sent to get was accounted for and the situation was under control. But things could still go to hell in a heartbeat.

With a slow kick and a long, deep stroke, I glided through the water. To try and keep the baby from crying again, I took the pacifier I had brought along out of its sealed bag and put it in her mouth. She took the pacifier, leaned her head back to look at me in that wide-eyed baby way, and . . .

Pooh! Spat that pacifier right back into my face. So much for the great big SEAL impressing the baby. But she did remain quiet for the rest of the swim.

Getting to the boat, I climbed aboard, careful to protect the child. The mother had already been placed in the bottom of the boat and I lay down next to her. We had brought light quilted poncho liners for just this purpose, and they were placed across the mother and myself so that both she and the baby would be protected from the elements.

As the boats fired up and headed out to sea, life became a little more interesting for Senior Chief Chalker, specially trained SEAL baby-sitter. The child became fascinated with my mustache. Here I was lying in the bottom of a rubber boat speeding through unfriendly waters with an M4 strapped across my back, a bandanna on over my hair, and my face all cammied up with black cosmetic. And now I had this small child on my chest absolutely determined to stick her finger up my nose or pull my mustache off.

Hey, even for a SEAL, having your mustache pulled can make your eyes water. And if I pushed the kid's fingers away, she might start to cry. Offering the pacifier just got it spat back at me again. What? Do these things come in flavors and I brought the wrong one? Everything I did just made the child more irritable. I wasn't about the let her go in case something happened and we had to swim. Giving in to the inevitable, I surrendered my mustache for the cause, thinking Hell Week never prepared me for this!

Then the mother put her head on my shoulder, close to the baby, and things quieted down. The ride back was very smooth. With the wind now at our back, we were moving with the sea. The baby went to sleep, and even the water spray stayed off us. Very quickly, it seemed, the ship loomed up and we were pulling alongside for recovery.

We had traveled only about half the distance we had covered on the trip in. The Navy ship had actually come into the harbor to pick us up and minimize our trip back out. Operating under complete blackout procedures, not a single light showing anywhere on the vessel, the big ship was nothing more than a large dark shadow on the sea. A particularly welcome shadow.

Hooking up to one of the lowered safety lines, I climbed up the caving ladder—a thin rope ladder made of cables and rods—hanging down along the hull. Additional lines with harnesses were attached for the parents. My teammates would follow the civilians up the lines and watch out for them. But with only the baby to be concerned about, I was quickly able to board the ship.

One of the SEALs on deck popped a chemlight (a soft plastic tube that glows when activated) and handed it to the baby. Wide-eyed, she held the dim light in her two pudgy hands, making *ooooh* sounds. The soft green glow barely illuminated the child's face on the deck of that darkened ship. Not another light was showing except the stars.

Some of the ship's medical personnel were waiting on deck for us and made kind of a mistake with me and the kid. "We'll take the baby now," someone said as they reached out for the child.

"You take your fucking hands off that baby!" I growled with no small amount of menace in my voice. "This baby's mine until we get to the medical room, and that's where I'll turn her over to her mother."

When he turned to one of the other SEALs on deck for support, the guy was told, "We'll see you in the medical room. Escort us. Other than that, keep your hands to yourself."

The other personnel were told in no uncertain terms to leave us alone and take us to the medical room. The plan was for us to move through the darkened passageways of the ship with the family and baby secured. Once in the medical room, we could have lights and the "cargo" would be turned over. That was what had been decided, and nothing was going to be suddenly changed by some self-important, overeager type.

The situation now clear, we moved through the ship, and once secured in a sealed room, I handed the baby back to a grateful mother. With our people officially turned over to higher authority, it was back to the fantail of the ship for me and my Teammates.

Inside our room, we downstaged from the operation. Stripping off our weapons and equipment, we cleaned up a bit and switched back to more normal uniforms. Our weapons and gear secured, we had other things to attend to. I hadn't showered yet; my face was still mostly blacked up, and I had that unique SEAL aroma of sea, salt, sweat, and rubber hanging around me. But no one noticed that as we headed to the chief's mess to eat and attend the little party that was waiting for us there. Everyone had a little toast to give for a successful operation. For myself, I lifted my glass and said: "To one perfect op, not one shot fired."

And all my fellow SEALs agreed.

CHAPTER 2

HOME AND HEARTH

Back when I was a kid, one of the things I always liked doing was playing Army. What I loved most of all was being able to sneak up on my playmates or campsites out in the woods without being spotted. We made forts out of wood and other scraps, like kids do. I would sneak up on the "enemy" position and scout out their organization.

The big thing in our game was to be stealthy, long before that word had anything to do with exotic aircraft. You had to be able to move without being seen by the other side and without making any noise that would give you away. Not being able to do that tended to lose the game for your side. Maybe that early stealth training is what inclined me toward the service when I graduated from high school.

When I was growing up, I was one of the smaller, lighter kids in my age group. People were always telling me that I was too small to do something, like play football. In fact, I was able to play football and other rough sports. The lack of weight hurt me, but I had the heart to make up for it.

It was that desire to overcome, the bet-on-the-underdog mentality, that helped me gather accomplishments that I otherwise wouldn't have. That didn't mean I liked being the lightest one my age around. That was what got me into body building. I built up my weight, and my strength, as I got older.

Growing up in Ohio, I was the second oldest in a family of five children and the only boy in the bunch. Maybe that's another thing that helped get me started wanting to see the underdog win: besides my dad, I was the only male in the family. I had one elder sister, Charleen, who was about a year and a half older than me. Then there were my three younger sisters, with about seven years between our ages: Cherylann, Roseann, and Darleen. It may be that my dad encouraged some of my sports pursuits to help increase the masculinity levels in the house.

We had a good family, and I enjoyed my family life growing up. My father, Harrison "Chuck" Chalker, worked hard as a milkman to support his family. I remember him getting up at three or four in the morning and coming home at five or six at night. In bed by nine or ten, he got up the next day to do it all again. In spite of his heavy work schedule, my dad found the time to take me to Little League baseball and do all the other things that came up as I grew older.

My mom was great to us, and I can attest to the fact that she kept us in line. When I was fifteen, for some reason I thought she wouldn't strike me anymore. She went to slap me for something I had done and I blocked her hand. "Man, I've got this nailed," I thought to myself. The arrogance of youth. I couldn't have been more wrong. At the supper table, as I was taking a bite of potatoes, Dad started to ask me how my day was, but just then, I managed to get struck by lightning. As the shock wore off and the room stopped spinning, I vaguely remembered seeing my dad's rock-hard fist flying at me right before time stopped for a moment. As I lay back where I had landed on the floor, tears coming to my eyes, I asked, "What was that for?"

"Now sit up and eat your dinner, boy," my father said sternly. "And if you ever do that to your mother again, I'll do worse."

Dad wasn't a real big believer in the new methods of child rearing that were coming into vogue back then. He didn't have to make his point very often, but he usually didn't have to repeat himself either. Getting knocked down wasn't fun, but listening to all my sisters giggling was a lot worse.

Our ethnic background was what you might called "mixed." My dad is English and German Dutch. My grandmother had some Mennonite and some Cherokee Indian. On my mom's side we're Bohemian, a term I remember well from my childhood. So all in all, we're good old American mutt. The bunch of us were all raised Catholic, and I attended Immaculate Conception Grade School.

After nine years of Catholic school, I moved into public school from the ninth grade until my graduation. I wasn't the best student in the school. All my sisters were honor roll students, valedictorians of their classes, slightly greater achievers scholastically than I was. I was lucky to get through as well as I did. In my senior year, I had to take Government over again. For some reason, the teacher for that course during my junior year thought my referring to him as a fat pig was cause to fail me.

I got into sports more heavily in high school. During my sophomore year, I was on the wrestling team. I may have been skinny, but I didn't give up very easily. No matter what pain was dished out to me during a bout, I got right up and came back. And I was fairly tall for my weight, which gave me a good reach.

One night my mom and dad were out and while I was sitting in the living room watching TV, my sister and her boyfriend came home. "Don't you think it's about time you went to bed?" Charleen asked/told me.

Heck, I was a sophomore, a man of the world, and knew

what was what. "No. If you two want to make out, why don't you just get into the back of the car?"

That started off a bout of shouting between my sister and myself. Her boyfriend decided to get involved somewhere along the line and told me I shouldn't talk to my sister that way. What I remember about how things turned out centered on my picking him up and dumping him upside down on the coffee table. That broke the table, put him on the floor, and damned near sent Charleen into hysterics. The full nelson I then put on him may have been a bit much. But that wrestling stuff really worked.

My parents came home shortly thereafter. I was standing in the hallway near my bedroom door when my sister went crying up to my mother. Dad came back to where I was, and he just drilled me right in the chest. I went flying back, right through my bedroom door, and decided that since I was already there, staying in my room for the night might be a good idea. At least that's what I did after I got up off the floor and caught my breath.

To this day my sister may not know this, but later, after the family got her boyfriend away, my dad came back to my room. "Oh man, it's not over yet," I thought to myself. "Well, I did break the table."

When my dad came into my room, he shut my badly cracked door behind him. "Are you all right?" he asked with real concern in his voice.

"Damn, Dad. Yeah, I am. Why?"

"Well, it's your sister's boyfriend—I had to make it look good, but you're okay, right?"

This physical acting bit isn't something I ever wanted to get into later. My father could make things look, and feel, a bit too real. But he was secretly glad that I upheld my sister's honor, or was just being a jerk for the right reasons, whichever works.

After high school I made the decision that I was going to pay for my own college education, and the easiest way to do that was to enlist. That wasn't the most popular option in the country at that time. The draft was still going on in early 1972, the year of my graduation (it ended before that year was over). But I was seventeen and had made up my mind.

At least I had made up my mind about where I was going after high school. In those days, I didn't really know what I wanted for my life. What I did want was to get away from home for a while, travel a bit, and serve my country at the same time. I admired and had a lot of respect for Charleen's boyfriend at the time, Ron Arbaugh. He had been an Army Special Forces officer, and it was due in part to his influence that I decided to go into the Army.

CHAPTER 3

FIRST STOP, THE ARMY

It was a really interesting time in the United States, from the late sixties and into the seventies, when it seemed every young person was protesting against the draft, the Army, and the military in general.

Direct U.S. involvement in the Vietnam War was ending. The troops were all coming home. When I enlisted, I didn't give any real thought to the possibility of going to Vietnam and seeing any actual fighting. I wanted to do some growing up, and I wanted to travel. The service was a way to do both. If I had to head over to Southeast Asia, that was just a chance I'd have to take. It came with the job.

Right before I left for basic training, the incident at Kent State University took place. Students were killed by National Guardsmen who had overstepped their authority in trying to control student rioting and protests. There was a lot of protesting at Kent State, in Ohio, and throughout the country. That incident at Kent State seemed to drive morale in the country to rock bottom, and any faith in the government and the military was pretty well gone, especially with the younger crowd. But I was already enlisted in the Army and couldn't have turned back even if I wanted to.

My family wasn't too thrilled with my decision to join the service, especially my father, who was a Korean War vet. My dad asked me, "What do you want to do, go out there and just shoot somebody?"

"No, Dad, I just want to go out and grow up."

He wasn't happy with what I wanted to do. But he respected my decision to do it.

Enlisting in the Army was an education. Basic training wasn't exactly Boy Scout camp with guns, but neither was it the most physically demanding thing I had done up until then. I was in a lot better physical shape than many of the other trainees, and the discipline was little more than what I had put myself through in high school sports.

Morale in the Army was different from what I had been told. Vietnam hadn't wound down completely yet, but the draft was over and it was an all-volunteer Army. All the men who were entering the service were there because they wanted to be, or at least thought they did. There were a few in basic and later who changed their minds about wanting a life in the service. But that had more to do with discipline and personal commitment than anything else.

After basic, I went on to AIT (Advanced Infantry Training) and from there to Fort Benning, Georgia, and Airborne (jump school). Ron, my eldest sister's boyfriend and later husband, had told me a lot about what he had done in the Army. So my immediate military objective was to try for Special Forces. The way into SF was through the Airborne, and that sent me on to jump school.

Jump school wasn't that bad for me. The instructors, what

we called the Black Hats, were all E-6 and above, senior NCOs (noncommissioned officers) who really knew their stuff. Many of them were veterans of the Vietnam War. They were strict and hard on us, but it was a generally applied kind of abuse and we all took our lumps in turn. Of course, if you had an Airborne tattoo of any kind, they gave you extra special attention to make sure you earned the right to wear it. Or wished you had never had it done in the first place. That was at least one mistake I didn't make.

Physically it was demanding, a lot more so than it is today. The amount of PT (physical training) was intended to build you up enough so that when you hit the ground, you landed on muscle and not bone. The "lateral drift apparatus" let you slide down a wire to build up speed and then practice those PLFs, or parachute landing falls. Going into the sawdust pit and rolling out your PLFs managed to get you a mouthful of dirt. The 34-foot tower was where you learned your counting: one one thousand, two one thousand . . . , to teach you the delay to when you were supposed to feel your parachute opening.

But it was the 250-foot tower that first gave you a feeling of height and a taste of what parachuting might be like. The rig hauls you up the tower under an open parachute and then drops you. The instructors shout up instructions through a bullhorn, telling you to slip left or right, pull on the risers, and cause the parachute to move to the side.

When I went up on my first tower drop, it wasn't too bad. You get hauled up in the air and there's nothing under your feet. Looking down, the ground goes away fast. You feel some excitement, anticipating the drop and trying to remember everything you've been taught about controlling the chute and especially the landing. And there's a little fear. It is a long way down to the ground, and you notice how the weight of your body strains down on the parachute harness. Some people give a little thought to just how strong the buckles are that keep you in the harness, but I wasn't one of them. You're really too busy just trying to get everything right to worry about what might happen that you don't have any control over.

The instructors shouted at me to slip left, and I was on the right. I landed softly, and the instructor was right up in my face quickly. He told me that I had failed due to not following instructions. You only got one fail out of three tower drops. But my other two drops went fine, and I stayed in the course.

When it finally came time for us to jump from an aircraft, we were weathered out. The plane couldn't take off, and we had to wait for three days. Nothing like getting all geared up and waiting in the pews for hours, only to be told your jump has been canceled. Nothing I had experienced in the service up to then was worse than that waiting for hours just to be told we weren't going after all. Eventually we managed to get our five jumps in fast, three from a C-130 and two from a C-141.

That first jump was much the same for everyone, I learned later. You just don't know what to expect. A lot of thoughts go through your head, including "What am I doing here?" You think about your life up to that point and what may be waiting up the line for you. But there aren't any thoughts about death. Mostly, thoughts about what might go wrong center on reviewing your emergency cutaway procedures. You're trying to be one of the best in the Army, and that honor keeps other thoughts at bay.

The first jump was amazing. Standing in the door, I was a bit nervous. There were butterflies in my stomach for all five of my Benning jumps. But I went out the door, and from there on, you don't have a lot of choice about which direction you're going.

After I exited the plane, my canopy opened, and it was down to the ground. The instructor was shouting up at someone who had a malfunction, a Mae West—where some of the suspension lines are over the top of your canopy. That kind of malfunction makes the chute look like a giant bra. That jumper was told to pull his reserve.

I had a good canopy, but I missed the drop zone. Instead I landed over on the duck pond. But even there I was a little lucky. It was so cold that the pond had frozen, and I didn't get wet.

I felt some concern, a little nervousness, and maybe some fear on all my jumps at Benning and some later in my Airborne unit. It wasn't until after I had completed ten or fifteen jumps that I started to like it.

With the rest of our jumps done quickly to take advantage of the weather break, we were Airborne qualified. They gave us our wings the same day we shipped out to our final units. "Here's your wings and there's the bus" was the order of the day.

The 101st Airborne, the Screaming Eagles, was where I had wanted to go, but the Army had a different idea. The 101st had been changed to an airmobile unit and now rode helicopters rather than jumping. My final orders were supposed to be to the 173rd over in Vietnam, but they had been badly shot up over there, and the unit was kind of in limbo. The 82nd Airborne Division was being built up at the time, and that was where I was finally sent.

After I had spent some time in the 82nd, my intention was to volunteer for either Special Forces or the Rangers. The Rangers had been decommissioned right after Vietnam, so that door was closed. It bothered me a little that I hadn't been able to go to a Ranger unit. That had been one of my goals. Ranger school was still going on, and the training was being offered, but only officers were being sent to the school at that time, and my chances of going looked pretty slim. So I did my Army hitch with the 82nd Airborne.

My first overseas deployment was as part of a NATO exercise in Turkey. After a long uncomfortable flight, we landed in Turkey and traveled to our campsite. One of the first things they had us do was meet our nearby NATO partners, the British troops. We met them in the usual soldier's place, the pub near the tent. And being young troops, it wasn't long before the brawls started.

In fact, we were just having a friendly boxing match, where our division Golden Gloves champ kind of danced all over the British boxer. He never had a chance.

Now we were going to do our drops as part of the NATO exercise. Before then, the lowest drop I had ever done was eight hundred feet. When you're too low, if your main doesn't open you won't have any time to cut it away and pull your reserve. In combat we could be tasked to jump from as low as four hundred feet. On this occasion, we split the difference and jumped from six hundred feet.

Our sergeant major let us know his opinion of the upcoming jump in no uncertain terms. As far as he was concerned, the only people who would get hurt on the upcoming drop didn't deserve to be in the unit in the first place. If we did everything we had been taught, everything would be fine.

The drop zone in Turkey was a freshly plowed farmer's field, and among the furrows of the turned earth were all the boulders and stones that had come up from Turkey's rocky soil. But only one person on the drop was injured—the sergeant major broke his leg on a rock. He didn't live that down for a long time.

In the U.S. Airborne, the heavy equipment is dropped in before the troops. That way, the troops can hit the ground, gather their vehicles and heavy guns, and move out. The Brits do it the exact opposite. They put in the troops first and follow that drop with the equipment. The British paratrooper who was walking off the drop zone was being watched by all the high-ranking NATO brass up on a hill overlooking the drop zone. They had a clean view of the multiton tank that streamered in, its parachute never opening, and landed on that Brit.

Once we had a deuce-and-a-half (2.5-ton) truck streamer in during an exercise. We could still eat the C-rations that were in the truck bed afterward, but the cans were pretty flat. Another time I watched an M551 Sheridan light tank plow into the ground and split in half like a melon. So I figured our technique of putting the gear in first was a fine idea.

It was the Israeli Yom Kippur War in October 1973 that took me back overseas with the possibility of facing combat for the first time. The whole division was put on standby and finally loaded on aircraft and shipped out to an airfield in the Middle East. We stayed on that airfield for two days.

All we did was unpack the aircraft, make a fast bivouac, and sit there in the sand, heat, and flies. Then we packed up and were flown back home. It was a frustrating first exposure to the possibility of combat.

When the end of my service time came up, I was ready to leave the Army and try something else. Things had changed a lot in the service. The Army was struggling to get through the post-Vietnam depression and drawdown in the military. One of the things they did was increase the opportunities for women. There were going to be women in the Airborne units. But the women were not going to go through the same training.

There was a new military phrase, "modified physical standards," and it was not something anyone was allowed to talk about. Basically, the brass and the politicians came up with a different set of physical standards for women who wanted to go Airborne. They didn't have to do all the same exercises and didn't have to have the same strength as the men did. Personally, I thought that cheapened the whole thing and made an elite unit like the Airborne less than it had been earlier.

When I finally decided to leave the Army, my commanding officer, Captain Black, made me a good offer to stay in. The possibility of a promotion to staff sergeant and an assignment to attend Ranger school were pretty good inducements. But I wanted to get out and go back to school. While in the service, I had finished my physical growth and was now six feet tall. Going to college would give me a chance to play football again. Maybe even make a professional career of it.

CHAPTER 4

AND NOW THE NAVY

My post-Army plans didn't work out the way I had hoped they would. While still in the service, I had hooked up with Markovich, a good guy from Wisconsin. We worked out every day and went on runs. Usually we ran about 2.5 miles up to the boxing arena and back to our barracks. That was our ritual, and I peaked in weight at around 210 to 215 pounds.

So when I got out, I figured I was in good enough shape to try out for football. Applying to Kent State, I tried out and was accepted for spring training. During a practice session, I injured my knee badly. Surgery took care of the ligaments in my knee, and it also took care of my college football career.

When the football went, so did my desire for college. I dropped out of Kent State and moved around a bit. Working as a laborer for a while, I figured I would eventually go back to school. But my goals changed.

Instead of college, I tried my hand at a number of jobs. I

worked for the railroad for about six months, driving spikes and laying rails. When I was laid off, I worked in a tire factory, but that really paled quickly.

One job I wanted to try was game warden. I had always loved the outdoors, and working among the forests and lakes sounded pretty good to me. So in 1976, at the ripe age of twenty-two, I moved to Colorado, where one of my sisters lived. While there, I worked as a rough carpenter in construction, basically building houses for six months. The astronomical costs of college for a nonresident put an end to my plans for the University of Colorado.

The head guy at the local National Park Service office spoke to me about my desire to become a game warden. What he told me wasn't encouraging: positions in the field were filled. There weren't any openings at the lower levels, and it didn't look like there would be for the foreseeable future. Besides, they didn't pay that well.

While I discussed the situation with the Park Service officer, he asked me what else I might like to do. I remembered meeting several UDT frogmen while at Fort Benning. They had been going through jump school after completing BUD/S, the Basic Underwater Demolition/SEAL training course. Those guys had impressed me.

One of my uncles had been in the SeaBees during World War II, and he had spoken highly of the frogmen back then. So I told the parks officer that I was thinking of going back into the service. Specifically, I would enlist in the Navy and become a frogman. The officer told me that if I joined the Navy, made it into UDT, and completed my degree, those qualifications would jack me up to the top of the list for jobs with the National Park Service.

My next stop was a Navy Recruiting Station, and in March 1977, I enlisted in the U.S. Navy. The general public still hadn't recovered from the dislike of the military that developed so strongly during the Vietnam War. But I had already spent time in the service and knew it for real, rather than from listening to rumors and stories put out by people who had their own agendas and were never there.

Boot camp was a waste of eight weeks, but it was a Navy requirement. So I spent two months learning how to march, wear bell-bottoms, swab instead of mop, and call the latrine a "head," the floor a "deck," stairs "ladders," doors "hatches," and walls "bulkheads."

Our training company commander was Chief Beard, a Navy Diver who recognized my experience and helped keep me going through boot. Chief Beard made me the RCPO (recruit chief petty officer) and master-at-arms, kind of the company sheriff. I was getting a bit out of shape because the physical demands of boot camp weren't much, and although I was a little anemic—I always have been—the Navy had taken my vitamins away. Again Chief Beard came to my assistance.

The chief ran me through PT in his office at night after taps had been played. He gave me one-a-day vitamins with iron and chatted with me about the Navy and the Teams while I worked out. He had a lot of respect for the UDTs and the SEALs. They were hard chargers who worked together and didn't take any shot from outsiders. And they were really dedicated to the jobs they did and the missions they performed. It was a very tight community that didn't welcome outsiders. If you wanted to be one of them, you had to dig down deep in yourself to bring out everything you had. That's why he had me in his office doing PT. He told me that he never had the desire it took to get through BUD/S training but that he would help me make it.

Chief Beard had enjoyed what he had done during his Navy career, and being at boot camp was his "twilight cruise." The chief would retire from this his last duty station. He was a man I had a lot of respect for.

What I will never forget from boot camp was going down

for my screening test to get into BUD/S. The SEAL and UDT training programs were volunteer only. That had been true from their earliest days in World War II. And after volunteering you had to pass these tests in order to qualify. So I went to the screening test and met Master Chief Tommy Hatchet.

Master Chief Hatchet may have been "only" six foot four, but he went sideways a whole bunch too. He was the biggest man I had ever met, and there couldn't have been more than a couple of ounces of fat on him anywhere. His thighs were twice the size of my body, his biceps were bigger than my thighs, and one of his hands could hold my whole face. If this is what it took to be a frogman, I was in real trouble.

The Team guys I had met in jump school had all been in great shape and had all been around six two or so. But SEALs and frogs came in all sizes, and few were as big as Chief Hatchet. There were about a hundred recruits trying out then, so the room was fairly full. But Master Chief Hatchet had his own way of emptying the room fast.

"Okay, all you recruits are here to take the BUD/S screening test," he said. "I want you to know one thing. First of all, you're going to have to get in the pool. You're going to have to do a combat stroke." He stopped. No one said anything.

"You will use a sidestroke or breaststroke, but it will be a combat stroke. I don't have any time to waste. We're going to take this test now."

"Master Chief," came a voice.

"What do you need, recruit?"

"What's a sidestroke?"

"Get your bags and get the hell out of here."

That let everyone know that the right thing to do was whatever the master chief told us. Then he talked about doing the PT test and running in our boondockers (heavy boots). He had the dive motivators with him, several of whom were wearing

Tridents. These were Team guys, but they weren't built to quite the same scale as the master chief.

Standing at the side of the pool was the master chief with his clipboard in his hand. "Go" was all he said. As the bunch of us were swimming along, I noticed that several of the recruits were changing to a freestyle stroke. I wondered what was going on. For myself, I switched from the breaststroke to the sidestroke, but that was about it.

The dive motivators were cheering the recruits on, including the ones who were freestyling. "Go, man, go!" they were shouting. As soon as those freestyling swimmers got to the other end of the pool, they were tagged by Master Chief Hatchet. "Get your gear and get out of here," was all he said. By the time the swim test was over, only about ten of us were left who had completed the swim properly and within time.

Hatchet passed out some more terse instructions. "Okay, jump in the shower, you have two minutes. Then meet me outside."

Two minutes were hardly enough time to dry off, but that didn't matter. Not getting Chief Hatchet upset at us in any way was important to the few of us left, very important. When we got outside, it was time for the PT portion of the test. I had no trouble with any of the push-ups, sit-ups, or pull-ups. But some of the others didn't fare as well. There were only three of us left to take the running test.

Now one of the few things I had never done in high school was track. But I started figuring out the number of laps we had to do and how fast we had to do each one, so I could pace myself. We had maybe a minute and a half for each turn around the track. The guy next to me had run a lot of track in school, and he told me just to follow him. When we were told to start, that runner took off like a deer.

At the beginning, I took off just as fast as our trackman. But then I realized what I was doing and slowed back to my planned pace. The third runner did the same, but he fell farther and farther behind me. The trackman did real well, but only for about two laps. Then he pooped out and couldn't keep going. I just kept going and I made the time, just barely. And the other guy made it too. The track runner? He was puking on the gravel for a while. It must have been the heavy boondockers dragging on his feet that did him in.

Then Master Chief Hatchet called us into his office. "You're going to sign these papers," he told us, and we did. "Now I want you to understand this right up front. These papers are no guarantee that you're going to make it through training. This doesn't mean you are going to be a SEAL or that you are a SEAL. It just gives you the opportunity to get in the program and gives you your chance."

"Chalker," he said, turning to me. "When you come up on your two weeks' duty, I want you to come down here so you can run."

"Yes, Master Chief," I said, and that was that.

A few weeks later, I was just about done with boot camp and I was pulling duty at the base. Every day, I went down to Master Chief Hatchet's office and ran with him and Chief Hall. Hall wasn't in the Teams, to the best of my knowledge, but he was in the Navy diving community. I ran every day, and then they had me run classes of recruits in training. So I kept going and got better at what I had to do.

When it was time for me to leave boot camp, I had to go down to the detailer's office along with everyone else. The detailer gave you your orders and sent you on to wherever you were going. As I waited in the detailer's office, I was excited. The Navy school I had chosen was Boatswain's Mate. It was a short school, and soon I would be able to go on to the Teams. Then that detailer came in and dropped a bomb on me.

"We're going to put you through a two-week Boatswain's

Mate school. I know you're supposed to go on to BUD/S, but to make sure you have an appreciation for the Navy, we're first going to send you to the USS *Guam* for a year and a half. Then you'll have a chance to try out for BUD/S again."

My Army service had already given me an honorable discharge. I already had an appreciation for the service. I told that chief to wait a minute. I hadn't come into the Navy to sail on a tin can. I had seven uncles who had done that during World War II. What I was there for was one thing, and that was to take a shot at BUD/S. If I didn't make it, then I would honor my contract and do whatever the Navy wanted.

But that chief didn't want to hear any part of it. I was going to the *Guam,* and there wasn't anything I could say to change his mind.

I asked him if I could have a moment to myself, and he said I could leave. Sprinting from the building, I ran to Master Chief Hatchet's office. Luckily he was there. "What do you want, Chalker," he growled. That was really the only way I had ever heard him speak.

"I'm being told that I'm going to Boatswain's Mate school but then they're sending me to the *Guam*."

"Get in my car" was all he said.

We drove over to the detailer's office, and Master Chief Hatchet walked right into that chief's office, not even knocking on the door. "Hey, Chief," Hatchet said.

"Yes, Master Chief."

"Two weeks' Boatswain's Mate school and then he's going over to BUD/S."

"You got it, Master Chief."

"Chalker, come here," Master Chief Hatchet said, leaving the room.

When I stepped into the hallway, those huge hands just wrapped around my neck and picked me up off the floor.

"I want you to know that I'm retiring soon," Hatchet said to me in a soft, quiet, deadly voice. "If you have any notion of quitting training, I will make it my personal business to hunt you down and kill you with my bare hands for making me come up here."

That was probably my first outside incentive not to drop out of BUD/S. Off I went to Boatswain's Mate school, and every night after class I ran and did PT to get ready. Boatswain's Mate was a good school. It was probably the most general school in the Navy; you learned a little bit of everything and what everyone else in the fleet had to do. A boatswain's mate was the most all-around and rounded-off sailor in the Navy. In the old days of wind sails, if the captain of a ship went down, it was the chief boatswain's mate who would take charge of the ship. He was the master of the machinery that kept the Navy afloat; and if that's not an important job, I don't know what is.

But that wasn't my path. It was time for me to cross the water and enter Coronado, where the Amphibious base was, for the first time. I was done with the gray Navy of big ships and slow days. It was time to attend BUD/S.

CHAPTER 5

BUD/S AND THE BEGINNING OF A SEAL

The lack of ligaments in my knee concerned the doctors at BUD/S. They wanted me to know that there would be a lot of soft sand running in the course and that my knee might not take it. If I was hit the wrong way, I would walk with a cane for the rest of my life.

All I wanted was a shot. My old football injury hadn't given me any trouble since the surgery, and I had followed the doctor's advice since then. They told me I had my shot, and I entered the BUD/S compound.

I arrived in July, just in time to miss Class 100, which had just started training. So instead of going into BUD/S directly, I went into pretraining. Personally, I thought missing the class was an advantage. Having just come out of boot camp and then Boatswain's Mate school, I hadn't been exercising as much as I should have. Even with the extra attention I had been given, I wanted to be in better shape before starting the most physically demanding course in the U.S. military.

Some of the instructors gave me immediate close attention, so I received a good indoctrination into what BUD/S would be like. While in the Army, I had gotten a tattoo on my arm that said "God is my Jumpmaster." Now my name was soon forgotten, but not me. Instead of "Chalker" being called out, it was "Where's God is my Jumpmaster?"

A group of us students were run through PT every day, and we did whatever other jobs the staff needed done. The PT and the running did me some good when it finally came time to class up.

Class 101 was a winter class at Coronado. We classed up in September for the six-month-long training course. Instructor Harry Kanakua, a big Hawaiian, was our class proctor. He was a well-rounded and experienced SEAL himself and he motivated us well. The class started off with three officers and soon dropped down to two, ensigns Ralph Penney and Robert Anderson, who entered Hell Week with us.

Boat Crew One was my first assignment, and Penney was the coxswain. Penney was the smallest guy in the crew, the rest being at least six feet tall. Lining up all the beef guys, we had John Shellnut, Bob Youngblood, John Hancock, James Lusher, and Mike Reiter along with Penney and me.

BUD/S had a lot to do with tradition. And one of the first traditions was the haircut party. There was a keg of beer, and everyone shaved everyone else's hair. You were going to be a Team, and no one was going to touch a Teammate's hair but one of his own. Besides, why pay a barber?

Some of the people who had been at BUD/S before I arrived were a little more knowledgeable and helped push us to do the right thing to start out. My Army time helped me remain motivated. I was an E-3, almost the lowest rank you could hold, but even so, I had a contribution to make to my class and my boat crew.

Then training began, and it was everything it was supposed to be. We were cold and we were wet. When we weren't cold and wet, it was because we were sandy, cold, and wet. The times we were dry were only spaces between wettings. And that was just the first week.

We were taught to prep our gear for a swim or an operation. And we learned how important it was to prepare properly for an evolution. An evolution is a problem, something you have to do. It can be as simple as a beach run or as difficult as a combat patrol. But every evolution has to be completed. Of course it was difficult to prep your gear with an instructor screaming down your neck. And any mistakes caused you to get cold, wet, and sandy again. Rolling in the sand when you were wet all over created the sugar cookie effect, a favorite among BUD/S instructors.

The sugar cookie effect is hard to describe, and harder to forget. Imagine a cookie in a jar, all covered with sugar. As it settles into the jar it rubs against the sugar from the other cookies until it starts to pick up that sugar too. Soon the cookie is covered all over—even in spots where the sugar shouldn't be. Now imagine the same situation, only the cookie is your skin and the sugar is nice abrasive sand. The top layer of your skin soon disappears, and then there's the soft, tender, sensitive new layer all ready for a good sandy rubbing. Believe me, it's a bitch to patch a rubber boat when you've become a sugar cookie.

When the sand gets into your ears, knocking it out won't work. And it doesn't feel very good. It doesn't taste good grinding between your teeth, or smell good as it clogs up your nose. The eyes more or less wash themselves out, but the irritation is still there. It's because of the sugar cookie effect that most frogmen and SEALs hold a lifelong aversion to wearing underwear.

During BUD/S, you quickly learned that underwear just gave the sand someplace to hide.

The other thing at BUD/S is the water, the cold sea water. It covers you in the morning, wets you in the afternoon, and keeps you moist in the evening. When you aren't swimming in it, you're crawling into or out of it. And then there's traveling on top of it.

Surf passage, or IBS (inflatable boat, small) appreciation, is another rite of passage at BUD/S. You have an inflated rubber boat and a paddle. On your head is a soft cap. And when you leave that water, you better have everything you went into it with still on you, so the cap is tied to your uniform with a piece of line. And you had better secure everything, because during surf passage you will be tossed from the boat, you will get wet, and the waves will see to it that these things happen over and over.

They made us turn our belt buckles inward to keep from scratching the boat. Buttons had to be buttoned and covered for the same reason. The heavy canvas kapok life jackets went on top of everything else. I hated those jackets. They could be like wearing a neck brace, which was helpful during Hell Week. Otherwise, they dig under your armpits, and the straps pull at your crotch and grind the sand into you. A number of SEALs, myself included, still have scars in our groins from those damned kapok straps.

Finally we got to hit the waves. We figured we'd have a nice sunny day. This was an exercise to give us an appreciation of the boats. They had to give us a chance to learn about them and get used to them, didn't they?

This is one of those evolutions where all you can do is look out at the ocean and think, "Oh, my god!" As we walked from the grinder—the exercise yard in the center of the compound— we could hear the crunching of those big kahuna waves pounding on the shore. The sound of those crunchers smacking down on the shore could be heard throughout the compound, like a cross between distant thunder and a volcano erupting some-where behind the barracks. The surf seemed to call out to the instructors, "Time for surf passage!" Apparently, an eight-to twelve-foot sea condition is considered excellent for learning to appreciate how much fun it is to push a boat through those waves with just muscle power.

When you saw that white foaming surf in the morning, the curling waves and rips flowing out, you knew it was time for a light breakfast. Going to chow that morning, you just knew it would be a good idea not to eat too much. Because coming back from chow, you would get the boats ready, march off to the ocean, and let the instructors see just how many students could be flung from their boats.

The boats would bend as we struggled to paddle them out to sea. When the boat folded in half, the trainees at the rear of the boat would have their heads shoved between their crewmates in the front of the boat as the two ends met. The men in the middle would be covered by a rubber canopy filled with struggling flesh. Then when the boat suddenly snapped open, all that could be seen from shore were little trainees flying into the water.

When the inevitable happened and your crew went flying from your boat, it was time to struggle against the water to try and save your life, while at the same time making sure your swim buddy was somewhere on top of the water as well. You had to swim hard and scramble fast to get back on board your boat before the situation got worse. If you landed on shore, things automatically got worse because the instructors would punish you before sending you out again.

We quickly learned that timing was everything in getting through the waves. One guy had to call the cadence so that we all paddled at the same time. Otherwise we would turn sideways and broach against the waves.

Finally we learned the timing of the surf, what the instruc-tors had told us we would have to do to get through the evolution. But it was a very tough learning experience. Then we learned that coming back was even harder. This time we were turned completely upside down. It was fun in its own way. But then we had to do the same thing at night.

Once you finally got the hang of moving a boat through the surf, you found out that it wasn't so bad. In fact, you kind of liked it when you finally timed it right on a good curl. There wasn't any feeling quite the same as sitting on top of a fifteen-foot wave and riding it in to shore just like the champion surfers.

And when your boat made it to shore correctly, the instructors would come up to you with grins on their faces and say, "Boat Crew One, good job. Now go back out and do it again."

And with big grins on our faces, we would all shout out, "*Hoo yah,* Instructor!"

A full day and night of that kind of training can be rough on you, and it was too rough for some of the guys. All you had to do to make it all stop was quit. There was a brass ship's bell that you could ring standing at the corner of the grinder. Three rings of that bell and you were done. Instantly you were back in the fleet and at the mercy of the regular Navy, but at least you were warm, dry, and clean again.

Hearing that bell ring meant that someone had "volunteered out" of the program. As the course went on, the ring of the bell got more common. It was unfortunate for that individual, but it also meant that someone had quit and you were still there. That could give your morale a boost, and sometimes you needed that.

During PT, I figured that if I was doing the exercise right, the instructors would leave me alone. Wrong. The Teams are called that because they work as a unit. And during training you learn that rule because you work as a Team and are punished as a Team. When one man did an exercise wrong, the whole class had to run into the surf zone and get wet. Then we would run back to the grinder to continue PT. If another man did an exercise wrong, we went into the surf followed by a roll in the sand to get a sugar cookie. Another mistake would move us to the sand to continue PT. A last error and we moved into the surf zone itself to complete our PT. Our first couple of weeks, we got very well acquainted with the feel, taste, and smell of the ocean.

We ended up swimming three or four times a week as training went on, with swim fins and without them, in the pool and in the ocean. You had to earn your face mask before you could wear one. That required a half-mile swim in under a certain time. You earned your swim fins with a one-mile timed swim. And finally, you earned the top of your wet suit with another, longer swim. The wet suit top was all the cold protection we were given against the water in those days.

One of the instructors had his own way of increasing your tolerance for working in the ocean. He would spit a wad of chewing tobacco into your face mask and then tell you he wanted the chaw back after your swim. Once you've swum with a big wad of used chewing tobacco in your mask, you can do an op through a floating mass of rotten whales and not get the pukes.

Games were played with you on a constant basis. And the training increased in difficulty too. We were getting ready for Hell Week, but first came rock portage. This evolution was like a killer version of surf passage. Down by the Hotel Del Coronado huge piles of rocks had been built up to protect the sand beach from erosion. The rubber boats had to be landed on these rocks safely and securely. During the day it was bad, but we did it. But this was a very dangerous technique, and an important one, so of course we also had to do it at night.

Fortunately, we managed to hit just the right wave at the right time and landed our boat smoothly the first time. This was great—we did it right and were going to get a break. Nope. They turned us around and sent us back out. I was the bow man and had to jump out onto the rocks each time and secure the line. During one of our attempts, our boat got completely turned around and I was sure we were all goners.

With our boat crew leader as the coxswain, calling out orders and trying to steer the boat with his paddle, we all dug in hard and dragged the boat around through the water. The bow was pointed toward shore as the waves rushed us straight at the sharp, jagged rocks. We paddled for all we were worth to get on top of the surf and use its speed.

Timing things as closely as we could in our exhausted condition, the coxswain called out for me to jump and I leaped out onto the slippery rocks. Smashing down on the stones, I ignored everything but scrambling across them and getting into a braced position. Leaning back, I took a strain to the line I held. The rest of the boat crew could now come over the sides of the boat, grab hold, and help me pull her in.

My shins were black and blue, I was pounded all over from the waves and rocks, and I was sure I had broken something. But we kept at it. We did our rock portage about four times. We finally got the technique down and were able to land the boat without any major injuries. The instructors deserve a lot of the credit. They made sure we knew what we had to do and gave us a break when they could see we were getting it together.

The expression at BUD/S is "It pays to be a winner." If you come out ahead, you'll be rewarded. We had to learn to be a team, and it was as a team that we received these rewards. They could be as little as a slight break before we had to continue with another evolution. Those breaks were going to be real important during Hell Week.

Outsiders tend to settle on Hell Week as the most important part of training. That's not necessarily true. But it is the most memorable single week of that twenty-six-week course. We received motivational talks and other incentives to try and help us get through that week. But when it gets down to it, all you can do is reach way down inside yourself and just keep going.

Your Teammates help; no one gets through BUD/S alone. But it's the heart, the "fire in the gut," that keeps you moving forward. Breakout was Sunday morning, and I have no idea exactly when it started. Suddenly M80 firecrackers were going off, M60 machine guns were firing blanks over our heads, and all the instructors seemed to be shouting at once. Confusion ruled, which was exactly the effect they were trying for.

Hell Week is intended to simulate as closely as possible the fear, confusion, and exhaustion of a major battle. That fact was impressed on me by a SEAL I spoke to years later. Joe DiMartino was one of the original members of SEAL Team Two. He was one of the few SEALs I ever heard of who didn't do a Hell Week. During World War II, Joe D was one of the Navy sailors who worked with the Naval Combat Demolition Units, the men who went on to become the UDTs. He helped blow open the beaches of Normandy on D-Day. Joe D would say that his Hell Week was June 6, 1944, and absolutely no one would argue that point.

So Hell Week was supposed to be a simulation of D-Day. For the whole week we only got a few hours' sleep. It wasn't long before we were shaky, cold, wet, and tired.

We hit the surf in the middle of that first night and did surf passage by moonlight. Then we brought the boats in and did another kind of surf passage. The instructors had the whole class link arms and move out into the water. We went out from shore until the chill water was about waist deep, then we sat down. The lighter surf was breaking over our heads, the waves having calmed down from earlier. We had to stay linked arm in arm for safety. Constantly we were told, "Don't lose your swim buddy." Getting separated from your swim buddy in some circumstances could mean the death of you both. That was another rule we were learning.

The cold was sapping our strength, and I started shaking. That shivering was something I had to overcome. Finally the instructors pulled us out of the water and had us take our shirts off. Then we went right back in. Taking us out of the water soon became the worst thing the instructors could do because the chill hit you, and then you had to go back in.

The whole line was shaking now. I could feel it through the men my arms were linked with. Looking up at the moon, I started thinking about the sun. Right there is the sun, I thought. And I started thinking about the Caribbean island that sun would be shining on. And I started to hum.

When the guys next to me asked what I was doing, I told them about the sun. Then they looked up and started to hum as well. Soon the whole line was humming. That really irked one of the instructors. He was shouting at us to stop humming. What was he going to do, punish us by making us cold?

But between breakout and that evolution, we had lost a large number of our people. The class was getting smaller, and we were getting more and more dingy. By Tuesday, most of us were so dingy we didn't know what evolution it was. Later in the week, when the hallucinations started, they couldn't hurt us much anymore. Sitting out in the boat on an evolution, I could see the lights of Coronado melting.

To bring us out of this, the instructors played games with our heads and bodies. They ran us through competitions that really woke everyone up. Everything was done as a team; none of the competitions were individual against individual. We did boat races as a crew, paddling all out against other crews over measured distances. We did relay races with the boat crews running along carrying their boats. Then we had to crawl through thick mud while explosions rang out all around us. Finally we heard the unbelievable words "Secure from Hell Week." We had made it.

There was a lot more training to do. We learned underwater work: how to swim long distances accurately underwater without ever breaching the surface, how to map beaches from the sea, and how to fire all kinds of demolitions, handle weapons, and conduct military patrols. A lot of my Army experience helped. And we all became good friends.

Today a lot of people claim to be SEALs or frogmen who never went through BUD/S. They say their class number is classified and they can't tell it to you. Or that they forgot it. A BUD/S class number is part of your open military record. It isn't classified, and anyone can know it. And you will never, ever forget the number of the class you graduated with. Those men will be with you for the rest of your life. That final day on the grinder when you have graduated BUD/S is one of the proudest days of your life. The moment when you join the ranks of the very select few who have gone before you is something that can never be forgotten.

When I graduated from BUD/S, I received my orders to report to SEAL Team One. A number of the guys went on to the different UDTs, but several of us went directly to the SEAL Teams. Now my real adventure was going to begin.

CHAPTER 6

SEAL TEAM ONE AND KILO PLATOON

Because of my previous Army Airborne status, I didn't have to go to Fort Benning and jump school with the rest of my class. Even though it had been about three years between jumps for me, the command said my qualifications were fine. My orders were to report directly to SEAL Team One.

SEAL Team One had its headquarters building just to the south of the training compound, right next door to UDT 13. So the physical walk to SEAL Team One wasn't very far, but it was a world away from BUD/S. There were about two hundred guys in the Team; the balance of the men were out on deployments, at schools, or on other duties.

SEAL Team One was one of only two SEAL Teams in the world then. They had been commissioned back in January 1962 at the direction of President Kennedy. They had been the first SEAL Team in direct combat in Vietnam. And they had been there a year before SEAL Team Two had come over to play in the game at their invitation. I learned a lot about the Team when I arrived and looked at all the pictures and citations around the quarterdeck. And then I checked in myself.

Once at the Team, I checked the bulletin board to try and find out what I was supposed to do next. As the newest man on board, I was automatically the bottom man on the duty rosters. Master Chief McKnight, who was the master at arms, sent me over to Rocky Cochlin for my plan of the day.

When you reported on board at a SEAL Team in those days, you were assigned to the master at arms as part of a general labor pool until you were picked up by a platoon and went through a platoon workup. You weren't doing all the high-speed SEAL operations and training yet. Instead you were painting the walls, cleaning the heads, and doing general maintenance work for anywhere from three to six months. After the big rush of getting through BUD/S, this brought you down to earth fast.

We were also sent over to the NAB (Naval Amphibious Base) right across the street to draw prisoners. The prisoners were sailors who had been put in the brig for some infraction. We would go get a group of ten or twelve of them, bring them back over to the SEAL compound, and direct them to clean up the area and do whatever other work had to be done. As the SEAL from the master at arms, I was in charge of the detail, which meant I had to direct the prisoners and make sure none of them ran away. This kind of thing, including the painting and other jobs I did myself, was called "snuffy work" and was done by the lowest ranking guys in a unit. It made you humble, and it put you in your place. That was me, new meat.

Needless to say, the glamour of being in a SEAL Team was fading a bit as I spent yet another day painting the walls of the head. That's where I was when Master Chief Gary Chamberlin changed my fortunes. Coming up to me as I was putting paint on the walls, he called out, "Chalker!" in that distinctive voice of his.

"Master Chief," I answered.

"You want to be relieved of doing this?"

"What?" I asked. "Of painting?"

"Yeah," he said. "Do you want to get out of master at arms?"

"Yes, sir!"

"Well then, tomorrow you report to me over there," he said, indicating an office area. "You're in Kilo Platoon."

Believe me, that helped speed up my painting job for the rest of the day.

Master Chief Gary Chamberlin, Chambo to everyone, soon became my Sea Daddy at SEAL Team One. A Sea Daddy is somebody who acts as your mentor as you start out in the Teams. He takes you under his wing, shows you the way, keeps you in line, and teaches you how to be a SEAL. This teaching includes how the community works and what it expects of you.

A Sea Daddy is somebody you can look up to and want to be like. Chambo fit that part for me. He was a well-respected Vietnam era master chief who had a direct way of speaking to his troops, usually unprintable.

In general, Kilo Platoon was a great way to start out a SEAL career. The guys who made it up included Jerry Bolland, Neil "Nelly" Nelson, Kurt "Stinger" Feichtinger, Bobby Just, Doug Tiedemann, Doc Warner, Gene Gardner, Lieutenant Mike Steinbaugh, who was our officer, Tom Bunce, the assistant officer, Billy Almond, Timmy Farrell, and I. Most of these guys had been in Class 100 just ahead of me and had gotten back from jump school in time to form up in Kilo. But the biggest surprise came in the form of the platoon's LPO (leading petty officer).

Checking in at Kilo as the LPO was Michael Faketty, the same gentleman I had known as Instructor Faketty back in BUD/S. There were a lot of new guys at the SEAL Team in Kilo Platoon, and most of us had been under Instructor Faketty's gaze at one time or another. There's a strange feeling when you find yourself working for an instructor who just a few months before was so high up over you he blocked out the sun. Faketty knew that and took us into a classroom to give us a heart-to-heart talk soon after he came on board at Kilo.

"Look," Mike said, "I know I put you guys through training and I'm your LPO now. But I want you all to understand one thing. I had to do a job over there, and I wanted to make sure we put the right people through. Someday, like now, I knew I might have to work with them. And I know you can all do your jobs."

That said a lot and cleared the air for us. The whole platoon became real tight, and all of us ended up being pretty good friends. Mike and I wound up as shooting partners when we broke the fourteen-man platoon down into two squads of seven men each. We were supposed to have sixteen people in two squads of eight each, but Kilo was running light at the start. Operating with Mike made us tight with each other, something I wouldn't have dreamed of just six months earlier.

Kilo Platoon started its workup going out to Niland in the California desert for STT (SEAL Tactical Training). We were prepping our gear, doing land operations, setting up point man courses, doing a lot of shooting, and conducting a lot of different kinds of ops.

Experience in the desert was new to me as well as to a number of my Teammates. On one op, we did a hit (ambush) up at the Chocolate Mountains. Bobby Just was one of our M60 gunners. We were on these sand dunes patrolling when we ran into one of the locals. This local was a sidewinder rattlesnake moving along the sand. Bobby decided to open up on the snake with his M60, which was loaded with blanks.

Blanks don't work too well on snakes, but they do manage to get their attention, and sidewinders can really move over the sand when they're pissed off, as Bobby found out when that snake started chasing him. We stood there laughing while we watched the snake chase Bobby all the way to the bottom of the dune.

That wasn't the only rattler we met while out at Niland. A guy back at the main camp had a snake from one of the earlier platoons that had been out there, a big rattler that was kept in an aquarium out near the fire area. One day this guy was going to show us how to handle the snake. He opened the top of the cage and stuck his hand in.

As soon as the snake was done biting him, we learned how to treat someone for snakebite. "Yup," we thought, "you're showing us." His arm started swelling fast, but the corpsmen started his treatment right away and he was fine.

One of the other things I learned about at Niland was a swamp cooler. Being from Ohio, my desert experience was limited to a couple of days sitting on an airstrip in Egypt during my Army tour. So I didn't know what to make of the tank of water and wet cloths at Niland that cooled the room through evaporation. Kind of a neat little field air conditioner.

At the end of a workday, after we cleaned the weapons and gear, we had some time for ourselves. We would take one of the vehicles over to where the canals ran along right behind the campgrounds, and going upriver about a mile and a half, we would get out our inner tubes. One of the tubes had a platform in it that would hold our cooler. Then we would just float down the canal on the inner tubes, wearing our shorts and drinking beer.

At Niland, we learned to work hard and earned the right to play hard. Besides, what else were we going to do in the middle of the desert?

When our training was completed, we returned to Coronado to get ready to deploy. Our tour was going to be of Southeast Asia and the Philippines.

Before we deployed, there was a little ceremony for the junior men from Class 100 and 101 that we will all remember to our last days. The graduates of BUD/S who were with me in Kilo Platoon, and the platoon officers, chiefs, and petty officers had held our performance board while we were undergoing STT. The board passed us all, and our six-month probationary period was officially over.

At Morning Quarters for SEAL Team One, when the whole team gathers to hear the morning orders, we received our Tridents. That was one of the happiest moments of my life. Before then, we had been allowed to wear Team shirts, called "Blue and Golds," that had a Trident printed on them. But they weren't the same as that metal device. That was something you became very proud of within seconds of pinning it on.

There wasn't any formal ceremony that morning. We were just in morning formation in our normal green duty uniforms, not even the blue and gold T-shirts. The rest of the Team were wearing their blue and gold T-shirts and blue shorts, so you could pick us out of the crowd easily. But standing there in front of the command, I felt like I was being gifted with one of the greatest honors that could be bestowed. The men standing around me were my Teammates, and they were welcoming me among them.

The commanding officer of SEAL Team One came up to each of us in formation, followed by our platoon officer and chief, and pinned the Tridents on our uniforms. Later, Chambo had his own way of pinning those first Tridents on us.

"Okay, missies," he told us after Quarters was over. "Into the platoon room." In the room, he placed our new Tridents on our chests and smacked them in solidly. A lot of men had bled for that Trident to build its reputation, and each one of us was going to do the same if only for that one moment to remind us of the men who had worn them before us.

That little weight felt good on your chest. It was the biggest, gaudiest insignia device in the Navy. And it told everyone who saw it just who you were and what you had done. You were a member of a very small, tight community of men. It had taken twenty-six weeks of unbelievable work and six months of proving yourself worthy before you could put that piece of metal on your chest. And it feels like your chest puffs out a bit to properly hold the Trident up where everyone can see it.

The traditions of the Team, those of Teamwork, dedication, and an ability to get the job done no matter what, were something that I intended to uphold to the very best of my ability. I didn't just want to wear the Trident; it was important to me to prove that I earned it, to give something back to the Teams. And the only way to do that then was to go operational. As a young SEAL, the last thing you wanted to do was develop the habit of sitting in an administration office. That kind of thing could turn into your entire career. So I wanted out into the field.

And I got my wish. Within weeks, my platoon had deployed to the Southwest Pacific. In the Philippines, Tim Farrell, Bobby Just and I went to Jungle Survival school. It was run by the locals, the Negritos. The first thing they did was take us to the local river and kill a big lizard. They tossed the lizard into the back of the truck, and then they took us into the jungle.

We began by learning about all the different things you could make from bamboo. One of the immediately practical lessons was how to make cook stoves for rice out of big chunks of bamboo. One of the instructors then took us down to the river, pointing out the wildlife and snakes that were all over the place. There was an area where bats filled the trees. Not your little winged mouse but huge fruit bats the size of small dogs.

Little did I know it, but I was soon to meet those bats face to face. Chambo, who knew well how the school ran, had told us that he would meet us that night at a certain point and have a case of beer for us. One of the instructors agreed to let us walk up the trail and meet Chambo at the prearranged spot. The only problem was that the meeting spot was right in the middle of that area full of bats. Chambo told us to "have fun" when he gave us the beer; as soon as it got dark, I knew what he meant. I only had to walk a couple of hundred yards through that area, but the bats were flying all over the place.

I must admit that beer hit the spot, though. The lizard that had been killed earlier in the day turned out to be dinner. They skinned it, roasted it, and we ate it. It wasn't bad; that reptile really did taste like chicken. The Negritos would only have one beer—they couldn't handle alcohol very well and knew their limit. The rest of us stayed up drinking. None of us had ever been in the jungle before, so we had hung our hammocks around the campsite, surrounding the fire. And pretty much all of us spent the night right around that fire.

The next day we started relaxing a little more as we learned about the jungle around us. The guides showed us how we could cut certain vines and water would drain out of them, pure and clean enough to drink. What little I knew about the jungle came from watching Tarzan movies as a kid. The real thing was a lot different. When I listened for all the sounds they always had in the movies, they weren't there. The jungle could be quiet and peaceful in its own way.

The vegetation was dense, and it gave me a good appreciation for what would be coming up. Eventually we would have to patrol though this stuff on operations. And we would have to conduct many of those patrols at night. When I was on point in a patrol, I learned that walking through the jungle wasn't easy. You had to take your time and choose your path carefully. Chambo showed me why he carried a small pair of wire cutters on patrol. When you got all tangled up in the little vines, you could finally just cut yourself free.

After completing the three-day jungle course, we conducted some further exercises in the area. Then the platoon continued on to Korea to work with the ROK (Republic of Korea) frogmen.

The ROK frogs were disciplined, and that's putting it mildly.

Their service is of the old-school military. If you screwed up as a trooper, you didn't necessarily get official punishment. Instead you could expect to be taken out behind the barracks and have your shortcomings discussed from the viewpoint of your NCO's fists. But there was also respect, very strong respect, in the ranks. An NCO didn't earn his position by just being the meanest mother on the block. He knew he had to do it better than the men, always. Leading by example was the only way to operate in the ROK military.

Our first dive with them was a simple open-circuit compass swim from one pier to an anchored landing craft some distance from shore. I was teamed with an ROK officer and their team's chief. The chief had the compass board, so he was doing the driving.

When we got into the water, I was glad I had an experienced ROK with me. Tiedemann was having some fun with his group of guys, just holding the end of the buddy line attached to the swimmers while they swam in circles. Meanwhile we took right off and were moving along well toward the landing craft. The swim was maybe fifteen hundred meters and didn't look to be any big deal. Then the ROK officer gave the out-of-air signal (indicating, of course, that he was out of air and couldn't continue to swim).

If it was possible to look determined and disgusted with a face mask on and a mouthpiece in, the ROK chief was pulling it off. When we finally broke the surface, he just cut the buddy line between him and his officer and wanted to go right back down. But we waited for the safety boat to pick up the officer. Then back down we went for the rest of the swim.

The current was worse than I thought it would be, and the swim was taking a longer time than I'd thought. As I watched the chief I saw his hand go up to his rig and turn on his reserve air. When you go on your reserve, that's usually the end of the swim, but not for the ROK chief. He just continued on.

About five minutes later I had to hit my reserve and signaled to the chief that I was on my last air. He just pointed to show we would continue with the swim. A few minutes later we saw the shadow of the landing craft and knew we had hit our objective. But that chief ran out of air well before we hit the boat. For the last hundred yards or so, I hadn't seen any bubbles at all. He must have been just holding his breath and pushing to complete the op.

What I found out later was that the air bottles hadn't been fully charged before we started our swim. Only a few teams made it to the target at all. But that chief was going to set the standard, so he made it. Later he chewed his men out, and I was very glad I wasn't on the receiving end of it.

On one night op, we were taking the Zodiac inflatable boats in on a compass course to the beach. The ROKs were navigating, and our guy was about fifty yards off the target when we finally beached. This was no biggie. You could misjudge distance over water pretty easily—that's why we practiced doing these kinds of things. Apparently the ROK chief thought differently.

The next morning, our navigator was standing in formation with his unit. We stood there and watched the chief whack this guy in the head with a boat paddle, not once but several times. The guy was just standing there taking it, kind of grunting with each strike. Finally he fell down and the formation continued. If it had been me, I would have hit the ground on that first whack. I did hope Chambo wasn't taking notes.

Before we left for another training site, the ROKs hosted a feast for us. There were a lot of dogs running around the ROK compound. When we came in for the feast, I noticed the canine population seemed to be smaller. During the meal, I wondered out loud to Chambo what it was we were eating. "Probably dog" was his answer.

After our Korean adventures, Kilo Platoon returned to the

Philippines and from there we went on to Thailand where we worked with their SEALs. The border situation with Cambodia was running hot at that time, and we could hear artillery and mortar fire off in the distance at night, but we never saw any action.

Working weapons with the Thais proved interesting at one point. I was running one of the stations on the M72A2 LAW (light antitank weapon) range while Billy Almond was running the whole evolution. As one Thai took a bead on a target, a teammate of his decided he wanted to see what the first guy was aiming at. So he slipped in behind the other, sighting along the LAW tube, and looking right up the exhaust end of the rocket that was about to be fired.

"Cease fire!" I shouted as I pulled the curious one away from the firing line. If that LAW rocket had been fired, the observer would have been missing his head. Billy caught the situation at about the same time I did. Afterward he just looked at me and shrugged.

We had given a full class on the M72A2 LAW rocket. We showed the Thais how it was used and made sure they knew about the safety procedures and the dangerous back-blast area. But there always seems to be somebody who doesn't get the word or thinks it doesn't apply to him.

Our tour in Thailand was a great time. We were staying near a resort area, and the beach looked nice. I wondered how much the local culture was like Vietnam's had been less than ten years earlier. The people were very friendly, and they lived in the same kind of hooches that were all over Southeast Asia. I learned a lot about the local culture. Then our deployment plans continued and we were on our way back to the Philippines.

Some of the trainings we conducted in the Philippines were real UDT-style operations. We spent a week on LPSS-574, the *Grayback,* a special transport sub for the Teams. The *Grayback* had two big hangars on her bow, with huge domed hatches that would open hydraulically. Swimmers could get into and out of these hangars from inside the forward compartment of the submarine, launching rubber boats, swimmer pairs, or even little submarines without ever breaching the surface.

On one night operation we came up to Horse Beach and launched rubber boats from the submarine hangars. Breathing from the multiple rigs inside the hangars wasn't anything special, but when those big doors opened up, it was a sight to see.

The moonlight filtered down through the water, and the natural luminescence of the water made sparks of blue-green light dance about in the silver-colored gloom. Then we had to release our air and move to the surface. The first guy let go and did a free ascent; I was the next guy in line. It wasn't any big deal, you just blew out the air in a steady stream as you rose to the surface. When we were all together, we climbed in the boats and moved to the beach.

The return operation to the *Grayback* was much the same. We paddled the boats out to the rendezvous point and dove down to the sub. The boats were pulled in later, and each of us just held his breath and swam into the hangar. Once in the hangar, we could breathe off the boat air from the regulators that lined the sides. I was down in the hangar breathing off a rig when one of our officers came into the hangar. Instead of taking the rig I was holding for him, he pulled my rig out of my mouth and started using it. We had a few words about that later.

But the crew of the sub were professionals. We locked in and out a number of times at fifty feet. The people were good to us, and we berthed in the forward torpedo room where arrangements had been made for transporting whole SEAL platoons. The food was everything we had been told submarine chow was supposed to be. When you can be stuck underwater on long cruises, even just mediocre food could crash a sub crew's morale, so subs were known to serve some of the best food in the Navy. The whole crew looked like moles with their white skins, and I soon learned why. After only a week on board, our "sun conditioning" (tans) started to fade and the light outside seemed awfully bright when we climbed off the sub.

There were little submarines that could also operate from the *Grayback*'s hangars, black-hulled SDVs, or swimmer (now SEAL) delivery vehicles. We never worked with the SDVs from the *Grayback*; instead we learned about them at their shore facility. The Mark VIII SDVs were a little over twenty-one feet long and a few inches over four feet tall and wide. The SDV has two compartments, one in the front for the pilot and navigator and one in the rear for the cargo. Since the SDVs operated while full of water, flooded in the wet condition, each person on board had to wear a breathing rig or use the boat air. Most of the time, the swimmers who were going on the operation breathed off their own rigs, and the two-man crew ran off of boat air.

The little subs were crowded, dark, and more than a little cramped. Riding in one was definitely not for the claustrophobic. But they could move a group of up to six swimmers and their gear a lot farther than you could push yourself with fins.

On my first workup swim in one of the SDVs, we just moved around in the bay during the day. Several of us hung onto the outside of the boat as it moved along through the water. It was like a normal dive, only we didn't have to kick very hard. Personally, I just watched the scenery, which really wasn't much, the water being murky.

But the night operational swim was considerably different. I was riding in a Mark VIII SDV, launching from pier side on an attack swim against an anchored ship. Moki Martin and Cooper were the driver and navigator of our SDV, both having a lot of experience in the little wet subs. We were breathing off Emerson closed-circuit rigs, which turned out to be a really good thing because what was supposed to be a ninety-minute ride turned into a four-hour underwater trip. Chambo and I were sitting in the very cramped front section of the SDV, behind the pilot and the navigator. The rest of our guys were in the rear compartment.

First we were almost run over by a destroyer. Then, when we reached the target, we were supposed to surface at pier side, leave the SDV, and attack the ship. We didn't come up to the pier, however. Instead we smacked into the keel of our target ship, and I swear it felt like those tons of steel hit me right in the back of the neck. We hit so hard the SDV hull cracked, and we had to do an emergency surface right there. Everyone got out okay, and we continued with our operation.

We finished out our tour in the Philippines with one really memorable parachute jump. Bordering the drop zone was a meandering body of water that got its name from having passed the town of Olongapo just outside the main gate of our base at Subic Bay. Olongapo didn't have the most modern sewage facilities, and the river picked up its name, Shit River, for just that reason. If you came into contact with the river, there was a series of something like fourteen different shots you had to get to guard against diseases they didn't even have names for yet.

To keep up our jump qualifications, we used an open field just to the right and inside the fence at the main gate as a drop zone. We had a CH-47 helicopter and were going to do a simple drop. Not all plans go as intended. Those dash-2 model chutes we were using could be steered, but only in a limited way. There was a mistake on the release point, and a number of us headed for Shit River.

The only reason most of us didn't take a dip in the river was that we slammed up against the chain-link fence surrounding the base. Mike Faketty managed to miss the fence, and the drop zone, but he didn't miss the river. When Mike hit that water, you could hear a groan come up from all of us. He was not a happy person, even less so when he received his shot series from the corpsman. The jump master who had given us the go on the release point was not Mike's favorite person after that. I believe the man went on liberty while Mike was getting his shots.

Still Mike survived his little mishap on the jump with little more than two sore shoulders and a sore ass. We razzed him a bit on his parachuting skills, which reminded me of my first Team jump not more than a few months before.

Soon after Kilo Platoon first formed up back in Coronado, we set up to do a parachute jump. It was going to be a static line water jump from a CH-47 helicopter. In a static line jump, the parachute opens automatically from a line anchored to the jump aircraft. You almost can't screw it up, and even if you do, you still have a reserve chute with you. Even though I still get butterflies before a jump, after more than 3,700 jumps, a static jump is easy. But the chutes don't steer very well.

I was going to be the man in our stick who carried the IBS, so they put me on the edge of the ramp at the rear of the helicopter with the big rubber boat slung from my front. On the way down, the rubber boat would be unrolled, inflated from a CO_2 bottle, and lowered on a tether line, so it would hit the water before I did. That way our water craft would be ready for us to climb on board and continue with the operation. But on this first jump, no one climbed in the boat after I landed, because on that jump I didn't even hit the water. I landed in the middle of the softball field near the base, where UDT Eleven and SEAL Team One were playing a game. Right out in center field, the new meat came down with his rubber boat inflated, his swim fins on, and not a drop of water nearby.

Some of the other guys hit the edge of the field, but most of them made the water, landing over by the sub pens near the base. The release point for our jump may have been the jump master's mistake, but I had to hear about it for a very long time afterward.

CHAPTER **7**

ECHO PLATOON AND A TASTE OF HIGH SPEED

It was early in 1980 when Kilo Platoon returned from the deployment to Southeast Asia. My career plan now was to work in the Intelligence Department at SEAL Team One and start going back to school. In the Intel Department, we gathered information and created reports to move up to higher command or disseminate in the Team. Making charts, taking photographs, and analyzing data all took place in the department. Working in a department would give me the time I needed to work toward my degree, and it looked like this was work I could enjoy doing. But another offer came up that completely derailed my plans.

There was a very select platoon at SEAL Team One that had been operating for a few years prior to my getting to the Team. Echo Platoon was the West Coast contingency platoon for counterterrorist actions. At SEAL Team Two on the East Coast, Mob Six (Mobilization Platoon Six) was assigned the same mission.

Both platoons had been operating since the late 1970s and were building up reputations as hard operators.

The mission for Mob Six and Echo Platoon was to react to any terrorist activity in our area of operations, centering on the marine environment. Both units would remain on standby at their respective Teams for deployment to any hot spot in their area. The units were the sharp edge of the Navy's counterterrorist program. They would kick the doors in, rescue the people, and eliminate the terrorists. If an oil rig was captured, a private yacht taken over, or a Naval facility seized, the men of Mob Six or Echo Platoon would be the first called on to take action.

The missions required very specialized training to board ships under way, climb, shoot, and swim. Stinger and I, along with several other guys, were asked to join Echo Platoon after Kilo returned, and we both agreed.

The counterterrorist mission required a hard-charging SEAL, and that was a description that fit Stinger and me. We knew a little bit about what Echo did, even though information on it was kept just to the command. After we got in the unit, they gave us a full briefing on the mission and what we would be doing.

Echo was only my second SEAL Team platoon assignment, but it didn't take me long to figure out that this was the kind of thing I wanted to do. The training was great and so were the guys I met there. In the platoon I met Pooster, Perdue, Faydog, Kevin Banker, Sluggo, Doc Luben, and T. K. "The Old Gummer" Davis, all of whom became lifelong friends. Stinger had another change in his life besides the new platoon assignment. He got married to Kathy, a girl he had met when she was working in the chow hall during BUD/S.

Marrying into the Teams was tough, but it wasn't as bad as trying to stay with a man through BUD/S. I can't remember one of my enlisted classmates being married in Class 101. It took a special woman to be married to a Team guy, and even then it was very hard to stay together during a Team career. But that was all something I was going to learn in the future.

Stinger wasn't going out with us on the weekends quite as much as he used to back when he was a wild bachelor. But training at Echo had introduced me to new actions that took up a lot of my off-duty time. Rock climbing was something I was really getting into, and Faydog, Pooster, and I would go up to the mountains on the weekends and indulge in this new sport. Both my friends were good climbers and taught me a lot.

A lot of new training came with joining Echo Platoon. Room entries—what we called door kicking—were something we practiced continually. Down at the helo (helicopter) base, we went in and hunted each other through some of the old buildings. Our operational handguns were usually customized M1911A1s, the venerable old .45 automatic. For a lot of our training, we used stainless steel Smith & Wesson Model 66 revolvers because we could shoot special ammunition through them. Wearing gas masks and using wax bullets instead of hard projectiles, we could safely fire on each other and establish hits with little question of just where the bullet had gone.

Training was hard and fast, but we still managed to have fun doing it. One of the things we would do was stage quick-draw contests where two of us would see who could shoot the other guy first. You had to nail the other guy quickly, so instead of waiting for the weapon to come into line before firing we would pull the trigger more than once as the pistol was coming up from the holster. You could watch the wax rounds kind of walk across the floor and up into the target. Okay, so it wasn't traditional Old West shooting, but it was a hell of a lot of fun. We also trained with shoulder-fired weapons, usually a carbine version of the standard M16A1 with a fourteen-inch barrel, what we still called in the Teams a CAR-15.

Besides shooting, there were other techniques that had to be learned, like how to get aboard a boat while it was under way.

The technique involved catching up to a boat, attaching a line, and climbing on board. This sounds easy, but it's a whole lot different when you have to do it. The first time you try and catch a boat is quite an experience, like trying to ride a bull. I was being groomed to be a catcher; in other words, the first guy to make contact with the boat we were trying to board.

Standing up in the front of a speeding small boat, I would have two guys hanging onto my ass to try and steady me. Runners also went out to either side of the bow to aid in my stability. There were foam cushions all over the bow of our Boston Whaler and at first I couldn't figure out what they were for. Maybe they were extra flotation in case the bow of the boat dug into a wave. When we hit our first rough water, I found out what the cushioning was for. It kept you from losing your teeth when you fell over and smacked into the boat.

I bounced off the bottom of the boat and got right back up. I liked the challenge and soon learned how to keep my feet. Once I had attached a line to the target, we would use a caving ladder to gain the deck of the ship. This was one of the very first boarding techniques we used, and it took a lot of time to learn how to do it right.

We spent six months in Echo Platoon learning the ropes and conducting local training. Range time to practice firing our weapons was included in the schedule every day, and we spent time keeping up our climbing techniques, studying possible targets and situations, and learning about terrorist groups and their preferred operational styles. The situation was still a new one, so it was flexible. We never stopped learning.

Other aspects of Echo Platoon caused some raised eyebrows among the rest of the command. We had relaxed grooming standards compared with the rest of the Teams and the Navy as a whole. We let our hair grow long so that we could blend in with a civilian crowd on a real-world operation. With a regular military haircut, you stood out. If you had what the East Coast

SEALs called a Rudy Boesch haircut—Rudy was a master chief and original member of SEAL Team Two—you stood out even in the Teams. Some of the old-school SEAL chiefs and officers didn't much care for our haircuts, but there was only a single platoon of us.

In June 1980 the word came out that Mr. Marcinko was coming to town and would be conducting interviews for a new Team. Everyone in the command prepped for the interviews. A number of people whose opinion I valued—Chambo, Gustaval, and T. K.—talked to me about the new unit. I was told that if I was given the opportunity to screen for the new Team I should take it. Some of those guys remembered when the SEAL Teams were first formed and what the first years had been like. It wasn't something I wanted to miss out on.

When you hear something like that, you have to take it seriously. Being in the Teams meant you already wanted to take on the hard jobs. This situation could mean a new field of skills to learn and missions to accomplish. This could be a case of my being in the right place at the right time and I wasn't going to let myself lose out.

A few months before, I had met Dick Marcinko, but only in passing. We had both been at an East Coast specialized demolition school at Harvey Point. Purdue and I had been sent to the school as part of our Echo Platoon training. I saw him there, complete with a beard and Rudy Boesch haircut, but no one talked about him in particular, and I didn't ask.

There was some scuttlebutt about then–Lieutenant Commander Marcinko. The stories centered on his having a platoon on the East Coast with the same mission as Echo, counterterrorism in a marine environment. He was the leader of Mob Six. And what he was doing was getting the schools lined up, buying the gear, and preparing his men for their mission.

Dick Marcinko wasn't well known to the West Coast Teams at that time. He had a long list of accomplishments as an operator in Vietnam, and he had been the commanding officer of SEAL Team Two from July 1974 to July 1976, but I didn't know him very well, a situation that was going to change drastically and soon.

At the screening interview, Dick Marcinko looked a lot like I remembered him but with longer hair and a mustache. He had a hard-charging style that he liked to use to keep you off balance. And his eyes held you with that hard, solid gaze so many of the old-school SEALs had.

The interview was not quite what I had been expecting. Dick had his new executive officer, Norm Carly, with him and they were conducting interviews in the SEAL Team One XO's (Executive Officer's) office. All of us hopefuls were waiting outside the office trying to look our best to make a good first impression.

From my Army days I knew how to spit-shine a pair of boots properly and had spent some time getting my uniform squared away. Going into that office was the first of my many adventures with the man I would come to call Skipper.

Walking in, I was told to have a seat. So I sat down. Dick was sitting behind the desk in civilian clothes. Those hard eyes of his immediately centered on mine and remained locked on their target for the duration of the interview. Then the questions came. Dick has a fast, staccato way of talking when he wants to keep you thinking. You never really get a chance to say much, and when he does give you a moment to respond, you're too shell-shocked to take advantage of it.

"What you doing?" he asked.

Before I could answer, he continued, "Who you fucking, what you fucking?"

"Excuse me?" I asked, a little stunned.

"I said, 'Who you fucking, what you fucking?' " and he continued just as quickly. "You used to be in the Army." He leaned forward and looked over the front edge of the desk at my boots. "Yup, must have been in the Army."

Norm just sat there looking at me as I underwent this weird set of questions. None of the interviews I had gone through in the Army or the Navy had prepared me for this.

"Here's the deal," Dick continued. "You're going to get your own rigs [parachute and diving]. You'll have your own weapons. You think you'll be working three hundred sixty-five days a year? Bullshit, you'll be working four hundred sixty-five days. You'll be going here and doing this. You'll be going there and fucking that. It'll be move, move, move, high speed, high speed. Any questions?"

"Ahhh, no sir," I managed to say.

"Then get the fuck out of here."

Whoa, I was out of the door before I had time to take much more than a breath. And you couldn't tell your waiting Teammates what to expect, not that they would have believed it anyway. Pooster and Faydog looked at me expectantly, and I just said, "Whoa!"

During the interview, I had managed to ask a few questions, like where we were going to be stationed. The answer was a straight one. We were going to be on the East Coast, but Marcinko doubted we would be seeing much of it. I wondered when we would find out who had made the cut, and he told me, "You'll find out when I'm fucking ready to tell you."

All in all, I thought the interview had gone rather well.

When my friends came out from their interviews, they had pretty much the same opinion I did. It looked like a wild ride coming up if it was anything like these interviews.

But the Old Man had come in with a pretty good idea of just who he wanted for the new Team. Our records had been screened closely, and he had probably gotten some insight into each of us from the command and the officers and leaders we had worked under. But everyone who wanted into the new unit was anxious for the next two weeks until the lists for orders came out.

SEAL Team Six wasn't commissioned yet and wouldn't be until much later in the year. But it was going to be a dedicated command with the mission of conducting counterterrorist operations for the Navy as a whole and being the point unit for all U.S. counterterrorist ops in a marine environment. It was a great expansion of the mission already being performed by Echo Platoon on the West Coast and Mob Six on the East. We were the contingent of men from Echo Platoon, and Mob Six would be absorbed into SEAL Team Six as well.

During the summer of 1980, the hostage crisis in Iran was still going on, and Mob Six was involved in the planned rescue operation. Even while we were building up SEAL Team Six prior to its commissioning, the Iranian hostage rescue was a constant contingency operation. If a follow-up to Operation EAGLE CLAW, the aborted rescue of the Iranian hostages, went down, one of our missions would be to go in and take out the radar installations near the coast of Iran. But that mission never materialized. Instead we worked hard to create the new SEAL unit.

The Old Man had a set of conditions he used as a guide to put together his new unit. The Team had to be up and running quickly, so he didn't have a lot of time for the more traditional problems with a new command. Mostly young single men were chosen to keep family problems to a minimum. We were going to work and train harder than we ever had before.

It felt good to see my name on that list. Stinger had made it too, and he was the only married man that I could see on the sheet. We got our orders to report to the East Coast and had a chunk of time to do it in. Several of us decided to make a caravan across the country, stopping along the way as we saw fit.

We hooked up Stinger's car to the back of a Ryder truck over behind SEAL Team One's building. Faydog, Pooster,

Stinger, Purdue, and myself were packed and ready. Dog was driving his old '55 Chevy truck. Pooster had a Jeep and was going to take Purdue with him. Stinger and I were driving the rental truck and pulling the car. Stinger's intention was to get settled on the East Coast and then bring his wife out there. It was going to be a new job and a new place to live. We were excited and looking forward to what was coming but not expecting anything in particular. Back in BUD/S we had all learned not to worry about the future. You just dealt with what you had right in front of you. And for us right then, in front of us was a coast-to-coast road trip.

We hit the road and left the West Coast behind. It would be a few years before I was stationed there again.

CHAPTER 8

SEAL TEAM SIX, 465 DAYS A YEAR

Our caravan arrived in Little Creek, Virginia, in late August 1980 after traveling on a whole lot of road. We checked in to our new company area right behind SEAL Team Two: two really unimpressive old World War II wooden barracks that looked like something used by the Boy Scouts. Apparently one of the buildings had actually been used by the base Cub Scout troop before we arrived. It was a busy few weeks as gear started pouring in, and that stuff looked like it belonged to the most lethal bunch of Boy Scouts you ever saw. We hadn't been commissioned as a Team yet, and there was a lot of work to do before we could go operational.

We started training almost right away. The men were broken down into two assault groups, one and two. The assault groups were further broken down into platoons and then squads. As the regular SEAL Teams had swimmer pairs, we had shooting partners to keep the two-man unit idea intact. Each squad would run a single boat for operations.

The Team area was actually on part of the SEAL Team Two compound, separated from them and the rest of the base by a chain-link fence. Inside that little compound we had to keep all ten of our boats on their trailers. There wasn't much room.

Our admin building was a small hut with no real room inside. We had Conex boxes for each squad's issue, but those quickly filled up as our gear came in. Conex (container, express) boxes are heavy steel cubes, about eight feet square, with a door on one side that can be securely locked. Common in the military, a Conex box can be packed, sealed, and moved as a whole on military transport.

By this time, Purdue, Stinger, and I had rented an apartment where we could live off base. Except for our weapons, the apartment became the place where we kept most of our gear. Even for a bachelor pad, it was sparsely furnished. There was one futon as a bed, and whoever got home first used it. The rest of us just crashed as we could. The one bedroom was where we kept all our gear.

As our gear showed up, we started doing some local training. One assault group would go to a training site, like Fort A. P. Hill in Virginia, for shooting, while the other group did their training someplace nearby. Our basic operational plan had two levels of alert status. One group would be on standby. If they were recalled, they had to be at our headquarters with all their gear very quickly. Within a few hours of the original recall, a full assault group could be on its way anywhere in the world.

The other assault group would be on a longer recall so that they could attend training farther away from Little Creek. Even so, if a recall went out, the group on training had less than a day to get back to the base.

In November 1980, SEAL Team Six was officially commissioned. We didn't have much of a ceremony, but we did stand an inspection. The relaxed grooming standards we had held to in Echo Platoon were even more relaxed at Six. We might have to join any population in the world in a very short time, and it was a whole lot easier to cut or trim hair than it was to grow it on a moment's notice. Also, we always wore civilian clothes in and around the base and at training sites. SEAL Team Six was a secret, covert operation and we weren't going to advertise it by having long hair and wearing Navy uniforms.

A lot of our training took us to different places, and most of the time we had to travel there on civilian transport. Our relaxed grooming standards let us blend in with the civilians on those trips. If we did stand out, it was because we looked like a professional football team due to our general level of physical fitness. Even that we tried to hide, covering our muscle with baggy clothing.

But the Army general in charge of all of the Special Operations Forces wanted to see his newest unit. We arrived on post in our usual civilian clothes and changed into our uniforms inside the admin building. It was full dress uniforms including all decorations and regalia. This meant the officers had to wear swords, which made us look like a bunch of pirates.

But our uniforms were spotless, our buildings clean, and our long hair, mustaches, and occasional beard combed. When the general came in our front door, he was a bit surprised by our doorman. The last SEAL officer on active duty to hold the Medal of Honor was the one to greet the general. He was also the only man who had gotten a haircut for the inspection. As per military protocol, the general saluted our lieutenant, as the holder of the Medal.

Purdue and I had made second class petty officer, but we still felt pretty funny standing there in our Navy Blues—what we called our "Cracker Jacks" because the outfit was the kind pictured on the candy box. The general thought we were all a bit of a sight as well. But he continued on his tour through our very limited facilities and left knowing we could do the job we were assigned.

The relaxed grooming standards caused us some trouble with the rest of the Teams, however, both UDT and SEAL. There may have been a little jealousy as well. I've been told that back when the SEAL Teams were first commissioned, there was the same trouble from the UDTs about the new Teams. The new guys seemed to have all the best toys and went on the neatest training. The UDTs were told that the SEALs were the same brothers to them they had always been, just with a different mission, and eventually things settled down. The same held true between SEAL Team Six and the rest of the community.

Our modified grooming standards also made for some fun during a demonstration we did for a Navy admiral. We had to do these demonstrations every now and then for the brass and politicians to show just what we could do that none of the other Special Operations Forces were trained for. We were going to do an underway takedown of a target ship in front of an audience that would be on the ship itself.

It was a stormy night when we approached the target ship. The Skipper was standing with the brass on board when we came out of the waters of Chesapeake Bay. With our boat being tossed about on the waves, the spray in the air, and it just being dark as hell, I couldn't see the spot I was trying to hit on the ship. This was an important demonstration, with all the brass on board watching us, but they couldn't see what was going on in the water. All they knew was that we were going to show up on board while the ship was still moving.

For a while I watched the ship, standing in our boat and keeping my balance as we were tossed in all directions. With my knees bent to absorb some of the punishing shock of the waves, I was going to have to make my best guess about how to secure to the ship. Then Mother Nature took a hand.

A sudden flash of lightning illuminated the ship, and my target. With one try, our caving ladder was secured and the squad clambered up to the deck far above us. When we assembled on the deck, we had impressed everyone who was watching, including the Old Man, who acted like this was an everyday occurrence. Then the admiral asked to see us.

As the Old Man explained our situation, the admiral asked to see the man who had caught the ship. The whole squad was standing there in our full equipment, including black uniforms and balaclavas covering our faces. Only our eyes showed. When the Old Man told me to step forward and unmask, I did. And then all the hair that had been stuffed up under my hood fell out.

"Good God, son!" the admiral exclaimed. "Are you in this Navy?"

"Yes, sir, I am," I answered proudly.

Then the whole squad uncovered. With the admiral staring at us, the Old Man explained the reason behind our long hair, mustaches, and beards. The admiral understood, but I don't think he ever quite got over seeing what had climbed up onto the deck of his ship.

The relaxed grooming standards were something we earned by working some of the longest, hardest hours of any military unit. We could easily go thirteen or fifteen days at a time, training straight through with long hours each day. Then we might get a day or two off. Officially, that first year we all got half a day off for Christmas. The second year we got half a day off for Thanksgiving and another half day for Christmas. That was about it.

The Old Man had a very short time to establish an operational unit and get it on line and mission-ready. The Army had established the same kind of counterterrorist team, but they had taken several years to get their unit up and running. The Skipper didn't have that kind of time. What he did was pick out people he could trust and then depend on them. While we did the nuts-and-bolts work of getting ready to operate—learning the skills, gathering the equipment, and training with each other—the Skipper was working twice as hard at his job as we were at ours.

The XO stayed with us in Little Creek to manage the situation on-site. Meanwhile the Skipper spent a lot of his time going from place to place, especially to Washington, D.C., trying to make sure we were keeping everyone happy in the command chain. A tremendous amount of work had to be done to create the first new SEAL Team commissioned since 1962, and a lot of that work involved meeting people and doing the politics. But whenever he could, he was right there with us on the range, pulling triggers, jumping, climbing, and doing what he loved—operating.

We were his unit. He treated us as individuals when the situation called for it, but he always looked at us as a Team. That was the ideal he was striving for. And it was what we wanted as well. You couldn't work for a man that driven and not pick up some of his enthusiasm for the job at hand. We all became close, a small unit of men with a single purpose: to defend the country we all loved from a new enemy, terrorism.

There were a few of the guys who didn't like the constant training. The Skipper put an end to the bitching in his own style. He put out what was referred to in the Navy as a "Captain's Call" to speak to all of us at once. Since we didn't have a building big enough to hold all of us in our compound, the Skipper held our meeting in the base theater.

"You don't have to like this," he told us from the stage. "You don't have to like that. But you *will* do it because that's what you get fucking paid to do! If you don't want to do it, you can walk out the door."

His speech wasn't much longer than that. The situation didn't call for a lot of words. Anyone who thought we were working too hard, moving too fast, or not getting enough time off was invited to leave. There wasn't any bell to ring like at BUD/S. You didn't have to say anything. All you had to do was get up out of your seat and leave. Like everything in the Teams, you volunteered in, and you could volunteer out.

No one walked out the door. The grumbling about the pace of our training stopped after the Skipper's little speech. The point had been made about what we were trying to do and how we were going to do it. Our continuous training was to get us up to snuff fast. Our standards had to be high in order to complete our mission properly. We trained hard and fast to meet those standards, and we kept up that level of training to maintain our standards.

How the Skipper picked the people he chose to make his Team, I didn't know. I do know that I was glad to be among them. That first muster of men were the plank owners of SEAL Team Six. In the Navy, each man in the original crew of a commissioned ship is considered to own a plank from the deck of that ship. That's where the term *plank owner* came from. And it was a proud and exciting thing to be a plank owner in our new Team.

The Skipper took care of his people, officer and enlisted. He was on your side and would always back you up. If he couldn't be there himself, he would see to it that the help you needed was there.

I got into trouble with the local cops one night shortly before my assault group was to leave on a training mission. Each squad had a panel truck to transport a boat and trailer and to pack full of gear for an alert. These were civilian-style trucks without Navy plates or government colors. There wasn't any room for us to leave the vehicles in the compound, so each truck had a designated driver who took it home every day. Drivers were also responsible for the maintenance and upkeep of the vehicles, since we couldn't take them to the base motor pool. I was one of the designated drivers.

One night I had dinner with some of my Teammates at a little place called the Raven. I had a few beers with the owner, but these were the seven-ounce bottles known as "Little Micks." During the whole night, I had maybe four or five of these little beers.

About 10 P.M. I went home to bed. We had to load the truck for the trip the next day, so I figured I would get up real early and go into the base to get a jump on things. About 1:30 A.M. the next morning, I was heading toward the base along a four-lane road, traveling in the fast lane far to the left.

Somebody came around the corner at me and I swerved the truck to the right. The guy moved in and was heading at me again, so I swerved to the left. The front wheel hit the curb, and the truck tilted over to the right. The right side wheel folded and the truck fell over on its side. The guy who had been coming at me just kept going. So here it was 2 A.M., and I had been in an accident with my squad's truck.

The officer who arrived on the scene was not in the best of moods. He had me blow up a balloon and gave me the standard drunk test. Nothing showed on the meter, but the officer must have thought I had been drinking, because all the bars had just closed. So he took me in to the station to take another test.

I kept asking the cop if he had found any witnesses. People had been coming out of the bars, but it wasn't the best part of town so not a lot of volunteers came up. I kept asking the cop the same question, and he started to get annoyed at me. The cop decided I wasn't cooperating fast enough and swatted me with his stick a few times. I told him I was sore from the accident and not to hit me again. When he pulled back his stick to nail me with it again, I responded.

He went for his pistol, and I prevented him from drawing it, smacking him back at the same time. Then another police car showed up, this one with two cops, one large and one small. They proceeded to help the first officer "subdue" me. With me stretched across the hood of the car, the big cop bounced my head off the metal once. Then the little one found he had some trouble getting the handcuffs on me. My comments to the smaller officer got my head bounced off the hood of the car again.

They kept me handcuffed and locked me in a cell. The little cop was still pissed at me and said, "I ought to come in there and kick your ass."

"Well, little man," I answered, not doing myself a hell of a lot of good, "why don't you come in here, take the cuffs off, and we'll lock the door."

Later they read me the list of charges: resisting arrest, assault on three police officers, and refusal to take an alcohol test. I made a call to our compound and just had to wait things out.

I figured my military career was over. The next day we had to load out for our trip, and it looked like I was going to miss it. If I missed a training op, I would be out of the Team. If I was convicted of assaulting a police officer, I would be out of the SEALs and the Navy.

Bob Schamberger, Scham, one of our senior chiefs, came and got me out. When I walked out of court, Scham was sitting on the steps of the courthouse with his ever-present cup of coffee in his hand.

"How's it going, mate?" he asked in that drawl of his.

"Bob," I answered, "not too good."

"Just get in Gracie there," and he indicated his blue Corvette.

Scham had paid to get me out of jail, and when he settled into the car, he told me that the Old Man had talked to the admiral and I was okay to go on the trip. I would do what I had to do, and we would deal with my situation when I got back.

CHAPTER 9

NOW HERE'S TO THE LAND DOWN UNDER

Just like the other SEAL teams, SEAL Team Six had an exchange program with our counterparts in other countries. This gave us the opportunity to learn new techniques firsthand and to teach what we knew to others. Overseas units such as the British SAS (Special Air Service) or GSG-9 would send guys to us for four or five months, and we would do the same with them.

For the exchange program, Purdue and I were sent to Australia to learn from their SAS contingency force. Not only did we get to spend time with their elite unit, we even got to see the Commonwealth Games.

The Aussies were really good people and they took care of us. Hospitality was something they all knew how to offer in a big, open way. They greeted us warmly and treated us like their own from the time they met us at the airport to the moment we left for home.

The beer in Australia was a lot better than in America, and

not just the taste either. If you ordered a "mini," you got a little glass of draft beer. A regular beer was a great big thing that would keep you drinking for a while. It was a very pleasant learning experience.

The local lingo, though, gave our hosts a chance to mess with the "Yanks" a bit. Not that it wasn't the same kind of thing we would have done if the roles were reversed. At the pub just outside the main gate at Campbell Barracks I had my first language lesson. One of the Aussies came up to me and said, "Hey, mate, you pissed?"

"No, I'm not pissed," I answered.

"No, mate," he went on, "yah pissed?"

"No, I'm not pissed at anybody."

"No, yah fuck'n idiot. Are you bloody drunk?"

"Oh," I said, the light finally going on. "Yeah, I am a little bit."

Slang can often be the most fun part of learning another language. For instance, "Do you want a root?" means "Do you want to meet a woman?" Then they call their girls "tarts." But those are more of the professional-type girls. The Aussies didn't tell me that bit, though. They just told me that was the way to speak with the local ladies. So I went up to a girl at the bar and started to talk with her. She asked if I was an American.

"Yes I am, tart," I answered.

She smacked me in the face and went off in a huff, while all the Aussie SAS guys fell all over themselves laughing. So I learned a lesson. And I soon learned that the term *Sheila* wouldn't get me slapped.

That wasn't the only time we had a run-in with the local culture. The unit was going diving, but Purdue and I had to wait for some gear to come in first. Then we were going to drive up to the base they staged from. The distance was only some fifty miles, so we figured there wouldn't be any problem. But we were about to be introduced to abo culture.

The Australian aborigines are usually very friendly, but they have certain places where they like to hang out and enjoy a cold drink and some company just among themselves. Apparently Purdue and I had found one when we stopped along the way. When we walked into the place, we were the only two white faces in view. Everyone just turned and looked at us. But as soon as we said something, they knew we were Americans. After that first tense moment, we had another good time, grabbed some lunch, and continued on our way.

Purdue was driving a bit over the speed limit, though, so we soon made the acquaintance of the local police. Fortunately, the cop who pulled us over used to be in the SAS himself. He was laughing at us as he came up to the car. "Okay, I know where you're going," he said. "Take your time, Yanks, and have a good one."

Like we said, it was a very friendly country.

The diving area was the Bass Straight off of Victoria near Melbourne in southern Australia. The water there was clear and clean. Normally when you dive you might be able to see as far as your hand. And that would be on a good day. In the Bass Straight, it was like diving in the best waters off Hawaii or the Florida Keys. You could see forever.

As good as the waters were, there were some problems. We weren't warned about the Great White sharks cruising around. Instead we were told that the sea lions were getting into their mating season. Apparently, as divers swam along with Draeger rebreathers, the local bull sea lions would come up from behind and smack into them, thinking they were a female, or maybe competition. If you were ever struck by one of these critters, you were supposed to turn around and smack him one right back. I guess that was to tell him you weren't in the mood.

The Australians swam a "W" compass course underwater with four legs and three turns. We were following the compass man when he got nailed by a sea lion. They didn't seem to hit very hard, more just brushed up against you. They didn't have any idea who or what we were; they just knew we were on their turf when they wanted to get down to some serious business. And we could understand their irritation.

At one point while we were in the Bass Straight, our SAS hosts took us to a pub right in the center of the town, next to this big Catholic church. While we were in the pub, a U.S. Navy guy from an American ship came up to Purdue and started giving him some grief. When I saw this going on I went up and jumped into the situation. I guess Purdue figured he could have handled it, so he started getting pissed (the American version) at me, and we started arguing.

The bartender looked us over, then asked, "Eh, what's going on here?"

I looked at the barkeep and said, "We'll have two Bundys and Cokes. If you'd like one, we'll buy you one."

Purdue just kind of looked at me and said, "Okay." That ended that argument, and soon we were hitting the drink pretty hard. By the time I got around to leaving, Purdue was nowhere to be found. This wouldn't normally be much of a problem, but he had the keys to the car. I couldn't find him anywhere in the bar so I started looking elsewhere. I walked around the streets a bit, but I was pretty well pissed (the Australian version) by this time. Coming up on some steps, I sat down and quickly fell asleep.

It was around three o'clock in the morning when I sat down on those wide steps. The sun was well up when I awoke the next day. Looking at my watch, I could see it was eight o'clock in the morning. It was people stepping over me that had woken me up. They were going into the big church on whose steps I had slept the night before.

I quickly hailed a cab and headed back to the sergeant's mess where we were staying. When I finally linked up with Purdue, I found out that he hadn't been in much better shape the night before. He had taken a cab back to the barracks thinking I had the car keys. When I told him he had the keys, he soon found them in one of his pockets. Another cab ride got us back to our car.

Up in Sidney, we had an experience with the SAS that would soon become very familiar to us. The Australians staged a mock terrorist takeover of a Quantas Airlines Boeing 747. "Passengers" had been gathered for the exercise, and they were a real cross section of people from all walks of life: government contractors, military personnel, and civilian families from eighteen years of age to sixty.

What these people were told was that they would have a free ride from Quantas to Perth, where the exercise would be conducted, and then a free return. The exercise would take about three days, and they would be involved with a simulated terrorist takedown of the aircraft. The idea was to give the SAS regiment some reasonably realistic field experience with a terrorist situation. Cooperation with the local police forces and negotiation teams would be part of the exercise.

The head pilot from Quantas was in charge of the 747. During a pre-exercise meeting, Purdue and I had a chance to meet and talk with him and the rest of the planners. It was decided to make my partner and me two of the aggressors. This would be my first chance to play terrorist, something I would do a lot later in Red Cell.

The two of us would do most of the talking for the terrorists who had seized the aircraft. To throw another twist into the plot, Purdue would play a "sleeper" agent and act like one of the passengers during the early parts of the scenario. Early in the exercise, Purdue would also be used to get the message across to the rest of the people about how things were going to be run.

During the initial actions, Purdue would react to the terrorists. When he jumped up to try and resist, a terrorist would nail him by punching him hard in the chest. That action should get everyone's attention real quick. When Purdue was knocked down, he would be taken to the rear of the aircraft, out of sight of the rest of the passengers.

Once there, Purdue could keep an eye on them without being seen. Good old Denny would be playing the part of the Dirty Yank and doing most of the speaking during the negotiations.

When we got on board the aircraft for the trip out, we were given specific seats at strategic points. All the other passengers were also given assigned seats, with married couples staying together. Once we had arrived at the planned execution point, the four of us who were active terrorists would put on balaclavas and pull out weapons. From that point on, we would be in charge.

As the Quantas plane started taxiing out along the runway, our balaclavas went on, weapons came out, and we started shouting out orders. "Freeze! Don't move! This is a hijack!"

We quickly took control of the aircraft. Purdue came charging up one of the aisles, and one of the Aussies elbowed him right in the chest as hard as he could. When Purdue was knocked back, the Aussie kneeled down on him and hit him a few times.

When my Teammate was "subdued," the rest of the terrorists dragged him into the back of the plane. Purdue was okay, but he was grabbing his chest and commenting on the realism of that Aussie's role-playing. I ignored him and started talking to the people on board the aircraft and the authorities who were trying to control the situation. Everyone knew that a Yank was now in charge.

We pulled the aircraft back up to the terminal but wouldn't let them bring out the gate to hook up to the door of the plane. Now negotiations started in earnest. When they gave us a phone, we put it away so that we could control when it would be used.

The pilot and crew in the cockpit played their roles and controlled their situation very well. I remained in the rear of the plane with the passengers, and the Aussie who was working the cockpit made sure everything up front went as planned. The hostage/skyjack scenario was planned to last twenty-four hours, so I would have my chance to interface with the pilot and crew.

The passengers didn't have the easiest time of it during the exercise, but we didn't abuse them either. About every six hours, we passed out orange juice and allowed them to use the sanitary facilities. As soon as we had taken control of the aircraft, we split up the married couples. Then we split up groups of people who knew each other and kept them separated. The other passengers who received special attention were the military people on board. Those we separated as well.

About halfway through the problem, I brought the captain out of the cockpit and moved him through the aircraft. Before we moved out, I spoke to him about what I was going to do with him. "Sir," I said, "when we get down to the bottom of the plane, I'm going to act like a different person. I'm going to manhandle you a bit if I feel it's necessary. I promise I won't damage you at all, but you are going to feel it."

"Okay," he said. "No problem, Denny."

The 747 has an upper and lower deck, the upper one being the lounge and flight deck where the cockpit is and the lower being where most of the passengers ride. A small staircase connects the two decks. When we got down to the lower deck, he started speaking to the people. He told them he was the captain and that everything would be all right—just generally doing his job and trying to reassure them. I felt the captain was talking too much, though, and I immediately grabbed him and knocked him around.

"Get going!" I growled. "And just say everything's okay. You don't have to say any more!"

Then I pushed him through the rest of the passenger area and we went back up to the flight deck. As we went up the stairs, the captain just kind of stared at me a moment. "Damn, mate!" he said, "you're right, you change one-eighty just like that!"

"Are you all right?" I asked, a little concerned.

He said everything was okay. Apparently I had just startled him. Back down on the passenger deck, I walked to the rear of the plane where some of the SAS guys were. One of the guys, Red, spoke up. "Hey, Denny," he said, "take a look at our army sergeant over there."

An Australian Army NCO who was one of the passengers had his shirt unbuttoned and his uniform open and sloppy. No air conditioning was running, and the plane was getting uncomfortable, but this guy was sweating a bit more than the conditions called for. It looked like the stress might be getting to him.

"You want me to mess with him?" I asked. It wasn't my show, so in general I just followed the leads I was given.

"Let's see if we can break him."

"Okay," I agreed.

Going up to where the soldier was sitting, I leaned over and said softly, "Hey, Sarge."

He looked up at me with these big worried eyes. He'd already seen us nail one of the "passengers" when Purdue got knocked down. Then he'd seen me rough up the pilot. The line between a fictional terrorist action and the appearance of reality was getting a bit thin.

"Button your fucking shirt!" I said softly but in a menacing tone. "I used to be in the military and I always took pride in my uniform. So button it up and make it neat."

Without taking his eyes off me, the NCO started buttoning up his shirt and straightening out his uniform. His hands trembled a bit as he worked the fasteners.

When I walked away, he gave me a look. I didn't see it, but my teammate did. Wearing a balaclava now and playing the part of another terrorist, Purdue went over to him. Whatever he said to the guy, it was enough to get a reaction out of him.

"If I had a chance," the sergeant said, "I'd break your arm."

Red immediately snatched the guy up out of his seat and moved him farther back in the plane. Shoving him into the cramped bathroom, we had that NCO spread-eagled and in a very uncomfortable position in seconds.

"You do that again and I will break your—," the sergeant started to say over his shoulder.

Wham! Red kicked the guy's knees out from under him and knocked him to the floor. Now he was leaning over the toilet, which isn't the nicest place at the best of times. But the sergeant was really starting to lose it now and we wanted to get him separated from everyone else.

It was a little past midnight and the temperature was starting to drop. A little fog was rolling in, so the situation outside was starting to get miserable. Opening up one of the emergency exits over a wing, we pushed the sergeant out of the plane and onto the wing.

Now our hardnosed army sergeant was stuck on the wing for the rest of the exercise. There wasn't any way off. The distance was much too great to jump, especially onto a hard runway surface. The takedown of the plane wasn't scheduled for at least four hours. So our hotheaded NCO could look forward to a cooling-off period out where he couldn't do any damage to us.

The sergeant just walked up and down the wing, peering over the side and trying to figure a way down. The authorities who were observing the situation had no idea what we were trying to do. All they could do was watch and report that they had a guy in uniform on the wing walking about and looking over the edge. There wasn't any way for them to get a ladder up to this guy without us being able to see them. So he spent a long, cold time on the wing of the airplane.

When the exercise started, we began our negotiations with the people on the ground almost right away. There was one guy on the plane, a sixty-year-old man, who was really not having a very good time of it. I suggested to Red that we get rid of this guy as soon as we could. He agreed and decided to negotiate a trade of the old man and a young woman for some food for ourselves.

The negotiators wanted to know how the passengers were doing. We told them everything was fine, and we let the captain speak to the negotiators to help reassure them. So the negotiators agreed to send out a tray of food in exchange for two of the hostages. The food was going to be brought out by a medic. What they wanted was permission to bring the walkway out to reach the aircraft door.

We agreed to this with some conditions. We wanted to see the walkway come out first with no one on it. We could watch this whole procedure through the windows of the plane. Then we told them that the medical guy could come out but that he had better be a medic and not someone pretending to be one. If we found a badge or a weapon on the guy coming out, we would kill somebody and it would be on their heads.

The walkway came out and we watched the situation carefully. Then a man in a medical uniform came along the walkway pushing a serving cart. Opening the door, we told the guy to wheel the cart a bit closer and to take the cover off it. There wasn't anyone trying to hide under the cart, and the only things in sight on it were food packages and containers.

Now there was the medic to deal with. We told him to turn around with his back to the plane and get down on his hands and knees. Now Red told me to frisk the guy to see if he was carrying anything.

Walking off the plane and onto the walkway, I patted down the medic. He was a big guy, something like six foot four and built like a rock. When I went up to him, I kicked his hands out from under him and he hit the ground hard, smacking his face on the walkway floor. If this guy got pissed enough, he could throw me through the wall.

Jumping on the guy's back to give me a head start if he

decided to get frisky, I continued with my role. I was silently thankful he didn't get up and clean my clock. There wasn't a weapon on him, but buried in his pants, I found a wallet with a badge in it. "Hey, we got a badge here!" I shouted.

In spite of the badge situation, we let the "medic" take the girl and the old man. Later, during the debriefing, I spoke to the "medic" and asked him if he was all right.

"Yeah. My nose is sore is all."

"I'm really sorry about that."

"Naw, that's all right," he cut me off. "I just never had that happen."

"Well," I asked him, "why did you have the badge on you?"

"I just forgot to take it out of my pants is all."

So that was the lesson he learned on the exercise. All the medic had been tasked to do was deliver the food and try to get a look inside the plane. He was to make note of the number of terrorists on board, how we were dispersed, and what we were armed with. The badge had simply been an oversight. He had screwed up and realized it.

The Australian Team came in and did a takedown on the plane. All our weapons were loaded with blanks, but they did their job so well we didn't have much of a chance to use them. The passengers were saved and the plane recaptured.

The terrorists were forced to sit down up front across from one of the big aisles leading to the door. The passengers walked by us on their way out, and one of them really let her feelings be known. As this girl walked by me, her face screwed up real tight. Then she spat on me and shouted, "You're a fucking bastard!"

"Hey, I'm really a nice guy," I protested.

But she wasn't having any part of my explanations. Red and the rest of his team were all cracking up and making their own comments on the situation. They could get away with it. They had made me act the prick during the whole exercise, and that girl wasn't the only passenger who didn't exactly look at me with love in her eyes. "I hope I don't run into any of these people on liberty," I thought.

With the situation over, it was time for the debriefing and analysis. Quantas treated us really well, taking us to a big hotel and giving us several adjoining rooms, including a few for us to crash in. Several of the tubs were filled with ice and beer, so it was obviously time to relax.

The head pilot from the plane showed up and made certain he had a chance to speak to me directly. "If they ever give an Oscar for playing a terrorist, mate," the captain said, "you damned well deserve one."

When it finally came time for Purdue and me to leave Australia and return to the States, it was on board a Quantas flight. We had coach tickets, but the crew moved us up to business class. Then the stewardess gave us a bottle of champagne each. We asked her what this was for, and she said that we would be asked upstairs after the takeoff.

Sure enough, after takeoff she took us up to the first class lounge and sat us down with drinks in our hands. Then the captain came off the flight deck. It was the captain from our terrorist scenario. And he sat down and started shooting the shit with us. Of course, that was after he stated emphatically that we weren't going to be taking that particular plane over. So for the rest of the flight to San Francisco, we went first class.

When we returned to Six, we gave a full report on everything we had done and what we had learned while in Australia. Reports like these made sure that all the men in the command had the opportunity to learn from each other's experiences.

CHAPTER 10

GEAR, GUNS, AND A LOT OF TRAINING

On our arrival back, the Old Man told me I had to deal with my legal problems. The DUI (driving under the influence) charge was the one I had to beat. Otherwise the Skipper would have to hold a Captain's Mast on me, kind of a limited Navy trial, and have more punishment come down on me than I was already facing. If things came to a formal Captain's Mast, I would certainly have to leave Team Six, probably the Teams as a whole, and maybe even the Navy. But I hadn't been left out in the cold. They saw to it that I had a good lawyer.

When I was in front of the judge, he looked at me and then looked at the three police officers that had to "subdue" me for the arrest. I had already admitted to having a few small beers that night and referring to the three officers by some much less than complimentary names. I even admitted to assaulting the officers, but only in my own defense after being struck.

The judge noticed that one cop was my size, one was smaller, and one was much larger. "The three of you couldn't handle that man when you say he was intoxicated?" the judge said. "As big as you men are? Charges dropped." But then he pointed at me and continued, "And you, Mr. Chalker. You owe this city fifteen hundred dollars, five hundred apiece for assaulting my officers. And your license to drive is suspended for ninety days. Case dismissed."

Yeah! I'd been saved, and I was still in the Teams. I didn't have all the money I needed to pay my fines, but Scham always seemed to have a couple of paychecks in his wallet. He loaned me the money and I was able to return to duty without any trouble. For several months after that, I would ride a bike to the base. The cops were watching for me, but they never found anything they could stop me for.

Marcinko had been tasked with putting together a maritime counterterrorist force, and he had been given a very short time to accomplish it. He didn't always have time to go through the niceties of the chain of command to get the job done, but he was able to get some money.

We were a "rich" Team. To accomplish our mission, we were getting state-of-the-art equipment, and we were receiving it in large amounts. Some animosity built up over that, but we needed the gear to get the job done.

In fact, we had so much equipment it started to turn into a problem. The boats and trailers parked in the compound made the place look like some kind of marina. Big steel Conex boxes took up most of the rest of the available open space.

The obvious excess of riches is part of what caused the friction between ourselves and the other Teams, which were still suffering under the post-Vietnam cutbacks. The military force of the United States had been severely reduced in size and effectiveness after Vietnam, with the Special Warfare Forces suffering the most. There was no funding for schooling, new equipment, and certainly not research and development. The Army Special Forces were reduced in size, the Army Rangers had gone away completely, and the SEAL Teams had taken bad cuts in their numbers.

With the creation of Dick's new command, funding became available from sources the regular Teams couldn't tap into. The allotment brought SEAL Team Six up and on line while SEAL Teams One and Two were still trying to work with weapons that had been almost worn out during combat in Vietnam. With our special mission and material requirements, the standard military guns and gear of just a decade ago were too outdated to do the job for us.

Our mission was secret and we couldn't talk about what we did, so all our Teammates in the other units could see was a handful of SEALs who could let their hair grow and had more equipment than a Team three times their size. But we all still had the same basic job.

Everyone in Six had been selected in part because of the different specialty skills each man brought with him. Each of us would teach what we could to the others. For example, the guys who ran Air Ops were all highly qualified parachutists. Several of them held different free-fall records that were still on the books. These were the men who taught us how to pack chutes, operate the equipment, and reach a high level of competency much faster than we otherwise could have.

Even with our top-of-the-line instructors, we had to push hard to reach the level of competency we needed. While at Eglin Air Force Base in Florida, we learned how to jump out of an aircraft and free-fall for thousands of feet before opening our chutes. This was new for me. All of us were jump qualified, but only a handful of guys in the Team were skydivers and free-fall qualified. During my first jumps, I mostly turned somersaults, seeing sky, earth, sky, earth as I tumbled through the air. It took about ten jumps before I became proficient enough to leave the aircraft in a stable position. But others in the Team had a much harder time than I did.

During one of our early free-fall jumps, Schamberger had to cutaway his main canopy. If your main canopy doesn't open, you have to pull a cutaway pillow, a small padded grip, that releases the main from your harness before you open your reserve chute. That keeps your last chance of staying alive from getting tangled in with your malfunctioning main. When Scham cut away his main and pulled his reserve, though, nothing happened. There's not a lot you can do in this situation. As far as Bob was concerned, it was the end of his life. But like any good SEAL or frogman, he was going to make death work to get him.

Falling through the sky, Bob followed the old frog rule: If you get in trouble, head for water. There was a river nearby, and Bob started to track for it. You can turn your body and control your direction of fall when skydiving. Properly done, you can track across a good distance, depending on how high you are when you start out. Bob figured if he hit the water, it would at least be a little better than auguring into the ground.

By turning toward the river, Bob changed the way the air was flowing over him. The slipstream grabbed the long tape that was to have pulled out his reserve chute and drew the canopy from the pack. Miracle of miracles, the malfunctioning chute opened up. With a good reserve over his head, Bob finished the job okay.

Later I had my first malfunction, and that's a heart-stopping moment. My reserve opened okay and everything was fine. But in that first moment, all I thought was "Here we go!"

Pooster had it a little different. In his first seven jumps, he had five malfunctions and had to cutaway on every one. Despite that he stuck out the training and became very good at jumping. Of course, that was after he had a refresher course in how to pack his main chute.

There was a strict level of discipline at Six, though an outside observer might not have been able to see it at first glance. We were relaxed in our military protocols for the same reason we had longer hair than most. It would be a dead giveaway if you saluted someone during an operation who was supposed to be a civilian just like you. Using "sir" could get you noticed fast too. We all knew who our officers were, and we respected them properly. We just called them by their first names.

There were standards we all had to meet, and we were still a military unit. Faydog screwed up once on some minor liberty incident and Duke came down on him: no liberty for thirty days. This wasn't much of a punishment as far as military discipline goes, except that there wasn't anywhere to live in the compound.

Our buildings were packed. We mustered the Team in the same room that held our weight-lifting equipment. Assault Group One was at one end of the building and Two was at the other end. Between us was the weight room. At the other building was the quarterdeck that held our one admin desk. Behind the quarterdeck was the Skipper's desk and then the XO's desk. The communications gear filled up most of the rest of the room. The only other space available was the supply room where we kept all our general equipment, which would be drawn for specific operations. We didn't even have our own armory to store our weapons. We kept them in cases in the SEAL Team Two armory.

The restriction situation with Faydog turned into a funny one. Coming into work one day, I saw a tent on top of one of the Conex boxes. Faydog had set up housekeeping in this little pup tent, and that's where he lived for thirty days. We all got kind of a kick out of that.

Harassment among ourselves never ceased at Six. We would play jokes on each other whenever we could. One time when I was getting a ride back with one of the other squads, they waited until we were just half a mile or so from the hotel before they kicked me out the opened door of the truck. And they did this without the benefit of slowing down first.

And we competed with each other on a regular basis. Sometimes things deteriorated into a brawl, with two or more squads rolling around wrestling on the grass. But no one got hurt, and the animosity was always light.

Our squad had a regular "choir practice," where we would gather at one of the guy's houses and start barhopping. One of the guys was a real pain about getting ready to go out. When he was finally perfect, we could move on to our next Teammate's house and pick him up. Nights like this, most of the public places were closed or close to it by the time we got there.

But the private clubs were open much later. The Fraternal Order of UDT/SEALs had their own place, and we often dropped in there. Some of the animosity between us and the regular Teams came out at the FO bar, but for the most part it wasn't too serious.

The FO bar was managed by Bob Gallagher, known at SEAL Team Two as the Eagle. He had built up quite a reputation as a hard operator in Vietnam and was a neat guy to talk to. But Bob was bald as an eagle, and our long hair sometimes rubbed him the wrong way.

There was one night when the White Rhino from our Team really got into it with Gallagher. This guy was short and stocky and looked like a rhino, and he was as strong as one as well. He wasn't the fastest runner in the outfit, but put a load on his back and he would out-hump you every time.

For some reason, Rhino started throwing his empty beer cans at the guy who was checking IDs at the door. Something must have just bothered him because he kept chucking these empty cans. Finally the guy had enough and Rhino was asked to leave. One thing led to another, and before long Gallagher and the Rhino were out in the parking lot squaring off.

The White Rhino told Gallagher to take his best shot, which

he did. The blow rocked the Rhino for a moment, then he came back and said, "Nice shot." They ended up rolling around together for a few minutes until we finally broke it up.

About three days later I was back at the FO talking to Bob.

"You know that friend of yours from a few days ago?" Bob asked me.

"Yeah," I answered, wondering what was up.

"Well, I'm getting too old for this shit," he said, reaching into his pocket. "That's why I'm carrying this now." And he pulled out a blackjack.

There wasn't another fight between the Eagle and the White Rhino that I remember. And maybe that was for the best.

Sometimes we had Team get-togethers, but we usually went out with our squads. There was this one place, the Casino, where we regularly met as a Team. The Skipper hosted a party there when Purdue and I were frocked for a promotion to E-5. There was a drink of the month for our groups, and that month it was schnapps. So the Skipper put down these drinks in front of Purdue and me, we belted them back, and he had the last laugh on us when it turned out to be water.

A real tightness developed in the unit from all this playing hard together, and we felt we had earned it. But like SEAL Teams One and Two, there would never be another time like this in Six. SEAL plankowners from that era told me what it had been like for them, and the same thing held true for us. Those early years, building something new, became the most amazing experience of our careers.

The heavy, high-speed training schedule also had a price. The Skipper had told us we would follow the rule: Train as you fight, and fight as you train. This meant live weapons on hard courses with fast-moving situations. Safety was always of paramount importance. We did a lot of dangerous things, and we always tried to stack the deck in our favor. But there were accidents and costs.

During one of our training evolutions, we were doing room entries down at Eglin Air Base. A wooden framework had been built where we could put up cloth walls and change the setup quickly and easily. For a room entry, you are right up behind the man in front of you, weapons locked and loaded. With the go signal, you move fast and hard. It's the only way to get the job done, clearing a room of bad guys while keeping any hostages safe.

There wasn't any body armor available then. It wasn't that we couldn't get any, it was just that no one made any we could climb in. During that training evolution it had rained, which it so often does in Florida, and the ground was wet around our cheesecloth building. On one room entry, Lee Chuey was the first man through the door and his shooting partner was right behind him to back him up. But Lee slipped on the mud and fell backward, hitting his partner. His partner had made the mistake of leaving his finger on the trigger of his weapon. The gun discharged, striking Lee in the back.

Our corpsmen were right there with us, and they immediately began treating Lee. When Scham said we needed a backboard, Doc Holliday and I just ran into one of the few plywood walls. Smashing down the wall and ripping a board free, we had our backboard. Lee was in the truck and on his way to the hospital as quickly as we could get him on his way.

In spite of herculean efforts on the part of the medical staff and Lee himself, we lost him a few days later. That loss hit the Skipper hard, partly because SEAL Team Six lost two men that day. Lee's partner had made a simple mistake, but it couldn't be allowed to happen again. He was shipped out of the Team within a day, and he left the SEALs as well and went back to the Navy to finish out his hitch. And that too made us a little less.

We learned a hard lesson that day, but we had to get up and continue with the mission. Safety procedures were tightened as much as they could be. But we still had to train live, the way we were going to fight. Constant trigger control was the only way we could conduct these operations and still come out intact on the other side.

Our battery of weapons increased constantly at Six as we adopted new ones and disposed of those that didn't work for us. Our accuracy standards were high. After our first practices with pistols, we started shooting at smaller and smaller targets. Finally we were using vertically oriented three-by-five-inch cards taped to a standard silhouette, one at the head and one at the chest, as our targets. The cards covered what we considered the most vital spots, the spinal column and central brain, for a one-shot stop. All your rounds had to hit the cards or they weren't considered hits.

There were also standards for drawing your sidearm from the holster. You had seconds to pull your weapon, aim, and punch out two rounds, what was called a "double-tap." And both rounds had to hit either the chest card or the head card. You had more or less time to draw and shoot depending on distance. From the close (seven-yard) line, you had three seconds from "Go" to "Cease fire!"

For our first set of shooting standards, we used the Practical Pistol Competition (PPC) rules. These were soon modified to fit our shooting situations. But on the PPC scale, we all had to shoot to at least the "expert" level.

The changes we made to the standards centered on accelerated pairs, firing two rounds very quickly and accurately. Double-tapping the trigger was the best way to be sure of immobilizing a target with a pistol-caliber weapon. It was two rounds fired on the same sight picture as fast as you could pull the trigger.

This standard was developed when we were using the Smith & Wesson revolvers. We started out with the heavy-barreled four-inch Model 66, a .357 magnum revolver made entirely of stainless steel. The revolvers would drain water fast if we came in on a swim, and they fired a powerful slug. Since we were going against terrorists, we didn't have to follow the Geneva and Hague Conventions in terms of ammunition. That meant we could fire the most effective ammunition available. So our revolvers were loaded with jacketed hollowpoints that would expand on impact.

Soon we switched to the Smith & Wesson Model 686 revolver, also stainless steel but slightly larger than the Model 66 and with a heavier barrel. The Model 686 had been developed for the demands of competitive shooters and police who were doing the same kinds of shooting we were.

Back in Echo Platoon, we had used accurized M1911A1 .45 automatics as our mission handguns. These were very accurate versions of the same pistol that had been used by the U.S. government since before World War I. The M1911A1 put out a big fat bullet that tended to stop a target fast. But the military was moving away from the .45 automatic, and ammunition started getting hard for us to locate. Also, the weapons would rust up with all the exposure we gave them to saltwater. When we moved over to Six, the .45 wasn't even considered.

The M1911A1 loaded from a magazine, which was a much faster system than the six-round cylinder on our revolvers. To speed up our reloading, we used speedloaders that held six rounds lined up to go quickly into the weapons. We looked like a bunch of banditos when we were geared up for ship boarding, with our revolvers and twelve or so speedloaders in pockets around our belts, plus a spare revolver strapped on someplace else as a backup.

We used the pistols as our primary weapons at the start because our shoulder weapons hadn't arrived yet. Our first submachine gun was the MAC M10 Ingram, a short, stubby weapon with a very short sliding stock that fired at a very high cyclic rate. But the M10s were too short to be practical as room entry weapons. We had picked them because of their size, and the fact that a number of terrorist groups were using them. If they were good enough for the bad guys, we thought, they should be good enough for us. They weren't.

Besides being too short and cycling too fast for accurate fire, the M10s couldn't take the environment we operated in. Coming up from the water, our M10s often jammed from sand or dirt. We had suppressors available for some of our M10s, but they didn't help in the accuracy or shoulder-firing of the little weapon.

The Heckler and Koch (H&K) MP5 family of submachine guns became our weapons of choice when they started arriving in the early 1980s. You could start with the MP5 in the high or low ready position, with the gun held up or down, and get it to your shoulder fast. Since the MP5 fired from the closed-bolt position, it was very accurate and you could keep all your rounds on target.

We had different kinds of slings and ways of holding the weapon for different situations. If you were wearing a gas mask, you could push the MP5 out against the sling, making a tension arrangement that increased the accuracy of your fire. If there wasn't a mask in the way, you could pull the MP5 tightly against your shoulder and fire it like a rifle instead of holding the trigger down and putting out rounds on full automatic.

With the MP5 set on full automatic fire, we trained our trigger control until we could fire and release the trigger for just one shot. If the situation got bad enough, all you had to do was hold the trigger back for the weapon to fire its ammunition at a cyclic rate of eight hundred rounds per minute.

Later on, after our first combat operations, I designed my own sling to carry all my shoulder-fired weapons. I had problems with all the different issue slings we used in combat and training. They could pull a gas mask off, get in the way when you were going through a small space, and not keep the weapon handy enough if you had to drop it to have your hands free.

Working on a chest harness idea, I developed a sling that

held the weapon on your chest with a single quick-release hook. The sling strapped on like a harness, and you could adjust where you wanted the weapon to hang. If you needed to dump the weapon, pulling the release let it go immediately. Reattaching it was almost as fast.

When I finally retired from the Navy, I patented my sling and use it in my training today. Metro Tactical Products, a company I have with my partners, Doug and Amy Kingery and Tim McGee, markets the sling commercially. Doug and Tim are both former SWAT officers I met while in California. Our sling was even used by Arnold Schwarzenegger in the film *The End of Days*.

With the adoption of the MP5 as our shoulder weapon, we switched sidearms so that we could use the same ammunition for both. The military was testing the Beretta Model 92 for possible adoption. We also picked up the weapon and used it for a number of years. The final model adopted, the Beretta Model 92-F, came about in part from our suggested modifications. In fact the *F* in the designation stands for a Teammate, Chuck Fellers.

There were some problems with the Beretta during our training: the slides cracked, and a couple of SEALs were slightly injured. The military and Beretta addressed the problem, and now the pistol works fine for them. Six didn't want any more difficulties, though, and switched to the SIG Model P226. Now all the SEAL Teams use that handgun as well as the MP5s.

We had a variety of different MP5 models to choose from according to the mission and our own tastes. Some of the guys liked the fixed stock standard model, while others, myself included, preferred the folding stock version. My favorite MP5 model was the very short K model. The K model was really little more than a machine pistol, it was so short. And that version had no stock. Later a folding stock was made for the MP5K and I used that version a great deal.

As the lead climber, I liked the compact size of the K model

MP5. When what became known as the PDW (personal defense weapon) stock arrived for the MP5K, I found it very accurate but still compact enough for my climbing. The last style of MP5 we had was called the SD model, with an integral suppressor. Some of the guys really liked the suppressed MP5 for its quiet operation. But the barrel and suppressor combination slowed the bullet to below the speed of sound and it lost a lot of its punch on delivery.

We also had carbine versions of the M16A1 for shoulder weapons early on at Six. But with our emphasis on shipboard operations, the danger of ricochets from the 5.56mm bullet was considered too great. The 9mm MP5s were our main shipboard assault weapons. For ground operations, the M16A1 carbine, what we still called the CAR 15, was our preferred weapon. Later, the M4 carbine was adopted by all the Special Operations units, and we got a lot of use out of that weapon.

Shotguns were used for room clearing and entries. The breachers—the men who opened the doors—packed 12-gauge pump action Remington 870s. These weapons could be used to blow out a lock or the hinge points of a door to open it for assault. The shotguns had short barrels, sometimes only fourteen inches long, and pistol grips taken from Remington Police folding shotgun stocks.

Before we used shotgun breaching to open doors, explosive breaching was our primary means of entry. A breaching charge involved putting standard detcord on a board covered with epifoam (a kind of Styrofoam) and then coating it with grease. The grease would hold the charge to a door, and the detcord would have enough explosive power to cut through most doors, both wood and light metal. The blast would create a big fireball and knock a hole though the door, if it didn't take it off the hinges. When the blast went off, in we would go.

Of course, it was best to wait until *after* the blasts.

During one simultaneous entry exercise, the countdown was

given and the charges fired. Only one charge didn't go off. Johnny Johnson, who was behind the breacher, thought both charges had fired and stood up just as the second charge went off. The blast stunned him into paralysis. The rest of the squad went around him and completed the exercise. When we took a look at Johnny a moment later, he was still just standing there, swaying a little. The blast had blown all his hair back, and the black grease covered everything from the top of his head to the middle of his chest.

Johnny looked just like a parody of the old Buckwheat character. That is to say, with his face black, his hair fuzzed and greased, he really didn't look too good. When we asked him how he was, all he could say was "Fuck!" The exercise was suspended for a moment while we took care of our Teammate—and stopped laughing so hard.

CHAPTER 11

A MOVE, SOME BOATS, AND SOME TIME IN THE WATER

Our training facilities grew in complexity and sophistication. Ranges were developed, room clearing and shooting facilities improved, and finally, after a year or so at Little Creek, our own headquarters were ready, and we left the little compound behind SEAL Team Two.

When we finally moved out of the old barracks to the new buildings about thirty miles away, none of us actually wanted a plank from any of those buildings. But we did take something with us from that site. There used to be a stump behind the buildings at our old compound that Schamberger would take you to when he wanted to talk to you privately. "Gather round the stump," he would say, and then he'd talk to you with one foot resting on that chunk of wood. When the command moved, we dug that stump up and took it with us. It finally ended up with a plaque on it that listed all the plankowners of SEAL Team Six.

By this time our heavy training schedule was taking a toll on our equipment. The Boston Whalers we were using had double hulls made of fiberglass. The fill between the hulls was Styrofoam. The boats were just about unsinkable, and we used them hard. The squad coxswains maintained their assigned boats, and they were rinsed out after every operation or exercise.

One time when the hulls were being hosed out, the guys noticed little white balls of Styrofoam coming out the drain hole along with the water. This was more than a little odd, so the hulls were checked for internal damage. Nothing showed much on the outside inspection of the boats, but X rays of the hull showed a big problem inside.

The constant pounding our Whalers took during exercises had shattered the Styrofoam filling. No longer a solid mass, the filler was turning into separate little beads of material, which were leaking out of the hulls. Some of the boats were little more than two fiberglass shells with nothing but air between them.

We had given the boats a rough go of it, but not any more of a rough time than we took ourselves when we operated in them. On the West Coast in Echo Platoon, we had padded the inside of the whole boat, especially the bow. The guys at Six had watched us pad up our boats back when we first started working in them. They started by giving us a hard time, laughing at what we were doing. After a few underways, they found out why. Ronnie Newhou was the one who really learned the hard way when he fell and broke his nose against the side of the boat during training. So it wasn't very long before all our boats were padded.

We had a rough time in our Boston Whalers, but that just came with the job. When they started cracking up, we had to move on to bigger and faster boats. The Whalers with their outboard engines just weren't up to going some fifty miles or more out to sea and crashing through the big waves.

We worked with the makers of a lot of our equipment to get exactly what we wanted. The folks who made the Boston

Whalers told us the boats could withstand what we wanted them to, but we had learned differently. They had also told us you couldn't flip their boat; they were wrong.

In Florida during a training exercise, we hit some heavy seas coming away from the shore. We had put seats in the boats for long transits, with heavy aviator-type harnesses to hold us in. To speed up the harness release, we had put golf balls on the latches. Now you could hit a latch quickly with either hand in very wet conditions and get out of the seat with all your gear on. The seats also had shock absorbers to suck up some of the beating.

On this exercise, I was up front on the right side. Pooster was behind me and Doc Holliday was on the other side. Rhino was to the rear and Gearhart was the coxswain. We hit that wave and went straight up. When we came straight back down, the stern went several feet under water. Looking behind me, all I could see of some of my Teammates were lips sticking up from the water, sucking air like a bunch of goldfish.

The boat didn't flip all the way over, and the bow did crash back down. Now we had a hull full of water to deal with. And when you stuck those outboard motors of ours under water like that, they didn't like it very much. So the motor crapped out on us. We ended up towing a lot of boats after incidents like that.

Before we put those modified seats in the Whalers, we had run them on ops without any way to secure ourselves into the boat. The coxswain and his assistant were the only two on the craft who had seats. Even with the seats, the coxswains did a lot of their work standing up so that their legs could absorb some of the shock of hitting the waves.

Coming back in on one exercise, I was acting as the assistant coxswain on our boat. We had been following a work boat, staying in its lee, with the rest of our squad having an easy ride on the bigger boat.

Senator turned from his coxswain's position and told me the bulbs on the gas tanks had to be pumped to keep the outboards running. I had gone to the stern of the boat to work the tanks when the work boat we were following suddenly turned. To keep his position behind the work boat, Senator also made a hard left turn. Oil on the deck made it slippery. The sudden turn caught me by surprise and I slid across the deck, hit the low gunwale, and flipped out of the boat.

We were about twenty miles out to sea at the time. The guys on the fantail of the work boat were waving at Senator, trying to get him to turn around. He just waved back and the boats kept getting farther and farther away from me. "Holy shit," I thought to myself, "I'm lost now." And I started out on a long swim for my life.

Finally Senator turned around and saw I wasn't there. Spinning his boat around, he started back looking for me. The work boat would have turned around eventually, but I was very glad to see that Whaler coming back for me.

Now that they could see I was going to be all right, the guys on the work boat started laughing at the situation. When I slid across and hit the gunwale, I did a really great somersault before hitting the water. This was, of course, considered hilarious by all my Teammates who had witnessed it.

Not all of our adventures with the Whalers took place on the water. Sometimes we had great fun with them just getting to the launch site for an exercise. Once, the boat wasn't even going into the water when the trouble came up.

One of the coxswains was hauling a boat to the marina in Virginia Beach to get it looked at. As he was driving the truck down Shore Drive, he looked to his left and saw the boat passing him. The trailer had come unhooked from the truck, and none of the safety chains were attached. Rolling on down the road, the trailer finally nosed into the median and came to a stop. It didn't flip or anything, just stopped in the grass. That could have been a much bigger problem than it turned out to be. And it gave us some great ammunition for the harassment of that driver. We had been following him and saw the boat trailer unhitch from the truck. There wasn't anything we could do but watch it roll on its way.

The trailers weren't the only way we transported our boats. We experimented with using helos to carry the boats to within range of a target and then release them into the water.

On one exercise Cheeks, Scham, Rhino, Doc Holliday, Pooster, and I were in our Whaler hanging from the helo by a single-point hook. I was wearing my wet suit with a UDT life jacket over it, Scham had his Gore-Tex jacket on over his UDT, and Rhino was manning the coxswain's position. There weren't seats for us to be secured in the boat, and in hindsight that was a mistake.

Once the helo picked us up, the boat began spinning underneath the bird. As the helicopter flew, we began spinning faster and faster like a top. As the G-forces built up, we began leaving the boat.

Scham was the first one to hit the side of the boat and go over into the water, not a great distance below us. Then Cheeks and Pooster followed. I was hanging onto the rail, and Doc Holliday was doing the same thing on the other side. As the spin increased, the rail finally broke off the gunwale and I went into the drink.

When I hit the water some fifty feet down, I still had that section of railing in my hands. "Well, this isn't great," I thought to myself. Looking up, I could see that Doc Holliday and the Rhino were still in the boat. The Rhino was hanging onto the wheel so hard he bent it. The crew in the helo finally saw what was going on and they started down to the water.

All of us in the water started swimming away from the boat so that it didn't come down on top of us. When we gathered up in the water, I could see that Scham wasn't with us but was struggling a short distance away.

When Scham had inflated his life jacket after hitting the

water, it pulled his Gore-Tex jacket tight around his throat. The pressure on his throat was so great that he was choking and in danger of blacking out completely. He couldn't reach either the release valve or the oral tube to his life jacket, and the Gore-Tex was pulled so tight he couldn't get the zipper down.

When we swam over to Scham, he was still struggling with the jacket and called out, "Stab me! Stab me!"

"I'll stab him!" one of the guys said, and he pulled out his K-Bar knife like he was going to plunge it into Scham's chest.

"No man! No! No!" we called out.

This guy looked a little too enthused about using his knife. But instead of stabbing down with it, he thrust the K-Bar into the jacket from the side, missing Scham and puncturing the vest. That was a near thing. For a while there, it looked like Scham's head was going to come off like a pimple.

With the immediate danger over, we swam there in the water thinking this technique wasn't the best one we had ever used. Later we used a dual anchor point on the lifting harness and that kept the boat from spinning.

Hanging the boats from helicopters was always a scary evolution when we were starting out. And it really got hairy when we started doing it at night.

Signals at night always caused us the most worry. Hanging underneath a helicopter in an open boat at an unknown altitude, you wanted to be sure the helo released you only when you were ready. We traveled in the bird and roped down to the boat when we approached our release point. The helo was supposed to be only about a hundred feet in the air when we went over the side and down to the boat.

Shining a single red light up at the bird was our signal to drop the boat. As the evolution continued, the signal changed a bit, and now a single red light meant we were ready to be lowered down to drop altitude. Several red flashes meant drop the boat.

On this exercise, we roped down to the boat and had troubles right away. Rhino was the first man down the rope, and he bounced off the engine cover, almost missing the boat entirely. The way the helo was moving, the slipstream had pulled the rope back to the stern of the boat. He recovered and clambered into the boat without any further trouble. Even though it was dark, we could see that we were much higher than planned. Instead of roping down at a hundred feet, we must have been five hundred feet or more in the air.

Thank god Rhino had the foresight to get into the center of the boat and anchor the line for the rest of us. Now we could get into the boat without much trouble. Once we were all secured, it was time to give the signal that we were all on board. All of us were thinking: "Oh God, please don't drop us. We're at five hundred feet!"

Crunching up a little bit, we gave the signal. There was a certain amount of relief when the helicopter started descending. Once we were good, we gave the flashing signal and they let us drop.

I don't care if you're only at ten feet, that is a solid drop down to the water. The hull smacks down hard like you're hitting cement. In spite of our level of fitness, absorbing that much shock takes a toll on your body. But we could heal; what we couldn't see was what the abuse was doing to the boats.

It was that dribbling Styrofoam that meant the end of the Boston Whalers for us.

The waters off of Louisiana, south of New Orleans, were a great area for some of our training exercises. The Gulf waters had a number of oil drilling platforms that we could work on, developing methods to attack them in case of a terrorist seizure.

On our first trip to Louisiana, we were flown down and then had to tow our boats to the exercise site behind our trucks. South of New Orleans, heading down the peninsula that jutted out into the Gulf waters, we had to pass through a number of smaller parishes and towns, and we stopped in this little town called Golden Meadow to get some breakfast. Sitting there in the restaurant was this big Cajun chief of police, just watching us. We had just ordered when he got up and walked over to our table.

"What're you boys doin'?" he asked us in a thick southern drawl.

"We just ordered some breakfast," one of the guys said. "We're going to sit here and eat."

"Not in this town," he said. "And you better go the speed limit gettin' out. See that man sittin' over there?" He pointed to another local sitting at a different table. "That's the judge and the mayor. He's my brother."

It wasn't like you had to drop a house on us. We got the hint and left.

It seemed we always had these little hassles with the locals when we operated in the deep South. They had their own customs and way of doing things that outsiders often didn't understand. With our long hair and high-speed boats, that chief probably thought we were drug runners, or maybe worse, customs agents. We were operating on their territory and they wanted us to pass through peacefully and not stop on our way.

Eventually we made it to the Governor's Resort where we would be staying. The Mississippi River was right across the street, with regular river traffic moving along it. We did get some attention from the work boats as they traveled the river. You could see the crews out with binoculars, watching us as we made our boats ready for operation.

We didn't like the attention, but there was little we could do about it. Down in that neck of the woods, guys like us weren't a daily sight.

The area got more and more built up as we worked there over the years. As more people came in, we moved farther south for our exercises. Finally we reached the end of the peninsula at Grand Isle. By then we had become familiar enough that no one thought much about us. Just those Yankees with their boats again.

Once, while working on one of the oil rigs out in the Gulf, we had climbed up into the girders and were taking a break when one of the guys suggested we try some high diving from the platform. We were about fifty feet above the water and the platform itself was about eighty feet up. Back when I was in the Army in North Carolina, I had done some cliff diving and knew my limitations. I wasn't about to jump from the eighty-foot platform, but fifty feet was okay.

Some of the guys with us had been competition divers back in school. They put on a pretty good show of flips, somersaults, and whatever. I was doing some diving myself, arcing out over the water rather than just jumping feet first. Doc Holliday didn't even want to jump into the water from that height. But that was okay, and the rest of us just continued with what we were doing.

Then one of the divers tried a one-and-a-half flip and didn't make it. We could see his eyeballs open wide as he realized he wasn't going to complete that last flip and smacked into the water on his back.

Doc Holliday, our corpsman, the guy who didn't even want to jump into the water, didn't show a moment's hesitation as he launched himself from the platform. Every second counted if our Teammate was injured, and Doc just took the fastest way down.

I dived in right behind Doc, and we got to our Teammate quickly. The guy was coughing up blood but kept saying he was okay. He had struck the water so hard that he'd bruised himself internally and was bleeding from his lungs.

We got him on the boat and contacted the Coast Guard over the radio. A couple of the other guys piled in the boat and took off to meet the Coast Guard cutter halfway. Every time our boat hit a wave, you could see our injured Teammate wince and cough up some more blood. He was all right later, but for a while it looked like a near thing.

Getting up onto the drilling platforms from the water required new climbing techniques. The lead climber during a tactical climb free-climbs. He may carry a runner line so he can rest at intervals, but he always carries a coiled caving ladder and then drops it down for the rest of the crew to come up. If the climber trailed the ladder behind him as he went up, it might catch on something and pull him off the structure.

On one climb up an oil rig to try some new techniques, Doc Holliday was leading and he had the ladder with him. We passed up an aluminum pole with a hook on the end. Doc was going to put the ladder on the pole and raise it the last ten feet, hooking it to the edge of the platform, but he snagged the platform with the hook. Then he couldn't get the pole untangled from the dangling ladder.

I was standing about five feet below and to the side of Doc. The rest of the guys were farther below us, and I called down to them to move away from below us and get over to the side. Moving up to Doc, I looked at what I could do to get the pole untangled. The best thing seemed to be just to go up the ladder and set the hook solidly into the platform by hand and ignore the pole. Putting out a safety line would let the rest of the guys come up the ladder and continue the exercise.

As I was going up the ladder, I heard a little sound that instantly rang in my ears. That sound was the soft *ting* of the hook breaking.

I was going to fall and there wasn't anything I could do about it. Kicking back from the platform, I tried to push myself far enough away to clear any obstructions on my way down to the water. I wasn't wearing a Pro-Tec, which was a helmet we decided to adopt for climbing soon after this incident. Balling up, I plunged eighty feet to the water. The White Rhino fell off the ladder and struck a stanchion but wasn't hurt badly. The rest of the crew were all safely on the structure when the hook let go.

When I hit the water, the broken hook and pole landed right next to me. The impact shook me up, but otherwise I was unhurt. Seeing Rhino in the water, I swam over to him. He was okay, but we bundled him into a boat right away.

The XO was peering over the edge of the platform and called down to see if I was okay. Shouting back that I was fine, I told him to unroll another ladder. I had to get back up the ladder just to get that fall out of my system. It was a shaky business going up that caving ladder, but if I hadn't done it right away, I might not have been able to do it as well later on.

That was the hairiest situation I went through while free-climbing. And I was thankful the fall was into water and not something less yielding. The lesson learned from that exercise was to wear headgear for protection.

There is a very large oil rig out in the Gulf run by Shell Oil. Called the Loop, the big rig is painted a bright yellow and you can see it a long distance away across the water. It was the biggest platform of its kind in the early 1980s.

To get ready for our operations on the Loop, we went out to take photos of the maze of pipes and stanchions that disappeared into the depth of the Gulf underneath the rig. Truck was doing the underwater filming, while Pooster and I were safety divers with him. As Truck took his pictures, we looked around through the water. We both nudged Truck to try and get his attention away from the pipes and direct it toward what we could see.

All around the rig were sharks. And not just little harmless varieties. This was a school of hammerhead sharks, one of the weirdest-looking killers swimming in the oceans. The wide flat hammer-shaped fin of their head has eyes at each end, and they could see us easily. But they just weren't interested, which I thought was a fine situation.

In all my time diving, I had never seen a school of sharks like that. And I didn't particularly want to see them again. We had our film and returned to the boats without any other casualties than my own rapid heartbeat.

That night we decided to do a training scenario where we would surface swim in to the rig. We had no rangefinder of any kind, so we were going to estimate the distance and go into the water from the boats about a mile from the platform. There were three squads swimming in on the op, and we all hit the water at the same time.

After the scenario was over, it was estimated that we had really been dropped off between five and seven miles from the platform. So we swam, and swam, and swam. The current in the Gulf of Mexico is circular. We stroked for hours and the rig never seemed to get any closer. What it did do was drift to the side as the current pushed at us.

The squads had all started out separately. But it wasn't long before we were all intermingled on that long swim. We hit the water at about 0100 hours and didn't get to the platform until 0500 hours, just as the sun was coming up.

One of the guys from another squad decided to mess with me a little bit as we swam along. He was behind me and grabbed my leg, screaming, "*Aaaaahhhhh!*" Maybe he had heard about the sharks we met earlier in the day and maybe he hadn't. But I sure remembered them. I thought I had been hit when he grabbed me.

The joke didn't last very long, though. As my Teammate watched, I turned around with my K-Bar knife in my hand. His eyes were a bit large as he looked at me, and I said, "You're lucky." Then we continued on.

When we finally got to the rig, we all crawled onto the girders and just kind of lay there, panting. We looked like drowned rats—yellow rats at that: we had these yellow long johns on so that we would blend in with the structure. Our own Mr. T really showed his feeling as he kissed the big steel beams over and over.

That swim was the second longest of my life. The only longer swim we had done was in BUD/S. All of us were pretty much exhausted, but we had to continue with the job. The only trouble is that with exhaustion come mistakes.

Pooster and I had to lead-climb up the structure. So huffing and puffing, we went up into the girders. In spite of doing one hell of a job, Pooster made what could have been a real bad mistake. While he was walking out on a girder, he reached out and grabbed what he thought was a yellow pipe.

The pipe Pooster grabbed turned out to be a rubber hose. Even though he had a good grip with his other hand, he swung out a bit over the long drop to the water. Smacking into that water and bleeding a little could convince those hammerheads we had seen to pay us a visit.

Pooster was scared for a moment there, and I was as well. We finally got up to a platform underneath the main one and secured one end of the ladder. Dropping the other end down to the rest of the guys, we leaned back for a moment.

The first guy up the ladder was Cheeks, and he immediately lay down on a grating. Cheeks was so drained, he passed out right there. We still needed to continue with the op, but the situation was changing. The work crew on the rig was starting to get up for breakfast.

Here we were in crappy-looking yellow underwear, wearing goggles and carrying stainless steel revolvers. Not exactly a sight you'd want to see right before eating. The revolvers had been carried at our hips in Bianchi pancake holsters, loaded with wax bullets for our training shoot.

But we were all so dingy we could barely operate. In spite of that, we completed the exercise, trying to stay out of sight of the rig's crew. We finished what we had started out to do, but only just. One lesson we learned was that you don't plan a long swim without a recovery period. That, and we soon got some navigational aids to help us better estimate our distance from a target.

You have to be fit to do an operation. If you overexert yourself just getting to the target, you won't have anything left for the action. And if you can't operate effectively, you can't do anyone any good. That was an important lesson we had driven home on that op.

That exercise on the Loop wasn't the only time Pooster and I had a run-in with sharks in the Gulf. There was the exercise when Pooster and I swam out from underneath an oil rig and came up on some local fishermen in a boat.

The fishermen called out to us, "Hey, what are you boys doing here? We're chumming for sharks!"

For those of you who don't know the term, or never saw the movie *Jaws, chumming* is where they throw scraps, chopped meat, fish guts, and blood into the water to draw sharks in. The smell of the blood is usually enough to set off the sharks' appetite and feeding behavior, which means they bite almost anything in the water: bait, fish, or SEALs.

Pooster and I quickly decided that we should practice our climbing techniques. Since we had become adept at our job, we moved out of the water quickly and worked from the first platform instead. And we were particularly careful not to fall back into the water.

CHAPTER 12

A DRY SPELL

There were also training trips where we didn't get wet at all. While out west for some parachute training, Duke asked me to see about setting up an E & E (escape and evasion) course for the desert. Researching what might be available, I met Dave Gancy in Arizona. He was a professor at Arizona State who was known as a desert survivalist. He had lived with the Indians, and he ran desert marathons.

When I met Gancy, it was pretty obvious this guy knew what he was talking about, and he was willing to pass on some of his knowledge. Arriving on site in a barren chunk of the desert, we broke up Assault Group One into two units, each doing a different course of training. I was in the first group, and we went north to work with Dave on a five-day, four-night desert trek.

Before we even started out, we broke the group down even further to a number of eight-man teams for the trek itself. This wasn't going to be the most comfortable walk I had ever taken.

We were starting out light, no food and only a quart of water each. But we had emergency supplies with us in the way of first aid gear, communications, and even IV packs for the corpsman to treat severe dehydration cases.

Just like a regular military patrol, each group had its own maps and routes with checkpoints along the way. We had to touch at each one of these checkpoints, most of which were supposed to have a source of water of one kind or another.

The first day we found the checkpoint without a lot of trouble. We had been out of water for about an hour, so we were getting a little thirsty. The checkpoint turned out to be a pipe coming up out of the ground with water dripping from it. It took half an hour to fill one canteen. But while the canteens were filling, we were sweating and losing even more water. And just to add some of nature's little irritations to the mix, there were small bees all around the pipe, and us. The insects were living on the moisture around the pipe, whether it was the dripping water or our sweat, they didn't care. While we were suffering through the situation, I talked to Dave Gancy about what more we could expect on our walk.

Before the exercise began, we had a safety briefing concerning what we might encounter. Emergency procedures, medevac of the injured, water conservation, and desert survival techniques were all covered. The lectures took a whole day, with a number of speakers, military and civilian, giving us different information.

One of the things we talked about was rattlesnakes. I remembered that run-in with a rattler back when I was in Kilo Platoon. But Dave told me not to expect much. He said his last class had gone though the same area without seeing any snakes at all. He thought we'd be lucky to see maybe one.

So here we are at the first stop, and Toad finds a little cove, kind of a miniature canyon in the rock, with walls about ten feet high. There was shade, and the area looked cool and smooth, so

Toad just walked in and sat down. The shade would help his body conserve water while we were all getting our canteens filled.

When Toad took his seat, he just stopped moving. A few minutes later, we looked over at him and called out, "Hey, Toad! Do you want to fill your canteen or what?" He didn't answer loudly at all.

It was hot and we were all sweating, but Toad seemed to have an extra layer of sweat all over him. Looking over, we could see a rattler curled up right behind his ass, softly rattling every now and then. The snake was calm, but it did look ready to change its mind in a heartbeat. Toad had heard the rattle and froze, figuring that if he even spoke out loud, the snake might strike.

"Hey, Dave," one of the guys called out. "We've got kind of a situation over here."

It only took one look at what was going on for Dave to step in and take charge. First he told all of us to relax and back away. Then, working his way in closer to see the snake clearly, Dave entered the canyon himself and started to talk Toad out of his predicament.

Dave had Toad sit up straight and then very gradually stand up. All the time Toad was moving, Dave was watching the snake. When the snake reacted or buzzed a bit, Dave had Toad freeze. When the snake calmed back down, Toad would move some more. It must have taken about fifteen minutes for Toad to stand up and get out of the little canyon. It was obvious that Dave knew what he was doing and had been around these kinds of snakes a lot.

Once Toad was in the clear, like all good SEALs and frogmen, we wanted to look at the snake, but Dave had a better idea, and we all just left the snake alone. Toad was relieved to have gotten out of that situation with his ass intact, literally.

After having drunk our fill, we continued on the course.

There were two very different ways of getting to Point B from where we were. The first way as the crow flies: climbing straight up and over about a 2,000-foot mountain. The other was around the base of the mountain, which would take a lot longer.

Our group decided to go over the mountain. As we climbed, everyone started to get dehydrated again. At the top of the mountain, we expected to find a cache site with water in it within an easy walk. We were wrong.

On the other side of that mountain was a ravine that looked like the Grand Canyon. It was on the far side of that ravine that we would find our next marker and the cache site. Now we had to go down the mountain, into the ravine, and back up the other side. It was starting to get dark by the time we got to the bottom and were traversing the ravine.

One of the other groups had taken the other route and gone around the base of the mountain, and they got through the ravine and to the site about four hours before we showed up. It was about 2100 or 2200 hours when we arrived at Point B.

Now we were really thirsty and looked for the cache site. The guy who met us there showed us the cache and what was waiting there. Instead of a source of water, we found a bunch of one-liter bottles marked "poison water." What was in the bottles was a mixture of half water and half beer.

The bottles were to simulate finding bad water. In real life, bad water could be poison or contaminated. If you got sick from the water and had diarrhea, losing that amount of moisture from your body could kill you fast. After being out in the desert, drinking that beer-water mix would relieve your thirst for a moment, but then you'd have alcohol in your system. As the body burned up the alcohol, it would use up the water in your tissues and dehydrate you worse than if you hadn't drunk anything at all.

A couple of the guys just said to hell with it and drank the bad water anyway. I know Kodiak was one of them, and there were several more. By the next morning, people were starting to get really dehydrated and tightening up.

By the time we were back on our compass course and headed on to the next point, one of our guys who had drunk the bad water was in physical danger. The dehydrated man was evacuated out of the exercise for a while. The corpsmen treated him, and he was back with us before long. But we continued with our cross-desert trek.

The next point had a well, a deep hole in the ground. Using 550 (parachute) cord, we could lower our canteen cups down into the fifty-foot-deep well and fill them about half full. Gradually we filled the canteens and had our water, so everyone was happy for the moment.

One of the things we were learning on this trip was to tank up whenever we found a water source. Tanking up was drinking your fill, until you felt you couldn't take another drop. Then you drank about a quart more. You got a little bloated in the belly, but the large amount of water hydrated your tissues. This way you built up a bit of a bank for when you were next on your way to dehydration.

We spent the night at the well site and were all freshened up the next morning when we started off again. Daylight was just breaking as we began moving along, and now we were entering a more severe desert environment.

Instead of more open country, we were walking along a dry riverbed. At turns in the riverbed, you could find shady spots where the ground was dark. In those places, we were told, you might be able to find water soaked into the ground.

When we found these dark spots, we dug in. And we never found any water. One of the guides, who could have been an ex-Army guy, was one of Dave Gancy's best friends and had helped him set up the course. While we were looking for the cache site, trying to find water, this guy was on a ridge line about five hundred feet away from us. Putting his hands on his hips, this guy called down to us, "So you were told there was water here, huh? Looks like you've been screwed."

It was probably for the best that he never heard Kodiak's comment. Looking up at the ridge line, Kodiak growled, "I'm going to kill that motherfucker!"

He probably would have too and eaten him afterward. We were all getting pretty dehydrated now. The IV bags in the medical kits were starting to look pretty good. But they were not "officially" part of our equipment. They were part of the emergency gear to be used only in case of an accident.

The next point we had to hit to get any water was a place called "the deserted ranch." At the ranch was supposed to be a well site. When we finally got there, we found a little pipe sticking up from the ground.

Water came out of the pipe, but that didn't mean it was any good. With our survival gear, we each had these little filter straws that let you purify the water as you drew it though the straw. Sucking the water through the straws, we found a heavy sulfur content that the filters did little to eliminate.

But water was where you found it and we used what was available. We had little pump rigs that would draw water through the straws and fill the canteens. So we pumped away to get the water we wanted so badly. The stuff still tasted like shit, but it was wet. I had brought some Tang powdered orange drink just in case we ran into unpalatable water. Mixing the Tang in my canteen, I found it still tasted like shit, only orange flavored.

When we had all filled our canteens, we decided on our next move. It was the middle of the day in the desert, not the best time to go traveling. We had a ready water supply and some scattered shade. We decided to spend the day at the well, tank up, and continue on when it got cooler toward nightfall.

Setting up a little bivouac, we found what shade we could. Staying in groups of two, we lay up for the balance of the day. When night fell, off we went. That night we reached our link-up point, where all the groups would come together. Now we were bordering a state park near an Indian reservation. With the whole group together, we moved on to the last watering site.

Tanking up again, we filled our canteens and then moved out. On this final part of the course, Dave was leading us himself and he would break us off in pairs as we passed points known only to him. We would camp out that night, then complete the last leg of the course into the state park on our own the next morning.

As we walked along a dry creek bed, we came across rattlesnakes three different times. The snakes were lying across the creek bed, absorbing the last bit of heat from the day. Amazingly enough, not one person in our patrol stepped on a snake. It was getting dark, and the snakes looked like small logs or branches. But it wasn't until one of the people toward the back of the patrol shouted, "Holy shit!" that the "logs" curled up and started rattling.

So as we walked along, dodging snakes, Dave dropped us off. The spot where I was left with my partner looked a little bit like heaven might. Here we were in the middle of the desert, and there was a barbed wire fence. Near the fence was this square patch of green grass, maybe twenty-five square feet of sod, like someone had laid a carpet down. Desert grass or whatever it was, it was soft and appealing. That was going to be my bed, I decided, and lay down looking up at the stars.

There was a moon shining a silver-gray light across the desert. The stars were brilliant, and there were more of them than you can ever see anywhere near a city. I had my water, was close to the end of the exercise, and just felt good. It was really something to be out there in the desert on your own like that.

It was about 0100 hours in the morning when I lay down. The last instructions Dave had given us were for the next day. In the morning, a shotgun blast would be the signal for us to start the last leg of our compass course. We would get up at the sound of the shot and start out on the heading we had been given. The path would take us into the state park.

In the morning, we all moved out. Gradually guys would link up as their paths crossed. The course was only about two hours long, so it wasn't any big final push. There wasn't much question of when we had hit the park. When we came up on a paved road, we followed the road and soon reached our last point.

Now we finally had the chance to get into some water. There was a river, and we could soak a bit. We hadn't eaten in five days, but right then the water was a lot more important. We probably looked more like a bunch of walruses than SEALs, everyone splashing in the water, letting it run off them, and generally tanking up. Later we went up to Pinnacle Pete's, a local steak house, to get our first full meal in a while.

We were told to tank up on water first, from a source that was right outside the restaurant. Since we had been so dehydrated, Dave told us, even one or two beers would be enough to put us right on the ground. A couple of the guys didn't believe him. Purdue and another Teammate even went so far as to have a shot of red-eye; since we were out west, they considered it a tradition.

Those old Western movies have it wrong. No one would come in off the desert, walk into a saloon, and have a belt of whiskey. Actually, Purdue and his partner were kind of interesting to watch. It wasn't more than two minutes after they had their shot that they wavered a bit, and then pitched right over.

None of us drank after Purdue's example, but Dave still had designated drivers for us all.

CHAPTER 13

A NEW GROUP AND SOME OTHER CHANGES

By the spring of 1983, it had been decided that a third assault group was needed to better fulfill our tasking. Our training pulled guys in and out of the area a lot. A third group would let us have a longer break between the standby group that had to remain in town and the training group that could leave the area for more distant schools.

Some of the people for the new group would be taken from the two existing groups, but the balance of the manpower was going to be brought up from the rest of the Teams. This was going to increase the manning at SEAL Team Six by a third.

Volunteers from Six were sought to start filling out the new group. The opportunity to form a new group was enticing, but most of us were reluctant to leave the positions we already held. The chiefs came down to talk to us. They wanted a good half-and-half mix from the old groups to make up the new one. There had always been a good-natured rivalry between the two assault groups, just as there had always been between the different squads in each group. But this would be for the betterment of the Team as a whole.

I volunteered for the new group. Duke became the first leader of what was now Assault Group Three, and Ho Ho became the group chief. There were two squads that had come over intact from groups one and two, and two that were mixed and hadn't operated with each other before. To build up some fast squad integrity, we came up with nicknames for our units. First Squad, where I was, we called the Bros. The unity formed up fast, and it wasn't long before we were as tight as we had been in our last squad.

One of the other squads was made up of a lot of guys with Latino backgrounds, so they picked up the name Los Hombres. Another squad tried to name themselves the Heat, but we kept calling them the Meat, and that's what stuck. The last squad was one of the mixed ones, so we called them the Spare Parts, which they didn't think a whole hell of a lot of, but that's the name that stuck.

A few years had passed now since Six had been formed, and concerns were coming down the pike about money and expenses. The Skipper ran too loose a ship to satisfy the Navy bean counters, and they didn't like some of the expenditures that had been made. Everything we had was for a reason, but we weren't explaining those reasons to anyone who wasn't in the direct chain of command and probably few enough of them. Top-of-the-line guns, electronics, munitions, and equipment were never too good for the mission, at least not according to the Skipper.

Time was also forcing changes at Six. The Skipper put in for an extension so that he could remain the commanding officer of SEAL Team Six. But the Navy has its own set of rules regarding commanding officer rotations. The Skipper had been at the helm of Six for three years. The Navy considers a two-year command tour sufficient for most officers.

So Dick's time was up for his tour at Six. None of us wanted to see him go, but rotating command was one of the things officers had to do. That was one of the advantages of being a petty officer or a chief: you could spend most of your career in a single command. That wasn't the case for officers, and Dick came under that rule.

Dick's rough way of dealing with anyone not directly involved with his Team or mission also burned a few bridges behind him. He just didn't have enough pull to beat the Navy rules. It was time for him to go and another officer to step up to the command.

There were mixed feeling among the men about the Skipper leaving. He had built the unit, selected us, trained us, and saw to it we had what we needed to get the job done. He had rubbed some people the wrong way, but he had always stood behind his men.

Dick was the kind of leader who always made sure his men and his command were taken care of first. He asked for everything that we could give, plus some more. But he also made sure that we had absolutely every bit of help that was in his power to give us. The style of command that Dick used was a lot different from that of any other officers I had known. It was almost like he was playing Lee Marvin's character in the movie *The Dirty Dozen*. To get the mission done, he fought against the established Navy way of doing things. He put his trust in all of us because he knew we were the ones who were crawling through the ditches, getting down in the mud, and pulling the triggers. He made us feel that we had more input in how things would be done than any other people. And he was also the man who made it all start to happen.

But finally it was time for him to go. No further time extensions were granted, and on July 8, 1983, Commander Richard Marcinko turned over command of SEAL Team Six to Captain Robert Gormly. It was hard to see Dick go, especially since we were only in our third year. It felt like we could keep going forever, us doing the job and Dick telling everyone else to leave us the hell alone. But all things change. It was a hard lesson for some of us young SEALs who had formed this unit to accept.

For every action that we had done, Dick had stood up to the higher command and let them know who deserved the credit. And when something went wrong, he also stood up and said he was responsible as the man in charge. When we had to complete an objective without clarification from higher command, Dick told us to just go ahead and do the job. If fire came down from on high for what we had done, he took the brunt of it. At Six, we were not like any other unit in the Navy. Even our Teammates in the other SEAL Teams didn't like us sometimes, and the regular Navy never seemed to care for Special Operations forces at the best of times. So with a new commander coming in, we wondered just how much things were going to change.

The new skipper, Bob Gormly, had also been a Vietnam era SEAL and seen his share of action. Captain Gormly had been the CO of SEAL Team Two, having held the command from September 1972 to July 1974, when he turned it over to Dick Marcinko. We were a little concerned about the new Skipper; he had been a hard charger in Vietnam according to those who had known him then. But had a couple of tours in staff positions changed him?

Turned out the answer was no.

It was a big moment when Dick left. But it wasn't like the Team was coming to an end. Dick came into where we were all gathered at the command and gave a speech. He spoke very highly of the command, of us, and of the man who was going to relieve him. He did say that he wished he didn't have to go, but since that had to happen, he said, Bob Gormly was the best man to take over the command.

Captain Gormly stepped aboard with both feet and immediately took charge. I had a lot of respect for what he did and how he did it. My assault group was on standby at the time of the change of command, so we had several months to get acquainted with the new CO, and he didn't make it hard for us to know him.

At that time, we were allowed to have beer messes within the compound after the working day was over. Once we secured from duty, we would often pop a few and relax. What was really amazing to me was that Bob came right down and became one of the troops. He would just sit down and shoot the shit with us, telling us some of what we wanted to know and learning a few things back.

He told us that he wasn't there to change anything about the Team. The one thing he did want to do was make sure the mission statement of Six—to be the maritime counterterrorist unit for the Navy—would carry on. We would keep training to be able to accomplish any mission that might come along.

We all have our own style of doing things, and Bob Gormly wasn't any different. He did things differently from Dick Marcinko. But the differences were in the details. Overall, the day-to-day running of SEAL Team Six remained the same. There wasn't a sudden flurry of haircuts or a blizzard of new orders and directives. We had been a functioning command for three years, so things were getting settled down and we had a pretty standard working schedule. That gave Bob a little more time than Dick had had to spend one-on-one with each of the different assault groups. And that was the only real difference I noticed.

The new Skipper worked right alongside us and did a lot of training of his own. He had to be able to operate as part of his Team, so he went through the same green (introductory) training as any new man coming in to SEAL Team Six. Within only a few months of taking command, he became the man who led SEAL Team Six into its first live combat operation: a series of operations in a little southern Caribbean island called Grenada.

CHAPTER 14

FIRST COMBAT AND FIRST COSTS

Grenada—Operation Urgent Fury—October 25 to 27, 1983

In the fall of 1983, a military coup on the small Caribbean island of Grenada deposed the government, and a new leader with definite Communist leanings took over. A buildup of Cuban advisers and construction crews had been taking place on Grenada, and an airfield big enough to handle the largest Soviet cargo planes was being constructed. Supplies were being brought into the small island nation for transshipment to Communist-backed rebel groups in South and Central America. Materials were also being forwarded to the Communist government in Nicaragua.

With the seizure of the last of the moderate government leaders on Grenada, and the threat against a large number of U.S. students attending the medical school on Grenada, President Ronald Reagan decided to act. There was no previous planning for the operation, at least not from our command. We didn't know anything was coming up. It just happened.

In October 1983, Assault Group One at SEAL Team Six was on standby and had a short recall. Assault Group Three was next in rotation and had a longer recall, but we were still in town when the call went out. Assault Group Two was out of town and didn't get back in time for the festivities. It was Assault Group One's party, but it looked like Assault Group Three was going to be invited as well.

I was living in Virginia Beach with my girlfriend Kitty. We had been together for eight months, and I was all of thirty years old. When my beeper went off signaling the recall, I was relaxing at home. Alerts had come in before, and we had rushed in, gotten our gear ready, and hyped ourselves up to go. Then there would come a big letdown when nothing happened. To keep the disappointment to a minimum, the command had finally stopped getting us all geared up for practice alerts. We still moved as fast as we could to get into the compound for any alert, though. For all I knew, this alert was another training exercise.

Arriving at the compound, we were all put into isolation. There was no outside contact. Things were happening all around us. When I realized this one was for real, I swear my mind went blank. All my training went right out the window. That lasted for about half a day.

Only two boat crews were going to be used on the alert op, a reconnaissance off the island of Grenada. The rest of the men in Assault Group One helped the boat crews that were going load out. It was just the luck of the draw that Assault Group Three hadn't been called up for a hot op, and we were a little disappointed about it. But that didn't slow us down when it came to helping Assault Group One get ready. When it comes down to it, it doesn't matter who does the job. The mission comes first.

Taking our trucks down to Fort Bragg, we prepped to board

the air assets assigned to the operation. The aircraft were at the yellow ramp location at nearby Pope Air Force Base. We were helping Group One prep their boats for a water drop. My understanding at the time was that it was going to be a semiadministrative water drop and the Team was going to link up with an aircraft carrier once they got on target. We would be prepared to go in on a combat insertion, but the crew of the aircraft would not be told that this jump was for real. For security's sake, they would be told it was a regular administrative training drop under peacetime rules.

Instead of going in on land, the team would parachute into the water. The guys would do a static line drop and conduct a standard water drop. Boats with their motors were prepped and rigged on drop platforms, packed to go out the rear ramp of the plane and be parachuted into the water. The men would jump from the rear of the aircraft after the boats had been pushed out. Once everyone was down, the men would climb aboard their respective boats and continue with their mission. We hadn't done a water drop at Six before, but it was something we had all done a number of times in the Teams in general.

The mission called for them to do a boat drop, link up with a carrier, and then set up for a further infiltration. They would use the eighteen-foot Boston Whalers and conduct a recon of the airstrips on the island. On a second op, they would insert an Air Force Combat Control Team that would direct the incoming air traffic during the invasion. Our Teammates would provide security for the Air Force CCT.

Like so many other times, there was delay after delay in getting the clearances—and the bird—off the ground at Pope Air Base. There was confusion coordinating support for the operation, and the schedule was thrown off before it even started. The aircraft took off late and it was dark by the time they arrived over the target area. Two C-130 cargo planes were being used for the insertion, each one carrying a boat and crew. At the last turn to line up for the drop, one plane separated from the other and went off on its own track. On top of being late, now one plane was off course and not where it thought it was. Instead it was almost two miles away from its target.

Mother Nature also took a hand in the deteriorating situation and the weather turned to shit. A rain squall had kicked up suddenly, accompanied by high winds. The boats and the guys were set up for a daylight rubber duck boat drop; now they would be dropping into a high sea state in the dark.

In spite of the situation, the mission was going to be SEAL Team Six's first hot op in a combat zone, and the guys would not fail to try. They made the drop into the darkness and rough seas. Out of the eight SEALs on that water drop, all of whom I knew as brothers, four drowned on the insertion and were never seen again.

Talking to the guys involved in the drop much later, it may be that one of the boats capsized or tipped over from the high winds. The one functioning boat was used to pick up everyone who could be found. The winds were so strong that the men who were lost were probably dragged through the water by their parachutes. The Capewell quick-release catches for the parachute canopies would be very heard to reach when being slammed around by eight- to ten-foot waves. It wouldn't be long before men beaten like that would be taken by the sea.

We lost four of our own during that insertion, the first SEAL combat losses since the end of the Vietnam War. Senior Chief Engineman Bob Schamberger, Quartermaster 1st Class Kevin Lundberg, Machinist Mate 1st Class Ken Butcher, and Hull Technician 1st Class Steve Morris were all lost on that dark night of October 24 in the waters of the southern Caribbean.

Searches for our lost Teammates began as soon as the weather cleared and daylight came. But in spite of days of searching, no sign was ever found of the missing men.

The shock of the loss sent a blow throughout SEAL Team

Six. Especially bad for me was the loss of Bob Schamberger because of all he had done for me personally. Each of the men was our Teammate, our brother, and we were made less for their passing.

Some of the Vietnam veterans we had in the Team had experience in the sudden loss of a Teammate in combat. Duke told us, "Hey guys, sometimes things happen. But what we have to do now is put our heads together and think about how we're going to solve this mission. Later we can go back and take care of this [loss] properly."

He was right. Though the loss of our Teammates was keenly felt, we had to continue with the mission.

In Six, a contingency plan was always being prepared even as another plan was going into action. This was true for the Grenada mission. When the original insertion turned disastrous, the contingency plan took effect. Assault Group Three was told to stand by, and we loaded out for a possible operation. Since we had come down to Bragg to help Assault Group One get ready, we didn't have all of our own equipment with us. Our bags were shipped down from Little Creek, and we geared up for whatever might be coming.

The word came down that we might be going to the governor's mansion on Grenada to secure Governor Sir Paul Scoon, protect him and his family, and bring them out of the combat area. A second mission was to capture and secure the island's sole radio station so that it couldn't be used by the local military to incite the population or coordinate military actions. The U.S. government wanted the radio station captured intact if possible so that Governor Scoon could broadcast to the island and tell the population what was actually going on.

The operation I was going to be a part of was the rescue of Governor Scoon at his mansion, where he was being held under house arrest. At the same time, another detachment from Six would be going to the radio station. The two operations were going to require more men than were in Assault Group Three, so we took on the guys from Assault Group One who hadn't gone on the original op.

A warning order came down to us, and we loaded out the required equipment, weapons, and ammunition. Reporting to a classroom, we received the final briefing on our mission and the available intelligence on the local situation.

Captain Gormly was very frank when it came to giving us our intelligence dump. Holding up a blank sheet of paper, he told us, "This is our intel on what you're going into."

That was fairly sobering.

We had all been down to the Caribbean at one time or another, to Puerto Rico, Saint Thomas, and other islands. We figured that Grenada couldn't be that different terrain-wise. Satellite images were shown that detailed the grounds around Scoon's mansion. Photographs—fax pictures really—of Scoon and his family were passed around so we would all be familiar with them. General Hudson Austin, who had led the coup that killed Maurice Bishop, the recent head of the Grenadian government, was also shown to us. Bishop had originally ousted Scoon some years earlier and turned to Cuba for assistance. His murder by General Austin had thrown the whole area into turmoil. General Austin was not listed as a target but was one of the people we could run into on the op.

This was going to be my first real exposure to combat. When Bob held up that blank sheet of paper, it did not make for a good feeling inside me. My only other exposure to combat had been while I was in the Army during the Mideast petroleum crisis. And all I did for that was sit on a runway in Egypt for two days.

Looking around the room, I could see my Teammates, several of whom had seen extensive combat in Vietnam. Johnny Johnson, Bubbaloo, and Duke didn't seem worried, just alert and attentive. Ho Ho had also seen his share of action in 'Nam, and he just sat there with a smile on his face. "Here we go," he said, and topped it off with his traditional Ho-ho-ho laugh. If they thought things were fine, that was good enough for me.

At one point in the briefing, a JAG (Judge Advocate General) lawyer came in to tell us what we could and couldn't do according to the rules of engagement. These rules about just how and when we could use our weapons had been put together by lawyers and politicians to make it easier for them to explain what we were doing in Grenada. Of course, those men would never have to put their lives on the line and actually try to survive while following them.

The strategic planners for Urgent Fury, the Grenada op, figured things would go so smoothly that we would never have to fire a shot. So they gave us very tight guidelines for the use of lethal force. We could fire back only if we were being physically threatened at the time. In other words, we had to wait until a weapon was being pointed at us before opening fire. If we encountered enemy forces, we had to first give them a chance to surrender before taking them under fire. And even then we could only fire if they threatened us with their weapons. If an enemy force was in a civilian building, we couldn't fire into the building to get at them. We would have to either bypass the building where enemy forces were hiding or go inside and move room to room and get them individually.

Okay, modern warfare at its best—our leaders directing us from wayyyy back at the rear on how we were to conduct ourselves in a combat zone. I don't think that JAG officer's words lasted much longer than the echoes of his footsteps as he left. Now it was time to get back to the real business at hand.

What we would be going into was called a semipermissive environment. Not everyone in the country would be against us. But the People's Revolutionary Armed Forces would certainly be against us. And we probably wouldn't be the most popular people with their Communist Cuban advisers either. We didn't have any solid numbers on how many Cubans might be on the island or exactly how they were equipped, but the large numbers of civilians on the island kept us from having any kind of free-fire zone.

By now I had long gotten over my earlier blank spot, where my training all seemed to go bye-bye. Things started clicking in just as they were supposed to. I knew what I had to take and prepped my gear accordingly. Even though we had been told how much ammunition to bring, I took more. I wasn't worried about being able to carry my load; I wanted to be sure to have what I needed. On top of my basic loadout, I slipped an extra bandoleer of 5.56mm ammunition in with my gear.

My basic loadout was a fairly light one, but I was geared up well for what we expected to be only a short time on the ground. My primary weapon was an M16A1 carbine with a fourteen-inch barrel. My backup handgun was a Beretta 92-F. For the carbine, I had ten thirty-round mags with me and five fifteen-round mags for the Beretta. My uniform was a standard woodland-pattern mottled green Army BDU (battle dress uniform). Instead of a cap, I wore a forty-inch OD (olive drab) green triangular bandage as a bandanna wrapped around my head and tied off in the back. The bandannas were something you could go into the water with and they wouldn't slip down over your eyes or float off. It didn't shade your eyes very well, but in a pinch you could use it as a bandage.

Like all good frogmen, we didn't wear any underwear. We did have on black Speedo swimsuits under our uniforms in case we had to E & E (escape and evade) through a public beach or whatever. Standard green jungle boots over green OD socks took care of my feet. Over my uniform, my equipment belt and H-harness were a standard nylon LBE (load-bearing equipment) setup. A K-Bar knife was on my left hip, my Beretta in a low-slung assault holster on my right hip.

Pouches of different kinds surrounded my equipment belt. I had three magazine pouches for my carbine mags, two pouches for my pistol mags, and three canteen pouches across the back. Two of the canteen pouches held standard one-quart military canteens. In the third pouch, I had folded up a black inflatable UDT life jacket in case of a long swim. The only thing we made sure everyone wore in the same place was their first aid pouch—attached to the cross-strap of the H-harness—in the center of the back so everyone knew where to grab the tan field dressing each man had in his pouch.

Some emergency gear was in my pockets. Besides a tin of Copenhagen dip (tobacco), I had a Silva Ranger compass and two pairs of flexible plastic riot handcuffs to secure a prisoner if necessary. The balance of my emergency gear was my E&E kit with a Mark 13 day/night flare and a strobe light for signaling. For communications I had a Motorola MX 360 radio with a spare battery for backup.

For the fast-rope insertion, I wore a pair of green aviator gloves under fingerless black leather sports gloves. I would put the aviator gloves in my pocket when I hit the ground; the sports gloves would help protect my hands during the insertion. Over all this stuff, I slung that OD cloth bandoleer of 5.56mm ammunition in ten-round stripper clips. And I still wondered if I had left anything out.

Things were moving so quickly I didn't have much time to think about what we were going to do. I had tried to imagine what Scoon's mansion might look like. All I could think of was a luxurious place, kind of an island version of our White House. Then I had to get to work, and my imagining ended.

Like any SEAL going into his first combat op, I spent a lot of time going over my weapons and gear. My weapons were broken down, cleaned, and carefully lubed. Each magazine in my pouches was checked and secured. The quick-tape I had attached to the magazines to get them out of the pouches fast was examined minutely and tested. I had ten thirty-round magazines on me, nine in the pouches and one in my weapon, each mag loaded with twenty-eight rounds to ensure functioning. The extra bandoleer I took along gave me an additional 140 rounds of 5.56mm ball to go along with the 280 rounds I had in my magazines: 420 rounds for my first combat. And I still wondered if it would be enough.

We had a chance to test-fire all our weapons before we left Pope Air Force Base. Each man checked all his hardware, and we had a good test-fire. From that point, our weapons were locked and loaded and set on safe. And they stayed that way until we landed on the island. That was all we could do with our equipment. It was time to get on with the operation.

ON OUR WAY: FLY THE UNFRIENDLY SKIES

Everything was working to get us on our way as quickly as possible, but we were still running about a day behind the originally planned schedule. The plan called for us to go in on helo assets, basing out of Barbados. Our birds would be part of a convoy of SEALs and personnel from our Army counterparts and the Rangers.

The Army detachment would take over Richmond Hill Prison while we would head into Government House, as we called Scoon's mansion. Three major targets were in a kind of east-pointing triangle, with Scoon's mansion on the north point, Richmond Hill Prison a little less than a kilometer away on the south point, and Fort Frederick a kilometer away on the east point. About six kilometers north of Scoon's mansion was Beausejour, where the radio station was located.

Of the nine Blackhawk helicopters we would all be flying in, four held SEALs and the remaining five held Army Rangers and other operatives. Two of the SEAL birds would head north to hit the radio station, while the remaining two SEAL birds would continue on to Scoon's. The five Army birds would head in to Richmond Hill Prison.

Our pilots were all from the Army's Task Force 160 and were very good with their birds. Having practiced night flying while wearing NVGs, the pilots could move through near total darkness and hit their targets. Night flying ability was important because our planned timetable had us hitting our targets right before dawn. That would put the element of surprise more in our favor.

The plan had us getting to Scoon by fast-roping down from the hovering Blackhawks. Once Scoon was secured, which was expected to take only twenty minutes or so, we would call the birds back in for an extraction. If we found the area too densely covered with trees or brush for the Blackhawks to set down, we would make a landing zone right on the spot. One of our guys would be carrying a chainsaw with him so that we could quickly "improve" the governor's landscaping. With Scoon in a bird, he would be on his way to one of the Navy platforms around the island. Max planned time: forty-five minutes from first man on the ground to last man extracted.

Even with the "simple" aspects of the mission, things were going to be tight. The Blackhawks would be going out to their maximum range to put us on Grenada and would have to get to a Navy platform offshore quickly to refuel. But that wasn't my part of the mission, so I wasn't given all the details.

One of our guys had been to individual training but almost wasn't there for the operation. As the loaded aircraft full of SEALs, Blackhawk helicopters, and pallets full of equipment started to taxi, charging along the runway came our missing man, Larry.

Our guy wasn't about to be left behind when the party was

finally going to start. His vehicle charged up to the aircraft, and Larry started pounding on the side door. The load master opened the door and we yanked Larry in, wearing his jeans and civilian clothes and not much in the way of military gear, but we always brought extra gear and weapons, so outfitting Larry wasn't a problem.

While in the air, some of the vets just settled in and grabbed some sleep. Most of the rest of us couldn't sleep much, maybe something like twenty minutes total during the whole flight. We were getting a bit jazzed up. It was 2100 hours, and the flight was supposed to be over in two and a half hours. By 0230 hours, we noticed the flight was taking longer than we had been told it would. Instead of landing in Barbados, we were circling the island.

Duke and the other guys on the plane were concerned about the flight being so late. They called up front to the pilot's cabin to find out what the hell was going on. The crews of the Air Force C5A Galaxy transport planes didn't know we were going in on a hot operation. They all thought it was an administrative operation and we were still under peacetime rules. The aircraft commanders hadn't known about the tight timeline to get us on the ground in Grenada while it was still dark.

Finally the huge C5A set down at a commercial airport. The original plan had us leaving Barbados on board the Blackhawks at 0400 hours, but it was 0330 hours before all the transport planes had finally touched down. The mission was already running close to an hour behind schedule and we had just gotten on the ground.

Duke wanted to try to regain a little of the time we had lost. Since my shooting partner and I were the fast-rope kickers and would be sent out of the helicopter first, Duke told us to get down to the Blackhawks and start hooking up the gear. At that time, only SEAL Team Six was using fast-roping as an insertion technique. Sliding down a specially made thick rope, a little like the ropes we used to have to climb back in high school gym class, a SEAL squad could be on the ground from a hovering helicopter in seconds. The special ropes were hung from the doorway of the insertion helicopter from a special bracket that had to be installed prior to the operation.

As soon as the plane had touched down, we were unbuckling our belts and getting ready to go to the helicopters. Most of the air crew, though, still thought we were on a regular peacetime mission. You know how the airlines have that warning about not unbuckling your seatbelt or standing until the aircraft has come to a complete halt? Well, the Air Force has the same rule.

A member of the flight crew took it upon himself to warn us to sit down and remain buckled up. Tempers were running just a tiny bit short, however, and we didn't have a time for this kind of nonsense. I believe it was Duke who convinced the crew member that leaving us alone might be the best thing all around. It might have been a threat about severe bodily harm that finally caused the crewman to go find something else to occupy his time.

The helicopters were pushed out the cargo doors as soon as they opened, and we were on the birds hooking up the ropes as soon as we could get down to the cargo deck. The Army crew chiefs were attaching the rotor blades, which are removed for transport, to ready the birds for flight. A number of us climbed up on top of the helicopters to help tighten down the bolts that secured the four blades to the rotor.

While we were working on top of the birds, the rest of the guys were moving below us. The M60 machine guns were mounted in the doors and the long ammunition belts carefully laid out in their cans and feed chutes. Now the adrenaline was pumping for me, and I imagine a number of the other guys also felt their hearts beating just a bit faster. Finally, at around 0500 hours, we lifted off for Grenada.

The helicopter formation flying across the ocean reminded me of the movie *Apocalypse Now*. That was the first time I thought to myself, "Here we go, this is the real thing." Up to that point, everything had been handled the way we had learned way back in BUD/S training: one evolution at a time, and don't anticipate.

The helicopters had metal decks inside with tie-down rings, much like in the older Hueys. We had the fast-rope rigs put up and securely in place, but this would be the first time we had used them without a safety rope. The training was over; it was time to put our learning to the test. And everything I looked at reminded me of that.

It started to get light while we were flying across the ocean, and our being behind schedule was looking more serious. The door gunner on the helicopter was newly assigned to the position, so my shooting partner and I tried to give him some help in setting up and operating his M60 machine gun. Unfortunately, we couldn't prevent him from making a bit of a mistake.

To make up time, the Blackhawks were moving along at near top speed. With his weapon stuck out in the windstream, that gunner opened the aluminum feed cover on the top of his M60 in order to load it. The wind immediately ripped the feed cover off the weapon. Now the right side of the aircraft was without a working machine gun.

The helicopter was pretty well maxed out as far as its load was concerned. And here we were with a couple of thousand rounds of M60 ammunition that was now nothing more than a big weight. In the back of the birds were large rubber fuel bladders to increase the range as much as possible. So we were flying along in a partially armed, fuel-filled bomb.

During that hour-long trip across the ocean to Grenada, I had time to think about my childhood, girls I had known, and Kitty back in Virginia Beach. But I couldn't dwell on such things. Thoughts like that can get in the way when you have to move and react fast. With a conscious effort, I thought about my part in the plan, how I would support my Teammates, and how glad I was that experienced guys were leading us in. I decided I was going to have a great time going into combat with these men at my side, and front, and back.

What we were heading into wasn't like taking down a bamboo hooch in Southeast Asia. We were going up against an old-world mansion, more like a fortress, with thick stone walls. Bullets wouldn't penetrate that structure. We would have to go in and cover it room by room. But that was what we had all trained for and why we were given this job.

Our training had been hard and dangerous for a reason: you train as you fight. We had done live fire exercises, stalked each other with revolvers loaded with wax bullets, and had learned from the best. We were tough, aggressive, and good. Where another troop would probably miss in a sudden face-to-face, we wouldn't. That's why we had the best chance of coming out on top in any fight.

We had been told to trust our training. That was probably one of the big differences between the combat veterans and us new guys caught on the sharp end for the first time. They knew instinctively that they could trust what they had been taught; we could be told that, but it took experience to settle the question at a gut level.

We may have lost one door gun, but we didn't have as much trouble as the other bird going to Scoon's mansion. Their doors were open, and all of a sudden we could see fluid flowing out the door and into the wind. After a few minutes, the flow stopped.

"What the hell was that?" someone wondered out loud. "A mass piss?" Later we found out the other bird had sprung a leak in one of the fuel bladders they had in the back of the passenger compartment. Our guys had joined in with the helo's crew to wrench down fuel fittings, finally stopping the leak. Now they were flying along soaked in fuel and not looking to light any cigars just yet.

The five Army birds were up front in the formation, with the

SEAL birds bringing up the rear as we arrived near the target. The island looked peaceful from where we were. There wasn't any noticeable movement. In fact, the whole place looked deserted to me.

We were blasting along just two hundred feet above the water, the birds trying to stay below any radar on the island. The daylight gave us a good view of the U.S. Marines coming across the water, getting ready to make their landing on the beach. We waved to them, they waved to us, and we continued on our way.

As soon as we had crossed the beach and were over Grenada proper, we started taking 23mm antiaircraft artillery fire. This was the first time I had heard bullets fired in anger going past my head. During range firing in training, I had been forward in the trenches and heard the snap and crack of different caliber bullets go past. That situation is enough to make you think. But now the bullets going past me were meant to bring down the Blackhawk, something I could do nothing about.

The bright green Soviet-style tracers looked like big Christmas tree bulbs or bright fireflies rising up slowly from the island. As the green lights came closer, they appeared to move faster and faster. The ZU-23 guns on the ground were being manned by Cuban or Grenadian crews, we didn't know which, and we didn't care a whole lot either. What we did care about was the four hundred rounds per minute of armor-piercing and high-explosive cannon fire the two guns on the ZU-23 could put out to a range of 2,500 meters.

We could hear the cracks of the projectiles going by. Those cracks were spaced out by the occasional sound of one of the shells hitting the helicopter. Nothing I had ever heard sounded worse. You didn't know what might happen. If one hit you, it was just going to be the luck of the draw.

As the number one kicker, I would be the first person out the door. I was at the back of the doorway with my shooting partner, who was the number two man, facing me. His elbow had to be only inches from my face, something I would be thinking about later. In spite of everything that was going on, I had to laugh at a problem I suddenly had. In my mouth was a big chunk of dip (tobacco), and my mouth turned dry as cotton when I heard the shells hitting.

My Teammates in the bird, Duke and some of the other Vietnam vets, were laughing, and it was pretty easy to see who they were laughing and smiling at. One of them leaned forward and shouted above the wind, "How's it feel to be shot at?"

Well, fuck this, we all laughed. It was about all we could do while moving through the air like a great big target. As we moved along, the AA fire would slow down and then build back up as we passed near another ZU-23 battery. Fortunately for us, we veered off to head for Scoon's mansion and didn't get the worst of the AA fire closer in to Richmond Hill Prison. Later we found out the prison was pretty heavily fortified and the Army took some losses getting to it.

Guns located at Fort Frederick were just pouring out fire at us and all the birds in the area. It was like we were flying into a bee's nest. At least four ZU-23s were on the ground, and all of them were aimed at us. As we came closer to the governor's mansion, we started taking more AA fire from both Fort Frederick and another spot closer to our target. To the east of the governor's mansion was another big house where there had to be at least one ZU-23 battery. Behind us Bob Gormly's helo was badly hit and had to veer off. They made it to a Navy carrier offshore, but it was a near thing.

In spite of the smiles and joking around, the pucker factor went way up on board after that. Even as full as that bird was, we snugged up so tight you probably could have gotten ten more people on board right then. You can't do anything to defend yourself; you just have to ride it out and trust in your pilots. And I hoped we had the best damned pilots in the world.

Since I was the first one in the door, thoughts about my

exposed position did run through my mind. Could this be it? Would I take a round? Would it hurt? Was there anything I could do about it? That last question I could answer: no.

Anyone who tells you they weren't scared when they were being shot at is handing out bullshit. Everyone is scared. It's how you handle it that makes the difference. I know I was scared in this first situation, with the rounds coming at me. But I thought about what was going on at the other end of those guns. Those guys on the ground were also probably brand-new to combat, and they were just as scared as I was. Two new guys going at each other in combat. And I knew I was going to react quicker than he would if it came to a face-off. There was no way I was going to let myself, or my Teammates, down.

Finally we recognized the governor's mansion from the air and split up for the insertion. Our two helos came in fast. My bird would be going in at the front of the building and the other would cover the rear of the house. Both birds were taking a lot of fire, and one of the pilots was hit. I never did learn how badly he had been injured, but he continued with the mission and survived the operation. In spite of this, both birds were able to get on station.

A few guys armed with AK-47s were firing up at our bird from the governor's mansion. All I saw were the muzzle flashes, but that was enough to let me know the guys were there. Since my side of the helicopter didn't have a working door gun, one of the SEALs in our crew leaned out with his carbine and returned fire.

Under the limited cover of our fire, we kicked the rope out the door. The Blackhawk was still ninety feet in the air, the full length of our fast rope, but that didn't matter. As soon as the rope was clear I was out the door with my shooting partner right behind me. Now that we were in the thick of it, the thought of bullets going by simply stopped, and it didn't bother me again. It was time to get into the game.

CHAPTER 16

VISITING WITH THE GOVERNOR: DON'T SPIT ON THE FLOOR

We were expecting flat land with the occasional tree and branch to contend with on the insertion. What we found was a lot different. The ground directly below us slanted off at about a 45-degree gradient. This was a steep hillside, not a flat yard! To make matters worse, instead of the small trees and brush we expected, we had large ponderosa pines that towered above the ground with their heavy branches.

When I went down the rope, I found out just how heavy those pine branches were because I broke most of them on my insertion. My web gear and equipment absorbed most of the punishment, so I was all right when I got to the ground. My shooting partner managed to smack into and break whatever branches I missed. Duke and the other members of our Team followed closely behind us down the rope. When we hit the ground, most of us, myself included, started rolling down the hillside, finally stopping when we hit a tree or were blocked by a Teammate.

So much for our first combat insertion. The only good thing about the hillside was that it protected us from any fire that could have come from Fort Frederick or the house. A five-foot-high stone wall was up the hill between us and the house. Behind us was an east-west road that led off to town. The driveway moved in a shallow U shape between the wall and the house, roughly paralleling the main road. At either end of the driveway was an iron gate in a wrought-iron fence that surrounded the property. The fence was about seventy-five yards behind us and maybe a hundred yards from the mansion proper. We were inside the fence, between it and the house, close to the center of the driveway, when we first hit the ground.

Moving up to the stone wall, we quickly regrouped and set up security with the machine gunners—Timmy, Johnny, and Bubbaloo—out on the perimeter. Holding security with each other as we moved, we jumped up and got over the wall and began moving in toward the house. There was a paved area with steps going straight up to the house. To our right was a covered porch with two balconies above it. To our left was a long two-story house used for the servants and crew.

Up against the wall of the house with my shooting partner, I was looking at the porch and saw a door in the side underneath it move a little. The door looked like it might lead to a cellar or some other space under the porch, but that wasn't important right then. Immediately I covered the door with my weapon. "Hey, Duke," I called out. "We've got some company under the porch."

"Okay, hold what you've got," Duke said.

Just about then the door opened a bit and the barrel of an AK-47 poked out. "Here we go," I thought. Clicking off the safety of my weapon, I switched over to full automatic and prepared to fire.

It was a very good thing that I didn't fire right then. I give credit to our training and my own discipline. The weapon came out the door, but it wasn't being held in a threatening manner. He had the rifle in one hand and the stock in the other, kind of like he was surrendering with it and just pushing the door open with the barrel. The man holding that AK was Governor-General Sir Paul Scoon, the man we had traveled so far and so fast to rescue.

"AK," I told Duke. "He's holding it out."

Duke just walked up with his shotgun in his hand, took the AK-47, and spoke to Scoon: "Mr. Scoon. We're U.S. Navy SEALs. We're here to get you out. Is anyone else in there we should know about? Any more weapons?"

"No," Scoon said. "Only my family and staff."

"Okay," Duke continued, turning to my partner and me. "Continue with the mission. Clear the rest of house."

Going up into the main house, my partner and I set up to enter the first room. Instead of following all the procedures we had drilled with for months, we kicked in the door and dove into the room. Landing on our shoulders, we did a ninja-style shoulder roll, came up with our weapons at the ready, and swept the room with the muzzles, clearing out fields of fire. Nothing was there but the furniture.

If anyone had been in the room, we would have put on quite a show. That dive and roll bit was straight out of the movies, and the only reason we did it was that we were both too nervous to think. The two of us looked at each other and laughed. Then we got our shit together and continued clearing rooms the right way. Somewhere in there, I finally managed to dig that dry wad of dip out of my mouth.

There had been some footprints in that first room, leading out toward the back. Whoever they belonged to must have beat feet into the heavy bushes behind the house. Our second unit had inserted into the yard behind the mansion, fast-roping into the tennis court. Anyone coming out the back would be their concern.

It didn't take long to realize we were the only people in the house. The footprints must have been from one of the people who had fired at us when the birds were coming in. Empty 7.62×39mm AK-47 brass told us which room the shots had come from. Apparently, while we had been kicking that first door in, the guards had bailed out and taken off.

Some of the guys from the front group had linked up with the guys who had inserted in the back and cleared the other side of the building at the same time. There were no threats in the mansion. All the problems that might come at us would be from the outside.

To ensure our security, Duke had us set up a perimeter from the house as well, covering the entire yard and the areas beyond. My shooting partner and I were joined by Pooster on a third-floor balcony. We had a good field of fire and could see much of the island around us.

Governor Scoon and his party were very glad to see us once they got over their initial shock, since we looked as much like a street gang as a military unit. My shooting partner was a good example, with his long hair mostly stuffed up under a red bandanna, his face camouflage of jagged lightning bolts, his wraparound silver sunglasses, and a camouflage jacket complete with several pin-on buttons of rock stars. I wonder what Scoon thought of the Adam Ant button on the uniform of one of his rescuers. The guy with the machine gun in one hand and the chain saw in the other also probably raised a few eyebrows.

Some incoming fire started up, just a shot or two from an AK-47 at first but then a constant few rounds. When some 85mm RPG-7 antitank rockets starting hitting the tile roof, that got our attention immediately. The first rockets must have come in at too shallow an angle to detonate the warhead. For the most part they just skipped off the roof and ricocheted away.

But one rocket went past the three of us, missed everyone along the way, and detonated deep inside the building, demolishing one of the sitting rooms. No one was hurt by the explosion, except maybe Lady Scoon in her concern for the house. This was a gorgeous old-style Victorian mansion furnished with French and English antiques. It was a nice place to look at, but we all felt like sitting ducks at that moment.

Duke must have felt the situation was a little exposed for the people we had come to rescue after that RPG went off. To protect Governor Scoon, his wife, and some nine other men, Duke moved them into the dining room since it was central in the house and the least exposed large room.

While there was a lull in the incoming, I looked over at my partner and noticed he had been badly cut at the elbow. I could see practically to the bone. In all the excitement of the action, he had never even noticed that he was hurt. I strapped a pressure bandage over the wound, which was about all I could do at the time. The wound didn't bother him particularly, and we continued keeping a watch from our balcony.

Later on, back at a hospital, the doctors dug out a fragment from a 23mm cannon shell. Apparently my partner had been hit even before we reached the ground. Some stray fragments probably nailed him while he was leaning on the fast-rope frame in the door of the Blackhawk. At the time, my head had been only inches away from his elbow.

Up on the balcony, we were laughing with nervous tension. The rush of combat, the adrenaline, gave us a good taste of what had been going on with the older vets. You keep your head on straight and follow your training—that was what we had been told, and it proved to be true. But the rush of combat also gives you a kind of ultra-alert high. You feel, hear, smell, and taste things with more clarity than at any other time in your life. At the same time, things that would normally slow you down if not stop you completely, like my partner's wound, you don't even notice.

We were supposed to arrive and leave fast, so we were running light in the way of weapons and equipment. Each of us had an MX-360 Motorola radio for communications among ourselves. For the longer-range commo with command, we had a 101 SATCOM radio. But in the confusion of coming in under fire, the SATCOM had been left on board the Blackhawk.

Lack of the SATCOM made our communications situation a bit tight. One of the guys came around and collected up all our spare batteries, and to save battery power, only one man of every shooting pair kept his radio on. You were normally within shouting distance of your partner anyway, so this wasn't a problem.

Things quieted down for a while after the initial excitement. The RPGs weren't coming in very often now, and we had a chance to consolidate our positions. Duke gave us strict orders not to challenge anyone unless they were in the compound proper. Everyone in our immediate vicinity had been accounted for, and our search of the house and grounds hadn't found any stragglers. A ten-foot-wide stone sidewalk extended about 250 yards to another mansion on our northwest. We knew there were some people there, since we had taken gunfire from that house during the insertion.

From where we were on the second floor of the mansion, looking southwest, we could see the port at Saint George's Harbor. Uphill to our southeast was Fort Frederick, where the majority of the antiaircraft fire was originating. A little closer than Fort Frederick and more to the east was Richmond Hill Prison where our Army counterparts and the Rangers were having a hard time of it. Down below us, toward the water, another bunch of antiaircraft fire was coming from a little fort. Behind Scoon's mansion was a tennis court, and then another mansion some few hundred meters away.

So we kept a close eye on the pathway and the other house as well as the wrought-iron fence and two gates in front of the house.

One of the new weapons we had with us was a bowling-ball-sized rocket grenade you could fire from an M16. The weapon was called a RAW, for rifleman's assault weapon, and it clipped on the front of an M16. To fire it you just pulled the safety pin and fired the rifle at the target. Firing the rifle launched the rocket, which carried three pounds of high explosive. This was about like firing a 90mm recoilless from the end of your rifle.

The RAWs were very new. We had only gotten them a few weeks before the op, and they looked pretty good. Only three of the new RAWs were with us; we had one, and the rest had gone with the second group to the radio station. We had all had a briefing on the RAW, but none of us had fired any except for the one SEAL in ordnance who had brought them to our attention.

We had several M72A2 LAWs (light antitank weapons), though, to give us some antiarmor capability. The LAW we had up on the balcony had taken some punishment during the fast-rope in and ended up a little bent. The fiberglass tube of the LAW is extended to fire. The rocket inside the LAW tube burns its fuel with a boom rather than a whoosh, all the fuel being spent before the rocket even leaves the three-foot-long tube. With the tube of our launcher bent, I wasn't sure the rocket would even leave the tube if it was fired.

But we did have some additional weapons to fall back on. One of the snipers had a .50 caliber RAI 500 rifle and twenty rounds of ammunition. That rifle could take out a man at well over a thousand meters and give most light vehicles a very bad time as well. One of the machine gunners had an H&K 21 light machine gun instead of an M60. SEAL Team Six had a couple of the H&K 21s, and a few of the gunners preferred them over the M60. The differences between the two weapons were mostly technical. Both guns could be handled by one strong man like a big rifle. From a practical standpoint, the M60s and the H&K 21 fired the same ammunition from belts, and that was all that mattered.

We also had some M18A1 Claymore mines. The sightly curved plastic Claymore bodies held over a pound of C4 plastic explosive and seven hundred steel ball bearings. When fired, the mine would launch those steel balls in a wide swath, cutting down everything in front of it. Just to be sure anyone who used the mine knew which end was which, the manufacturer put "FRONT TOWARD ENEMY" in big raised plastic letters on the front of the mine. The rear of the mine says "BACK" just to be sure.

We had used some of the Claymores to cover the driveway and gates, putting them in front of several large trees and camouflaging the electrical firing wires that ran back to the security posts. A couple of the M60 machine guns had been set up below us on a second-floor balcony. Anything we couldn't handle with our M4s would be covered by the M60s. Our security had been set up quickly, according to our training, but not so quickly that we were sloppy about anything.

It was still early in the morning. A little over four miles away to the southwest, we could see the Rangers jumping onto the Salines airstrip to capture it. Their parachute canopies were blocked from clear view by the black smoke of antiaircraft shells detonating in the sky. They were jumping so low they weren't wearing reserve parachutes, because if their mains didn't open they were too low to deploy a reserve before impact. These guys were getting shot from the sky and there wasn't a damned thing we could do to help them.

Cobra helicopter gunships were flying right over us, turning and wheeling through the air, covering the Rangers and other U.S. forces. The 23mm antiaircraft fire was intense, and the inevitable happened. We saw two of the Cobras get hit and go down. My hat is off to the pilot of one of the birds. He dumped all his ordnance, ejecting it away rather than chance hitting his own troops. Then his stricken bird crashed into the bay, killing him.

A Marine CH-46 pilot came in to rescue the crew of the other shot-down Cobra, which had made it to the beach. The pilot of that big CH-46 did a perfect high-speed flare, tilting back as slowing down before landing very near the Cobra. A CH-46 has two large multiblade rotors both fore and aft on the fuselage. It can carry a hell of a lot of troops or a big heavy load but doesn't maneuver all that well compared with the smaller birds. Most of us didn't know a CH-46 could even do that maneuver, and that pilot may have wondered as well until he saw a fellow deep in the shit. The wounded pilot of the Cobra was picked up and carried to the CH-46 by that same great flier. He was wounded himself in the exchange by the Grenadians who were coming up on the downed Cobra to take out its crew.

We didn't have much time to watch the action, though. There was some movement down by the iron fence near the gates. Three guys were walking up to the driveway. Two of them were in Cuban uniforms, one of them in civilian clothes, all of them carrying AK-47s. My Spanish wasn't very good, but I knew how to shout "*Alto!*" (halt).

You could see the three men over the stone wall, through the few trees and scrub. When we yelled, their weapons came up. And that was the last mistake they made. Two M60 machine guns and at least three automatic rifles opened fire.

All our training shooting at each other with wax bullets had given us the edge. Those wax projectiles stung, and you learned fast. What you learned was target acquisition, accuracy, and speed on any individual you saw with a weapon. When we saw their weapons come up, the threat was there and the training took over.

The fire seemed to go on for at least a minute. Probably it

was more like a few seconds. I suppose that we may have been a little more excited than we were during training. We seem to have put out a little more fire than usual. The foliage wasn't blocking our view anymore. The storm of bullets cut a window through it. One guy tried to climb the fence but didn't make it. He was almost cut in half by the M60s. I wasn't sure if we had gotten all three, but we had a sign later that we probably had.

Three nurses in white uniforms and caps were walking down the road around an hour after the incident. Life goes on, even in the middle of a war. We were watching them when suddenly one stopped, looked at the side of the road, and clamped her hands over her mouth. The shredding that 7.62mm and 5.56mm bullets do to a human body is a little hard even on the strong stomachs of people in the medical professions.

Now, of all things, the phone rang inside the house. Governor Scoon picked it up. It was somebody checking to see if he was all right. The noise of our little firefight had probably gotten someone's attention back in the city. When the governor was asked who he had with him, Duke said, "Tell them you have a battalion of Marines up here." The governor relayed the message. We weren't in a mood to trust anyone on the outside right then. Apparently the answer was sufficient, and the conversation ended.

In that short fire we put out, I had used about three magazines, and a couple of the other guys had used about the same. Now that bandoleer of extra ammunition came off my shoulder and we all started reloading our magazines. In just a few moments our loads were full again, which was more comfortable.

Very soon afterward we had other visitors at the gates. Two BTR-60PB eight-wheeled armored personnel carriers showed up, one at each gate. The BTR-60PB is a big angular steel box that carries a crew of two and up to fourteen armed troops. In a turret on top are two machine guns, a 7.62mm PKT, much the same as our M60 machine gun, and a very large 14.5mm KPV heavy machine gun. That large gun could send huge two-ounce slugs at us, traveling at over three thousand feet per second. It would literally chop its way through a target.

According to our very limited intel dump, there were only supposed to be four BTR-60PBs on the whole island. But when we asked Governor Scoon, he said there were more like twenty of the damned things rolling around. Now one of the BTRs sat on the road while the other started toward the gate.

One of the guys with the RAW must have decided to open fire on the BTR. The RAW rocketed off the end of his weapon and flew straight up into the air. We watched this high-tech ball of explosive fly up into the air and then come right back down. All we could say was "Holy shit!" as this bomb smacked into the front lawn. And there it lay, a big dud. For the rest of our stay at the governor's mansion, we avoided that particular spot on the lawn. Lesson learned: Test your new weapons before going into combat.

Duke called up to us, "Get the LAW ready." The LAW was a proved piece of ordnance, only ours didn't look so good just then. "Here," Pooster said, handing me the bent LAW. "You've fired more of these than I have."

Oh, great. So I prepared the LAW for firing, extending the launch tube and arming it for use. I was wondering just what would happen if I fired that weapon with the exhaust tube practically bent behind my head. It looked like a big, dangerous green banana.

The BTR coming up to the gate stopped and opened fire with its 14.5mm. It may have been just a single shot or a short burst, but there was a big explosion in the front yard. It looked like the round fired from the BTR had hit and detonated one of our Claymores.

That stopped the vehicle for a moment, but then it moved forward again. We weren't supposed to take a shot unless we were directly threatened. This BTR had threatened us, but I didn't have a clear shot. Besides my not trusting the LAW, trees and brush were between it and me. I only had the one shot and had to make it good. If I missed, the BTR would know where we were and could open up on us with its heavy machine gun.

But I never had to take the shot. For whatever reason, the BTR moved a little farther forward, then backed off. The other BTRs also backed off, and the troops that had been reported as accompanying them couldn't be seen. Things became very calm again, with only the occasional shot to add a little excitement.

CHAPTER 17

A LONG DAY AND A NIGHT

The Navy was making air strikes on Fort Frederick to knock out the antiaircraft guns that were making the skies so dangerous and helping to prevent the helicopters from picking us up. Our sniper with the .50 caliber spotted someone up at Fort Frederick, either an officer or maybe a spotter who was helping direct their guns. Either way, the sniper figured he could nail the guy with the big .50. Duke recommended against taking the shot. Rules of engagement and all.

But one shot with even a big .50 wouldn't have made much of a difference a few moments later. Navy A-7 Corsairs showed up and made several gun runs, strafing the fort with their 20mm cannons. Then their bombing runs, when they dropped 250-pound bombs into Fort Frederick, caused a bunch of secondary explosions. There was a grim satisfaction for us in seeing the explosions. The Fort Frederick guns had brought down the Cobra gunships earlier.

The only communications we had were through our Motorola MX-360s. Captain Gormly and his team had gone into the airport that the Rangers had taken and set up a SEAL command post. Now our radios were starting to go dead and the communications were getting weak. But we did manage to call in our own air support, relaying the request through Captain Gormly's team and on to whatever air assets were available. Gormly's radio operator, after talking to us, called out to a ship on his SATCOM, which directed the aircraft. Not the most efficient way of getting commo, but it worked.

The strike we wanted was on the mansion near us, from which we had been taking fire off and on all day. Several of us were told to go up to a higher window and spot for the air strike, directing their fire onto the targets we wanted hit. Originally we were going to go up to the roof, but the occasional RPGs still bouncing around made that option a poor one. Instead we watched from a high window and called in strike effects over our radios.

In the room there was a can of Coke that looked mighty tempting. We shared it and watched the aircraft come in. That Coke made a big difference to the taste in my mouth. It was considerably better than canteen water and dried tobacco.

The air strikes leveled the house. But the troops inside must have had bunkers. Later we saw them running away from the rubble like ants from a big footprint.

Night started to fall by 1730 hours, and we got word from one of the gunships overhead that about thirty people were penetrating the area around the house. My shooting partner and I were told to move to a forward position. We got down low in front of a big tree. The M60s were behind us. If we saw the enemy coming we were supposed to open up on full automatic and stay low. The M60s would be firing right over our heads.

Shooting over our heads. Okay, right. We each knew how

hard the others had trained. We trusted our Teammates. That was a confidence builder.

But my partner was wounded in his elbow. The arm was stiff and he was concerned about being able to reload fast. I thought about the M60s backing us up. "Don't worry about it," I said. "I don't think we'll have to."

While we were getting ready, Duke was busy inside the house. The radios were running down, and most had gone dead. We needed air support as soon as we could get it. Using the governor's regular telephone, Duke just called back to Hurbert Field in Florida and eventually got connected to the right people.

It was early in the morning, 0100 or 0200 hours. We could hear a single Specter gunship circling above us. The AC-130 Specter was a heavily armed version of the C-130 cargo plane. Out of the left side of the bird extended two 7.62mm Miniguns, then two 20mm Vulcan cannons, the Minigun's big brother, two 40mm Bofors cannons, and, near the tail, a 105mm howitzer.

All this firepower could be concentrated on a fairly small area, directed by a full suite of optical and electronic devices. What we couldn't see, Specter could both see and hit.

When Duke called in the air strike, Specter opened up. Out by our tree, my partner and I didn't know the air strike had been called in, since our radios had been dead for a while. Suddenly we both heard the quiet *POOP, POOP, POOP* of the Specter's 40mm gun opening up. I hope they're coming this way, I thought.

Then the ground erupted in front of our position by the tree, the shells appearing to impact only thirty yards or so from where we lay. In spite of being as low to the ground as we could get, we dug in a little deeper, willing our bodies to become flatter and make a smaller target. Just the pressing down, I think, dug us in a good four or five inches. Each of us outside the building could be seen by the AC-130 because we all had glint tape sewn into the tops of our hats. The tape reflected more than enough to make each of us stand out clearly to the gunners on board the bird. Still, I didn't feel entirely safe.

The roar of those 40mm and 20mm shells exploding cost me a good part of my hearing in later years. But at the time we didn't care about the noise. Whatever targets were creeping up on us in the dark were no longer a problem after the Specter's one or two gun runs.

The gunship had only enough fuel or ammunition for a few runs. Then it had to return to base for refueling and rearming. Before it left, the pilot relayed to us that two targets were running away from the governor's house, the rest not being in a position to ever run again.

After the gun run we were pulled back to the house as the perimeter was tightened up. But I had to go back out to the tree where we had been lying. When we had been in that position, I had taken out an extra magazine and laid it down next to my weapon, thinking I just might have a chance to reload if it came to a firefight. When I got back to the mansion I realized that I'd left that loaded mag back on the ground. "Well," our chief said, "go get it." So I had to work my way back to that tree and find my ammunition.

Eventually we were all back at the mansion. Everyone had to be close in as protection against the darkness. The guys who weren't on watch were supposed to catch whatever rest they could. I don't know about the others, but I couldn't even try to sleep.

I don't smoke cigarettes as a habit, but tobacco can help keep you alert. One of the guys was smoking and I bummed a couple of drags from him. He was one of our Vietnam vets, and I asked him, "How does this compare to Vietnam?"

"Vietnam was fun," he answered. "This ain't fucking fun! This is for the Marines to dig in and hold." He handed the butt over and continued growling. "And the next time you come to combat, bring your own damned cigarettes."

We had a laugh over that.

The morning finally came, and with it came word that a unit of Marines had landed nearby and were making their way to the governor's mansion. Grenada was almost secured, and the Marines would escort us out of the area. Some young Marine recon-type walked up to one of our guys who was out by the back fence. The kid was all of maybe eighteen years old, and his eyeballs were bulging as he came up to a SEAL just sitting on a rock.

"Hey," my Teammate called out. "Are you in the Marines?"

"Yeah," the kid answered.

"You coming here to get us?"

"Yeah."

"Okay."

Easy, right? So much for conflict between the Navy and the Marines.

Governor Scoon and his party made up the nucleus of our group as we extracted from the area on foot. With the Marines keeping a wide perimeter, we maintained our own fields of fire and stayed around the governor's party.

One of our M60 gunners was escorting Scoon, so I swapped him my weapon for his M60. Walking on the outer edge of our group, I kept the M60 loaded and ready. As we walked down the street, you could see this one local sitting in a rocker on his porch, a blanket covering his lower body. He had bloodshot eyes, so we knew he had gotten about the same amount of sleep as we had the night before. He could easily have been one of the few survivors of the Specter strike.

"Hey, guys," we were told, "don't take your eyes off him."

There could have been a weapon under that blanket. Or he could just be a local who had stayed up to watch the show. Either way, we weren't trusting the situation.

As we left the grounds of the governor's house, we saw burned-out trucks at the side of the road. Weapons, especially AK-47s, were scattered all over. In one truck were the remains of one of the ZU-23mm antiaircraft guns that had caused us so much trouble. The vehicles were destroyed, and blood was spattered everywhere. The Specter had done its job and just hammered the area. Someone had gathered up the bodies, but it was obvious to all who could see the scene that men had died here.

For us, though, the situation was finally a good one. We approached an open field, and a halt was called to our little parade. Helos were coming in to pick us up, but there weren't enough available to get us all in one go. So the plan was for the governor and his party to go out in the first bird and the rest of us to be shuttled out a little later.

This wasn't a problem. Of course, the sudden loud explosion nearby made it seem like there might be a problem. After that long day and night, we were a bit jumpy at loud noises. But we were told that it was simply a cache being destroyed by the Marine Recon people.

Lady Scoon was trying hard to show her appreciation for everything we had done for her and her family. She had a number of charm bracelets on and was breaking them down, passing out the trinkets as souvenirs. I still have the one she gave me. It says *Te Amo,* I love you in Spanish. That little bit of jewelry is in the shadow box I had made for my retirement, among other mementos. The family must have felt well protected, in spite of our appearance. A report written by Governor Scoon arrived at the command later and praised us for everything we had done.

Those bits of jewelry weren't the only souvenirs we took from Grenada. We came up to a flagpole flying the Grenadian flag as we were leaving the area. "Denny?" one of the guys said to me, looking at the pole.

"You've got it," I answered, and I laid my weapon down and climbed up the pole.

That flag hangs at Assault Group Three today, a trophy of our first combat.

Now the first bird arrived, and Governor Scoon was ushered aboard. Several of our guys, including a couple of the officers, went with him. The bird soon returned to pick up the rest of us and get us to the airport. The crew chief of the returning bird, who was manning the door gun, put on a big smile and lifted his visor. It was one of our officers who had left in the first bird. He had come back to help ensure that the extraction went okay.

We regrouped at the airport, which was securely in U.S. hands. The 82nd Airborne was in now and securing the area. The confusion that had dogged the operation hadn't been limited to us. Most of the guys from the 82nd had thought they were on a training operation, just like the Air Force C5A pilots on the way out. They were short of gear, and we ended up stripping out our ammo and giving them every magazine we had. It wasn't like we were going to use it now.

While we were waiting at the airport, I had a sobering reminder of the cost of this little operation. A jeep pulled up with a stretcher on it, holding the body of a U.S. Ranger killed in the fighting. This was the first time I was ever close to a dead body in combat, especially one of our own. Bodies that I had seen in car accidents and mountain climbing just didn't have the same impact as that dead Ranger. We were all a little quiet for a while then.

A C-141 landed and picked us up for the trip back to the States. We landed and reported to a U.S. Army base for a debriefing on the op. We were back in isolation and couldn't contact anyone outside our little portion of the base. They had chow and some beer for us and put us into one of their transient barracks. This was a chance for us to decompress a bit from the combat high we had been on for the last two days. They told us to get a good night's rest, but we were still way too hyped up to get much sleep. For most of the night, we just sat up and talked.

CHAPTER 18

OUR TEAMMATES

The next day, our debrief actually began. It was a full mission debrief from the captain on down. Now we learned about how Gormly's bird had almost been shot from the sky. Then it was the turn of the guys on the radio station op. The site itself turned out to have been only a transmitter; the main studios were back in Saint George, the capital of Grenada. But the transmitter had been taken and secured without any problems. People who had been manning the station were secured, and the site went off the air.

While our guys were waiting for helicopters to come in and pick them up, a large number of Grenadian soldiers showed up, along with a BTR-60PB armored personnel carrier. That's when the shit started to hit the fan.

From a guard's booth near the chain-link fence that surrounded the station, the guys took out one of the trucks with a 40mm grenade from an M203. The local troops weren't too excited about storming the station after that. But they had a Cuban adviser with them who had one of these command sticks, and he was swatting his troops, getting them into a line to assault the site.

With the BTR approaching, one of our guys fired the other RAW, which worked a whole lot better than ours had. The rocket fired straight, but hit the chain-link fence and detonated before it got to the BTR. Still, the blast was so strong and the RAW warhead so close to the BTR that it jammed the turret. Now that KPV heavy machine gun couldn't be aimed at the buildings or much of anything else.

But the remaining Grenadian troops lined up behind the BTR and prepared to assault the site. With the increasing fire coming in on them, the leader of the SEAL detachment decided to abandon the site. There was no way our guys had enough firepower to go force-on-force with the much larger group of Grenadian troops. It was time to E&E. They pulled out through an open field, toward the ocean. Before they left, they rendered the station inoperable.

Leapfrogging away from the station, one group of SEALs would protect the others as they pulled back. Then the unit that was farthest away would cover the first guys. But that Cuban adviser was doing his job too, swatting his troops on the rump and getting them to lay down a base of fire.

In spite of their movement, some of our guys were hit as they pulled out. One guy took a round from an AK in his leg, high up near the hip. Another was hit in the triceps. The radio man had the SATCOM shot right off his back.

When they got to the water, everyone followed our standard operating procedures, breaking up into shooter pairs and making their way out to sea, stripping down and caching their first-line gear so it couldn't be found by the enemy. Some of the men went to a local marina and commandeered a small sailboat. Others hit the water and swam out to sea where they were picked up by Navy assets. The guys in the boat were rescued by a Little Bird helicopter that lowered a caving ladder to them. That gave our wounded comrades an airlift out that kept them from a long swim. Everyone was recovered safely. The E&E plan had proved itself. And it all proved the worth of our training.

Then it was our turn to talk about the op at Scoon's mansion. In spite of the seriousness of the debriefing situation, some of the guys still found time for a gag.

We were waiting around in a lounge with padded chairs and a couple of pool tables. We had been told to stay awake, but that was a lot easier said than done. One of the guys stretched out on one of the pool tables and promptly fell asleep. Not wanting to see a Teammate get in trouble, or to let a good opportunity for a gag go by, one of the guys made it look like sleeping beauty was paying attention. Taking some chalk and a pen, he whitened the lids of our sleeping Teammate's eyes and drew in open eyeballs on the chalk.

So much for being in a heightened state of tension and having those combat-tuned catlike reflexes. Our guy never woke up. But it was pretty funny to see him lying there with his "eyes" wide open.

The debrief at the Army base reminded me of something else: why I got out of the Army. When we first came back from combat, our Army hosts treated us well. They hosted a steak cookout that evening, and we indulged in a few beverages after the official work was done. We were all pretty beat and slept soundly in the transient barracks they assigned us. But the next day, before we were allowed to leave the barracks, we had to clean the place up as if we were preparing for an inspection.

Buffing floors and polishing bathroom fixtures was not what we expected to have to do after getting back from a combat mission. It was like being back in basic training again. The guys grumbled, but the work was done. Only it wasn't done quite to the master sergeant's satisfaction. We failed the damned inspection and had to clean up some more! Now the guys were seriously pissed.

We ended up cleaning that barracks three or four times before we could finally leave. The situation was so ridiculous it was funny. But we looked forward to the next time we hosted some Army guys up in our neck of the woods. Finally, by the middle of the afternoon, we could turn the building back over to them and leave.

There were Greyhound buses waiting to take us back to our compound. We stopped at the nearest Kmart and bought two trash cans, filled them with ice and beer, and were on our way back to Virginia Beach. We enjoyed ourselves, to say the least.

Back at our base in Virginia, I found out that I had been out of the Navy for a day and a half. My time in service had expired while we were isolated, and I had been officially a civilian during part of the Grenada operation.

Grenada wasn't over yet. The SpecOps forces were trying to regroup, and the word was out that we might be sent back to the island to stand by on a contingency basis. A lot of stuff was going on right then, so Duke came up to me and asked if I was ready to go back down.

"Yeah," I told him. "I'm ready to go back."

"Well," Duke continued, "you're going to have to be back in the Navy to do that."

Things were moving so fast, I hadn't even taken the time to shower. My long hair was dirty, I still had the remainders of cammie paint on my face, and my uniform wasn't quite up to inspection standards. Looking like a dirtbag, I followed Duke into Captain Gormly's office, where he had everything set up and, I reenlisted in the Navy on the spot.

Now I was ready to return to Grenada for more action. We loaded out and were all set to go when the word came back to stand down. Some of the guys hadn't liked their first taste of combat and were a little shaky about going right back.

Some of the older vets said this uneasiness had occurred every time a Team had first gone into action, back in Vietnam and probably well before that. I asked Duke about it and he told me, "Hey, that happens. Once they get back out, do some patrolling, and get a good indoctrination, then they're back." We weren't in a position to do that right away, but things worked out for everyone eventually.

Personally, I was ready to go. I had proved to myself that this was what I wanted to do. Operating was something I would do at every opportunity that was offered. It was something I loved.

Back at the base, we had an award ceremony at our compound. We all wore three-piece suits rather than uniforms. That was quite a moment, though it led to a far more serious one. It was then that we started making arrangements for the memorial services for the four Teammates we had lost that first day.

These had been the first combat losses any SEAL Team had suffered since the end of the Vietnam War ten years earlier. Other SEALs, including members of our own Team, had been killed in training accidents, but that didn't help when it came to our feelings about the four men lost in the waters off Grenada.

Losing Bob Schamberger hurt a lot, but losing the others was just as bad. Kenny Butcher had been one of the most easiest-going of guys. A little fireplug of a man when it came time to do his job, there wasn't anyone better at it than Kenny. And he was very good at air operations.

Kevin Lundberg (Kodiak) had a bald head and a full red beard. People used to look at him and wonder. Not that he cared much what others thought. Kevin didn't care for a lot of people. I first met him back on the West Coast and I don't think he immediately liked me a whole hell of a lot. But things changed. Later, when I was dating Kitty, he would meet her and let her know when I was going to be late. And he made sure no one else took up Kitty's time until I got there.

Steve Morris had been one of the newer members, joining

SEAL Team Six shortly before the Grenada operation. I never got to know the man as well as I would have wanted; he was a very quiet guy. Steve was sturdy and built, but he didn't talk much in the short time I was able to know him.

We gave those men, our brothers, a proper SEAL going away. Just like in the old tradition of the Teams when they were in Vietnam, we had a beer mess where we toasted our lost brothers. Funds were put together to care for the men's families, especially the children. I believe a college fund was put together for Scham's son, and he received Gracie, Scham's Corvette, when he was old enough.

Some of the Team guys went to the homes of each of the men to attend their family services and show our respects. I went down to Florida and met Bob Schamberger's parents. While there, I learned a bit more about Bob, saw the books he had grown up reading and the Purple Heart he had earned while in the Teams in Vietnam. It was good for me to be there, and Bob's family was comforted by our being there, which also meant a lot.

About a year and a half after Grenada, the Naval Amphibious Base at Little Creek named a new barracks structure after one of our fallen. We were all in attendance when Schamberger Hall was dedicated. Bob would have liked that, no doubt about it.

CHAPTER 19

RED CELL AND
A NEW MISSION

The year after the Grenada operation went down, I had a number of changes in my life and career. In January, Kitty and I got married. Then in the summer of 1984, I was offered another challenge by the same man who had brought me to SEAL Team Six in the first place. Dick Marcinko opened the door to several of us at the Team with an offer of a new position, new challenges, and a very new mission statement.

Vice Admiral James A. "Ace" Lyons, Deputy Chief of Naval Operations for Plans, Policy, and Operations, had directed Dick to design a unit to test the Navy's vulnerability to terrorist attacks. Admiral Lyons well knew the dangers of terrorist attacks.

On April 18, 1983, an Islamic Jihad suicide truck bomb blasted the U.S. Marine barracks in Beirut, Lebanon. In the final body count, 241 Marines were killed along with 58 French Legionnaires. The U.S. military had taken steps to harden our sites to attacks like the one in Lebanon as well as to the more insidious terrorist hostage-taking and smaller bomb attacks.

Admiral Lyons wanted Marcinko to test the effectiveness of those measures and to prevent further attacks. To do this, Marcinko officially created OP-06D, the Naval Security Coordination Team, which we all called simply Red Cell.

The name Red Cell came about in part because it was being set up much like a terrorist cell. It would be a very small unit of men, smaller than an Army platoon, and pretty much autonomous in its actions. It would report to a very limited chain of command with only a few steps between an operator in the unit and the chief of naval operations himself. Because the color for the highest level of alert status was red, that became part of the name.

Dick had come back to his old command at SEAL Team Six to gather the kind of men he wanted in the new unit. He was looking for volunteers. A number of us interviewed with Dick, and he told us what would be expected of us and what we would do. The interviews were different this time only in that Dick already knew all of us and we knew him. So this time, instead of knocking us off balance by his staccato questions, he already knew how we would act and answered our questions instead.

We would be testing security at Navy facilities around the United States and throughout the world. There was beginning to be great concern about terrorists getting their hands on weapons of mass destruction. So we would test sites that held some of the Navy's most secret materials to make sure neither a device nor the materials to make one could be stolen.

The new assignment was going to be a different one, and it sounded like an exciting ride. A lot of traveling would be required as well as a lot of new training. I really liked where I was and what I was doing, but this had a lot of appeal to me. In a heart-to-heart meeting, I told Bob Gormly that I was thinking about the assignment.

Dick Marcinko and Bob Gormly had butted heads a bit during the change of command at SEAL Team Six, but I didn't think that was due to any personal problems between the two men. It was more that they both saw the problems that had to be addressed and had different styles of leadership to get the job done. Captain Gormly told me something that made me feel pretty good about the whole thing.

"Denny," Bob said, "no, I don't want anyone to go, and yes, I don't want you to leave the command. But I will not hold your going against you. If you feel a little devoted to—"

"It's not that I feel devoted," I interrupted. "I think it's an opportunity to expand on what I've done here. Hopefully, I can eventually come back and bring those skills with me."

"If you decide to go," Bob continued, "and you don't like it up there, I don't care if it's a week, three months, four months, or six months, you give me a call and you'll have orders directly back here."

That made me feel really good. It had been a hard decision to make, but I made it. And a number of others had made the same choice. Pooster joined me on the move as well as a bunch of our Teammates. We were all going to join the Old Man and his new unit up in Washington, D.C.

Pooster and I went up to D.C. to get settled in. Kitty stayed in Virginia Beach to pack up the household and come up later. D.C. was only a four-hour drive or so from Virginia Beach, so the separation wasn't as bad as for some Navy families. We all stayed in a civilian hotel while looking for our own places to live.

Johnny Johnson had come up from Little Creek to visit us at Red Cell. Soon after his arrival, we had a get-together in the lounge at the Marriott in Arlington. It was a big room, with tiered seating going up from a wooden dance floor. Brass rails separated the tiers, and a wooden rail topped with brass surrounded the dance floor itself. Out on the dance floor was Pooster, and he managed to get into a hassle with somebody.

Punches were thrown, and Pooster probably would have come out the better for it if he hadn't missed with his second swing and nailed the brass rail with his fist.

Kitty and the Old Man were sitting on an upper level watching the floor show. Down on the dance floor, I was backing up Pooster and had a hold on the guy who had been fighting with him. While I was holding the guy on the floor, I could see Pooster's boot coming in from the side. This wasn't something I wanted to be meeting, so I turned my head out of the way and Pooster nailed the guy on the floor.

Now things were growing fast. The guy on the floor wasn't going to be bothering us, but he had a number of friends in the immediate vicinity. They decided that picking a fight with Johnny Johnson might be a good way of introducing themselves. Since Johnny had boxed on the All-Navy team earlier in his career, this wasn't the smartest choice they could have made.

Bouncing lightly on his feet, Johnny was making short jabs at anyone who cared to mix it up with him. He'd nail somebody, and the rest of us would watch the guy fall down. Duke was busy himself, and he learned a valuable lesson about clothes. Duke was holding one guy and grabbing at another when somebody came up and grabbed him by the tie. Duke's head was pulled back, but he managed to deal with the situation quickly. Another lesson learned, this one on the value of a breakaway tie.

The guy who originally picked the fight with Pooster held some position with the hotel. After that evening, we learned that he no longer held the same job. But after we had tossed him out, he decided to return. This time he brought along a fire extinguisher, with the intention of hosing us all down with it. That didn't work too well. We held him down and took his little toy away. Then hotel security came up and took the guy away, and the fight was over.

But the evening was far from finished. Johnny had a bad cough. He was a heavy smoker, and he used to hold his hand to his chest when he had a bad episode. After the fight, we decided to go out and get something to eat at a local Denny's. I thought Johnny looked a little beat. His cough was acting up, and the fight seemed to have gotten to him. Maybe he had taken a blow when none of us saw it. I asked him if he wanted me to drive him, but he turned me down.

Saying he was okay, Johnny climbed into his own car and joined our little motorcade. As we were traveling along to the Denny's, Johnny cut off and started back to the hotel where we were all staying. Looking back, I figured Johnny was just tired and had decided to turn in for the evening.

On his way back to the hotel, Johnny Johnson suffered a heart attack and died. We had lost one of our own to something none of us saw coming. Purdue, Pooster, and others joined the rest of his Teammates in escorting the body to Johnny's home town in Oregon. We held a wake for Johnny down south at SEAL Team Six. It just went to prove to some of us that you can never take anything for granted. But to go out after a good time with a bunch of your friends isn't a bad way to leave.

Even without Johnny, we had to continue on with our mission, and finding our own living quarters was part of it. The first place Pooster and I could find was on Duke Street in Alexandria, a Virginia suburb of D.C. The place would have been too expensive for just Kitty and myself, but it was big enough so that splitting the space and the rent with Pooster made it affordable. We had one whole corner of the building and it worked out well for all of us.

There was a nice little pub, Shooter McGee's, which we all just called Shooter's, across the street from our penthouse apartment. Shooter's quickly became the unofficial second home and meeting place for Red Cell. Many of the guys that we dealt with regularly from the rest of the Special Operations community also dropped by our watering hole.

The new official home for Red Cell was in the E-ring at the

Pentagon. It was a little room, secured with a combination-lock steel door, more like a vault than an office. At the beginning there were only four of us—Don Hubbard, Truck, Pooster, and myself—working at the Pentagon, but right behind us came Ho Ho, Knobber (who had reenlisted in order to come up to Red Cell), Sundance, and Butch Cassidy. Stevie Wonder, whom the Old Man had met during his time at the Washington Navy Yard, an ex-Marine with more than a little experience behind him, also came on board.

Eventually we were eleven enlisted men and three officers, but we didn't look like any military unit anyone had ever seen. We held to our relaxed grooming standards, and the long hair, mustaches, and beards did tend to stand out a bit at the Pentagon.

Our uniforms were different too. Slacks and mostly pullover shirts were as close to the uniform of the day as we wore at the beginning of our time on the E-ring. But a lot of eyes would look at us as we walked up to our office on the ring, and that was more attention than we wanted. Red Cell was a very classified operation. We couldn't do the job we were tasked with if people knew who we were. Slacks and a collared shirt became our regular outfit, and maybe a tie as well. But for a long time, the dress code at Red Cell was relaxed. Even jeans were worn. We were a lot more concerned with getting the unit together and following the Old Man's mission statement than with following anyone else's personal dress code.

Our goal was to test Navy facilities in the most realistic manner commensurate with safety. After a test penetration—a hit—on a facility, we would go back and survey everything we had done. It was only by showing them how we had done something that the security could be improved to prevent it from happening again. We also had the personal security of admirals, naval commanders in chief (CinCs—pronounced "sinks"), and other important or highly visible people to consider. These people could be a target on their respective bases or in a motorcade far from a government facility.

Prior to conducting any scenario, we would study the different terrorist groups that were interested in the area, or a specific group that might come to a new area and target a site. Once we had an idea of the terrorist groups that could be involved, we would adopt their known methods of operation and techniques. Making case studies of different groups was something we did almost constantly.

It was a number of months before Red Cell was fully operational to Dick Marcinko's, and our, satisfaction. It was at least four months before we did our first real exercise. In the meantime, we had been building up our intel and equipment levels.

Heckler and Koch showed us the latest in firearms, and the basement range at their Chantilly, Virginia, facility was where we kept up our pistol and submachine gun qualifications. We incorporated Bill Scott's Racing School into our defensive driving profile. Defensive driving was not only something we could use in beating pursuit, it was also something we could recommend for drivers of those same high-ranked individuals we targeted.

We needed to learn how motorcades worked, how barricades could be breached, and what you could and couldn't expect to do with a vehicle. The training was a challenge, and thrilling. Racing around a track at ninety miles an hour will get anyone's blood pumping faster. But then learning how to take that same car at speed and drift it sideways, or spin it 180 degrees and head it the other way, that brings out a whole new level of excitement.

We learned about ramming, both how to do it and how to survive it. And we held competitions between ourselves to see who was picking up the material the fastest and the best.

Distance races might not seem so interesting, but they are when you're learning how far you can drive a car without its tires, just on the rims.

Jerry Smith ran the defensive driving program at the school. He had worked with a number of other government agencies, such as the State Department, teaching them the skills we wanted to learn. Working with Jerry and the other people at the school was very rewarding. We became good friends and even helped his facilities with our training. Building a range on his site, we were able not only to practice ourselves but to extend the training he could offer.

We also put together an obstacle course for physical training. That wasn't our most popular construction project. It wasn't having an O-course available for us that was a bother; we were looking forward to that. But the fact that almost every one of us came down with poison ivy after working in a field full of it was less than fun.

We all completed both the driving course and the instructor's course. By working as instructors for the State Department guys at the school, we helped them and got better ourselves. There are few better ways to learn something than to teach it.

And we kept practicing all our other skills as we got ready for our first operations. My rock-climbing abilities even got a little workout outside of duty hours on occasion. In our penthouse apartment in Alexandria, you had to push a button to be let in if you didn't have a key. Kitty had my key most of the time, and somehow Pooster could never manage to keep one.

There was the occasional evening when Kitty thought the two of us were arriving home at an unacceptable hour, or in an unacceptable condition. It didn't really matter which, the results were the same. We'd push the buzzer and she wouldn't let us in. The building was seven stories up to the penthouse and constructed of brick. So when Kitty wouldn't let us in, we just climbed up the outside of the building. If she was really mad at us, the balcony door would be locked. So we would end up spending some quality time on the balcony, jimmying open the door.

The apartment building was managed by a retired Navy captain. There was one neighbor who didn't think a lot of us climbing past his window at night, and he complained about us regularly to the manager. That captain finally told us we couldn't climb up the outside of the building anymore. What he said was something along the lines of "If you do that one more time, I'm going to have to evict you!" So we tried to behave.

That wasn't the only time Pooster and I had adventures at the penthouse. He had his own style of living that made things kind of interesting. There was one particular night when I came home later than he did, and I knew he was already pretty well wasted long before he got home. When the elevator doors opened outside the penthouse, one of Pooster's boots was lying in the hallway. The other boot was just outside our door, which was open a crack.

Apparently he had been trying to get undressed to save a little time before he went to bed. He didn't make it. Inside his bedroom was Pooster, pants around his ankles, kneeling on the floor with his head on the bed. Kitty and I picked him up and heaved him the rest of the way in.

More details on how Red Cell would operate were worked out as we went along. Soon we were fully equipped to conduct any operation necessary. All we would need was transportation to a target area. Even our communications details were worked out by the use of code names.

During an operation, we would have to be able to address each other both face-to-face and on the radio, but not with our real names. This not only maintained our anonymity, it made it harder for our captives or security to get a fast handle on who we were. The psychological factor of "unnatural" names would also help raise stress levels for our hostages.

Everyone came up with a name. Dick Marcinko was the Silver Bullet, his old call sign from his SEAL Team Two Vietnam days. We never called him Dick anyway. He was always the Skipper. Pooster picked his name up because his hair stuck up much of the time like a rooster's comb. Our corpsman was Doc, but that hadn't been much of a stretch. Then came me. The Skipper couldn't think of a name for me right away, so I went home to think about it.

When I was first at SEAL Team One, I had been called Macho Man from the popular song of the time. My first leading petty officer had tagged me with that. But that wasn't going to be my handle at Red Cell. That night I watched *Escape from New York* with Kurt Russell. With the earring, long hair, and mustache, Russell's character seemed to fit. The next day I was just joking around when I said a line almost straight from the movie: "You can call me Snake, Snake Chalker." And it stuck.

CHAPTER 20

A VISIT TO NORFOLK

Our first Red Cell operation was in familiar territory, the huge Naval base at Norfolk, Virginia. Knobber had his own pilot's license, which made for some interesting transportation possibilities. He wasn't the only pilot we had in Red Cell—Butch also had his license—but Knobber was an ex-cropduster and one of those people who could fly anything. And he flew everything with the same lunatic abandon.

In the early spring of 1985, we rented a plane, a twin-engine 401, and flew it down to Norfolk, landing at the air station there. That got us on the base in an easy penetration. The commander's house faced the air strip, so we just taxied to the front of the house.

The Skipper kind of sat to the side and observed the developing situation rather than taking an active hand in the action. He would make the report to the higher command at the base, telling them how and what we did. To make certain we didn't cross the line legally, a lawyer observed with the Skipper, recommending or advising against a course of action as it came up. It was supposed to be a test and a training operation. We were acting the part of terrorists, but we were still Navy personnel working for the general good of our service.

One exercise the Skipper wanted to see was a hostage-taking scenario. The captain who was the base commander knew what we were going to do. He just didn't know how we were going to do it.

That morning, the captain was sitting at his breakfast when six black-clothed, balaclava-wearing terrorists burst in through his front door to take him and his family hostage. While this was good experience for the Navy base's security team, it was also an opportunity for the local civilian security forces. Hostage negotiation is a tricky thing, and any practice or practical experience that can be obtained without someone's life actually being in danger adds to the overall quality of the security force.

A couple of people from the FBI negotiation school had been sent to the Norfolk area to gain experience through our exercise. These guys had the excellent luck to be sitting at breakfast with the base commander when we barged in. Knobber, Butch Cassidy, and I were assigned to put these two individuals through some stress to see if they would break.

We knew who the negotiators were; we had a picture of one of the pair who wore glasses. Grabbing one of them, I shoved him into a kitchen cupboard, knocking pots and pans out of the way as he went in. It was manhandling, but we were being careful not to injure anyone. Still, injuries weren't the only mistakes that could be made.

As I was shoving my man into the cupboard, Knobber called out to me. "Snake!" he said, indicating the man he had secured. Knobber had the glasses-wearing FBI man in his hands. Well then, who was it I was shoving into the pots and pans? Pulling the man out of the cupboard, I found out. It was the Navy captain who lived in the house, the commander of the base.

Oh, that was really good.

Pulling the man back out, I shoved him down into his seat. He sat there a bit stunned. He wasn't the only one who was in shock from the suddenness of our little encounter. The captain's wife was standing at the kitchen stove, frozen in the same position she was in when we all arrived. At the table sat a younger woman, the other member of the negotiation team.

We isolated everybody, putting the young woman in the dining room and the man in the living room. Butch secured the guy in the living room and started a little modern torture on him. Turning on the TV set, Butch set it on a station showing cartoons and left the guy there watching them.

Knobber and I had a different assignment: we were running a Mutt and Jeff routine on the young woman. I was the bad guy, Knobber was the good guy. It started out with Knobber being nice to the girl, asking her if she was okay and saying that she shouldn't be scared. Then I would barge into the room, being a badass and manhandling the woman a bit.

There wasn't any physical abuse, no slapping or actual striking. But it doesn't take much shoving around from a guy who's been working out with the Teams for the last five years to make you feel physically intimidated and helpless. I shoved her down on the floor, holding her there and telling her how I hated females and all that kind of shit. Then I put her in one of the chairs and pulled a bag over her head. This was all intended to get the woman riled up and upset so that she wouldn't feel in control of the situation.

Then Knobber would come back into the room and shove me away from the woman. Slapping me—no one cared if we hit each other—Knobber would holler, "Snake!" I would just answer with a nasty "Fuck you" and storm out of the room.

Then Knobber would turn to the woman and ask her if she was okay and act all concerned for her welfare. This show went on for at least two hours.

The negotiators were one aspect of the exercise, but it was primarily a hostage rescue situation for the security personnel. We kept our hands off the captain and his wife; at least I wasn't pushing him into any more cupboards. The Skipper was talking to the captain, keeping him informed of the situation and what would be coming up next. The captain wasn't too upset with me for roughing him up, not even when he found out I had broken one of his dining room chairs when I was playing bad guy and shoving the woman around.

Meanwhile we had secured the house and put up barricades as best we could. Base security had been brought in, surrounding the area and keeping outsiders away. They had even brought up an ambulance and had it on call, showing good foresight. Negotiations began and continued throughout the incident.

There was no real physical abuse in any of our simulations. All the military personnel involved had been through far worse in their own training. SERE (Survival, Escape, Resistance, and Evasion) school, which all the pilots and many others had gone through, was many levels worse than anything we did. But it didn't take very much for some people to break down or just feel completely helpless.

The woman said the nasty talk had gotten to her the worst. Later I had shoved her into a closet, still with the bag over her head. With a cigar I was smoking, I would blow smoke into the bag. This was irritating but hardly dangerous. It still got to her. Minor irritations can grow out of all proportion if you think about them too much.

The woman did really well, we all thought. We went through almost the whole exercise without any trouble from her, though toward the end she was reacting to the stress a bit. We had one of her own people with us to observe the situation, but she didn't know that. Finally we ended the situation with the woman and the guy.

We called up the ambulance and told them we were going to release somebody and medevac them out. When the ambulance arrived, we took it over. Using our hostages as a shield, we escaped the area in the ambulance. Once we had gotten out of the area, the exercise was over.

The whole incident lasted about six hours. Afterward we debriefed and explained to them what we had observed and how we had conducted our operation. A film unit made up of ex-SEAL Team Six operators had been hired by Red Cell to video-tape all our operations. Being ex–Six SEALs, the camera crew could keep up with us and maintain our security during an operation.

The base security unit had done a good job. We had never given them a chance to do a dynamic entry on our position, so they held the position secure and let the negotiators do their job. Our first Red Cell operation turned out to be very productive for all concerned. The Skipper talked to the negotiators and the security people, telling them how the negotiation went and what else could have been done to manipulate the "terrorists."

We explained to them that they would want to hold us secure and in position for as long as possible. Once the site was secured, a specialized team should be called. These specialized teams trained for these situations constantly and should be brought in to deal with the situation directly. Usually there would be a problem over one security agency or group calling in another one, especially a military base calling in a civilian organization. No security chief wanted to admit that there were actions his team couldn't deal with. This wasn't always true, however, and Red Cell went a long way to point this out to people.

A local security force couldn't be trained in one day on how to do a dynamic entry. Entering a hot area and dealing with hostages and targets all mixed in with one another is very hard and takes specific training to have any chance of success. We had trained for years at SEAL Team Six just for that kind of operation. So we could explain the situation well to the security forces we were testing with Red Cell.

The main thing we tried to do with our exercises was demonstrate site vulnerabilities and how to set up perimeter security and begin negotiations. The idea behind perimeter security was to leave no holes through which we could escape the area, as we showed the Norfolk security team during that first op.

For the hostage, it was a different kind of training situation. It might be compared to an advanced SERE course for possible targets and for the negotiators who would have to deal with the situation. We worked hard to give the hostages a feeling of not being in control, something that's very difficult for senior Navy officers and other VIPs to accept. What was even harder to accept for some of the individuals was how they reacted to the stress.

The physical intimidation added greatly to their overall feeling of helplessness. The language we used, shouting, fast constant movement, and general intimidation didn't give the individuals time to think. It was a lot like breakout, the first hour of Hell Week in BUD/S, where the instructors are all shouting orders, firing blanks, and causing confusion among the students. Red Cell's students were the hostages we took. Only they couldn't quit the course.

To the hostages, our planned confusion and actions seemed a lot worse than they actually were. Shaking someone by the shoulders or grabbing them by the back of the neck or the shirt was usually all we did. The barking and shouting normally intimidated them enough all by itself; it was never necessary for us to throw a punch or anything more.

The force we did use was actually so minor that most of our hostages didn't believe it later on. They would swear we did a lot more than even the observers would tell them we did. The fact that we videotaped all of our actions, the better to review them during the debriefing, helping prove our points.

In addition, some of the hostages couldn't believe we were only playing a part. The evening after that first exercise, we went out to a Pizza Hut on the beach to get together and relax with all the parties who had been involved. Sitting at the table with us was the same woman I had been dealing with that morning. It was obvious she didn't mind sitting next to Knobber, but she also made known her feelings about me by giving me dirty looks all night. "Hey, look," I finally told her, "I'm really a nice guy. We're just doing our job."

That explanation fell on deaf ears, except for those of my Teammates (Cellmates?), who got a good laugh out of it. I decided that was the last time I was going to play bad guy for a while.

We continued with exercises in the Norfolk area. We did a number of moderate hits, penetrations at different points of entry on the base. We found weak spots in the fence, dark areas where there should have been more security in the form of roving guards or other measures. We gathered our own intel on such spots for later use or pointed out examples to the security force during a post-op debrief.

HUMINT (human intelligence) was something we also gathered for our own use. Women were very good for this—wives or girlfriends or women recruited from on the base proper. They would gather intelligence on the target for us, especially on open penetration points where they would talk to the gate guards around the base. Who knows, maybe today it wouldn't look out of place for a guy like me to be engaging a gate guard in conversation. In the mid-1980s, my flirting with a military gate guard would have stood out. The ladies, though, could do that very well.

There was one security building on the main base that we considered a primary facility target. The base held the headquarters of the Atlantic Fleet as well as the Second Fleet, so their facilities had to be secure. Now we were going to test that security.

One of our targets of opportunity for the exercise was a building that held a vault full of classified materials. The office adjoining the vault was full of various pieces of technical gear that were also highly classified. The security level of the room next to the vault would be Top Secret, very limited accessibility, and certainly not open to the likes of us.

We studied the structure, gathering intel on the building itself and its internal layout. None of this information was given to us beforehand; we had to develop it all on our own at the site as part of the exercise. It was this intel gathering and target analysis that made some of our earlier SEAL training and experience so valuable. Without our skills, we couldn't have pulled off the operation or kept it as controlled and safe as we did.

Going up and over the fence gave us access to the base. Getting over the three strands of barbed wire at the top of the fence took a matter of seconds for Pooster and myself. Penetrating the building itself was a direct result of my SEAL Team Six training. At a dark corner of the building was an old-style iron drainpipe secured to the brick wall. The two of us free-climbed up that drainpipe, quickly gaining the roof after several stories.

We knew where we were going from our studies of the base. During the daytime we had scouted the base by just driving through the gate. There hadn't been an ID check, so a simple sticker on the windshield got us in. Looking at the outside of the different buildings located our targets for us. When there was an opportunity, we just walked into some of the buildings, took a look around, and walked back out. No one challenged us or even asked if we needed any help.

Going up the drainpipe was a fairly easy climb. We had done far worse ones going up wet girders on oil platforms in the Gulf during our Six training. Once we were on the roof, we located a vent that was held shut with a padlock. No alarm systems were evident, so we found our way in. My lock-picking skills weren't the best in the unit, so we adopted a simpler solution. A small pair of cutters eliminated the padlock, and we climbed in the vent.

We came down into the rafters of the building, stepping carefully above a false ceiling. Lifting one of the ceiling tiles showed us an open admin-type office below us. We had a good idea of what we were looking for in the way of the vault room. Moving around on the ground brought us to a door set into a brick wall. On the other side of that high-security door was the office next to the vault itself. The door would be a bitch for us to open, and there wasn't any other way through the wall. But there turned out to be another way into the room.

Whoever had constructed the brick wall had built it solidly, but only as tall as it had to be. Climbing up on a desk and raising one of the ceiling tiles showed us an almost three-foot gap between the top of the brick wall and the solid ceiling itself. Going back into the false ceiling and over the wall put us inside the office we had targeted.

We weren't going to target the vault itself. We would have had to take over the building completely and either use a lot of equipment or blast with demo, damaging some expensive government property in the process, to breech that vault. Instead Pooster and I just settled in for the night. Making ourselves comfortable, we waited for the office to open in the morning.

The Navy chief who opened that secure office in the morning was more than a little startled to see us. His eyes bulged out as he stared at us and the special Naval Security Coordination Team badges we held out to him.

This action brought big attention from just about everyone. We debriefed the situation, and the Old Man explained our actions. "But how did you get in?" we were asked. "Our walls are solid."

"They're solid all right," we told them, "up to within three feet of the ceiling."

I lifted up a panel of the false ceiling and pointed out the big gap at the top of the wall. "See where your wall is?" I said. "Three feet. We crawled right through there, and here is the panel we came through."

There was still some dust and debris on the desktop where we had climbed into the secured room. There wasn't any way they could deny the situation. A lot of other times we would just leave calling cards or signs saying "Red Cell was here!" This time, because of the sensitivity of the target, we decided to stay and wait for someone to come in, preventing any possibility of denying the penetration.

We were not out to bust anyone's chops. We didn't have a vendetta against the Navy. We were all career Navy people and this was our service. But we could make a base commander or security chief look pretty bad. So a lot of the time we would be told, "No one got past my post!" or "That couldn't happen here!" Out would come the videotapes, and everyone could see exactly what had happened.

Some of our scenarios involved detaining the CinCs of an area or command. Our objective on one exercise was to secure the CinC from his house, remove him from the area, and detain him at a location of our choosing. This would force the local security unit not only to react to the loss of their CinC but also to track us down and work in unknown territory. This would force them into closer cooperation with local authorities if our hideout was off base.

Good plan. Only trouble was we didn't get our hands on the CinC. Mr. Murphy showed up, and Plan A kind of fell through. Butch and I had been tasked to commandeer the CinC, a three-star admiral, while on his way to work from his home on base. Even though the home was on base, and there were roving guards around, we had no trouble scouting the place just driving around in our own car.

The house was by the water, and water is the natural home of a SEAL. There was a small inlet near the base, lined with civilian housing on either side, that we were going to use as our way in. Running off the inlet was a canal that bordered the base proper. Slipping into the inlet late one night, we swam across to the canal and followed it along the base up to a small bridge.

There was some late-night traffic on the bridge, but those people weren't looking for anything in the black waters below them. And I'm sure no one would have expected to see two swimmers moving up the canal.

Near the bridge was a partially submerged sewer pipe, a storm drain really, without a grate over its end. The pipe led into the base proper, and we knew from our earlier scouting that there were manholes near our target. A section of metal fencing had been placed in front of the pipe, but that was more to keep critters and junk out than any real protection. Just by lifting up the fence, holding our breaths, and ducking under, we gained access to the pipe system.

That pipe was one of the nastier ways in we ever used on an operation. We worked our way up the pipe, slipping through some very dank and tight areas, counting manholes and storm drains, until we came up at the side of the road near the house. We just lifted up the hatch cover and moved along carefully to our target.

The admiral had a large house with pillars in front facing a tree-lined side street on the base. This was a residential area of the base, so there was little in the way of regular military traffic. In front of the house, the admiral parked his official Navy vehicle. In addition to the Navy car, the admiral was known to have a classic convertible that was his pride and joy.

The convertible was kept in a garage near the house but not

attached to it. Usually the admiral would take his Navy car in to work, but occasionally he drove his private vehicle. Our plan involved making certain that he drove his classic convertible to work.

Having slipped up to the garage near the house, Butch quietly picked the lock and broke into the building. The admiral's garage was going to be the staging area for our little kidnapping. I climbed a tree nearby and kept watch on the house.

It was getting toward four o'clock in the morning, and we had a feeling for what the roving guards were doing. They didn't have a real routine, but we figured we had a window of opportunity. We slipped up to the admiral's official car and let the air out of several of his tires. One tire we flattened completely, and the others we let down partway. Now, even if the admiral decided to have the tire changed, he would only have one spare in the car.

The Navy car was in a wide-open area, and it would have been very hard if not impossible for us to grab the admiral without attracting a lot of attention. But if the admiral came into the garage to use his personal vehicle, we would have our best chance to grab him while remaining under cover.

Lights started coming on in the house, and we knew we wouldn't have long to wait. The admiral went to his official car, started it up, and began to drive off. As he started to slow down, we figured we had him. Then he picked up speed and continued down the road, the flat tire flopping along.

Either he suspected something, or he just didn't care about the tire. Either way, he continued on to his aide's house, where he got a ride in to work, and we stood there in the garage wondering what to do now.

Here we had been waiting all night and now nothing. Suddenly we heard a dog making noises, and there were sounds coming from the house. The admiral's wife wasn't part of the problem, so we didn't want to startle her or anything. And we certainly didn't want to be detected in the admiral's garage by his family dog!

Then the wife started jogging down the street, taking her dog with her. The animal hadn't been excited about detecting us; it just wanted to go on the morning run. Now that the immediate excitement had died down, we had to decide on our next plan of action. It was daylight now, and we would have to work our way off the base, hoping we didn't get caught along the way.

On the bounce, being ever resourceful Navy SEALs, we came up with an impromptu Plan B. We would commandeer the admiral's personal vehicle and use it to make our escape off the base. It would be a good test to see if the gate guards stopped us or let the car go on through.

So we hot-wired the admiral's classic convertible and drove it out of the garage. We had the top down and didn't exactly look like the admiral's normal friends, not in our black sweat-shirts and with our long hair and my Fu Manchu mustache. The Marine guard at the gate was doing his job and checking the vehicles ahead of us. Pulling up to the gate, we were ready to brazen it out with him.

It turned out we didn't have to worry about anything at the gate. Instead of stopping and questioning us, that Marine guard saw the three-star sticker on the bumper of the car and immediately snapped to attention, rendering a nice hand salute as we drove by.

We drove through another gate and on to the compound at the rear of the base where we were staging our operations. Pulling the car into the back, we told the Old Man, "Hey, look what we brought you."

Marcinko got a kick out of our bringing him the car, though I think he would have preferred the admiral. We took some pictures of the bunch of us with the car, and then thought about what to do next. The Skipper was fairly certain the car would be missed soon and someone would be pissed that we had it.

Phone calls were made, and we received a message regarding our recent acquisition: we had an hour to get the car back in the garage and there would be no repercussions. Presuming, of course, that there was no damage whatsoever to the car. We got the car back quickly, and it was unharmed by its little adventure. I think we brought a little heat down on the Old Man for that adventure, not that he seemed to mind very much. But when in doubt, go to Plan B.

The point we had been striving for, and pretty much proved by taking the car, was that we had been there and the admiral was vulnerable. He could easily have been in the trunk of that car as we took our salute and went out the gate. If violence was our game, an assassination would have been simple for the admiral and his whole family. And the proof was, we had taken the car.

The whole operation had pointed out a common choke point. Security could be tight everywhere else, but people tended to relax once they got home. Most assassination hits or kidnappings, as we had found during our studies of terrorists, took place at or around the home.

Taking the admiral's wife wouldn't have been a problem: the noisy little dog would just have been an irritation. The dog might have tried to protect his mistress, but it sure wasn't a German shepherd.

Still, the admiral himself had been the objective. If the right opportunity had come up, we would have rushed the house and snatched him right there with just the two of us. Our original plan had been to grab him and move on to the main base to run the rest of the scenario. I have to give the admiral credit for continuing to drive on his flat tires, even though it wrecked our plans for him.

Even though we hadn't completed our mission, we had

made a number of points. In spite of the area having good fences, there hadn't been a grate over the storm drain. A heavy grate would have kept us out, but the simple bit of cyclone fence that had been there was insufficient protection.

That snatch wasn't the only Red Cell operation we went through in Norfolk where we had to adapt to a changing situation quickly. Butch Cassidy and I were targeting one of the Naval bases in the Norfolk area where the destroyers and other major fighting ships are. We were walking in the area of the piers, scoping out the base. Our plan was to go through one of the strategic gates, where all the personnel are allowed on and off the more sensitive areas of the base, and set some devices.

For our attacks, we made up IEDs (improvised explosive devices), relatively simple bombs put together from components we could easily buy on the open market. A number of us had gone through Explosive Ordnance Disposal (EOD) training, in addition to our demolition training in the Teams, where we learned to make these devices and have them work and look real. There was never any explosive in our IEDs, but they had some red sticks or blocks to simulate live explosives, with "RED CELL" written on them plainly, along with a timer, batteries, and usually a flashbulb to simulate an explosive. Using these devices stepped up the realism of our exercises and allowed EOD units to play their part in the scenarios.

So we had a device in a paper bag and we were going to leave it by one of the gates. The trouble was, security was doing its job pretty well, and we figured we had been made. Before we could be picked up, we commandeered a Navy van at gunpoint.

Like our explosives, our guns were real enough but had a lot of safety built into our using them. The muzzle and the front of the barrel were blocked and covered in red tape, so the guns were closed up, couldn't be loaded accidentally, and were well marked in red to show just what they were. In addition to our blocked guns, we always carried our creds (credentials) with us in the form of our Naval Security Coordination Team badges along with our Navy ID cards.

When we seized the van, our rules of engagement for the scenario immediately took effect. We told the two people in the van that we were Red Cell and that they had become part of the problem. We took them hostage and got in the van ourselves. Driving down to the gate, we planned to go off base.

Gate security was doing a good job, checking the vehicles going through the gate. We wanted to develop the scenario further, so we got out of the van along with our hostages and began moving them along at gunpoint. "This is Red Cell. This is Red Cell. Exercise. Exercise," I called out. "We're taking these people hostage, and we are taking them off base."

All of a sudden this civilian security guard came up and pointed his pistol directly at me.

"This is an exercise," I said.

"Drop the weapon!" he shouted. "Drop the weapon!"

"I'm not dropping the weapon," I shouted back. "This is an exercise, and this person is my hostage. You either let us pass or I'm going to shoot him."

We eventually worked our way to the edge of the gate. The scenario didn't go much further; they had us cold and we weren't getting past easily. But their reactions were something we were trying to test. It was during the debriefing later that we found out just how interesting those actions could have been.

That civilian guard told me, "I didn't know there was an exercise going on. The word never got down to me, and I had live bullets in my weapon."

This was not good news. I just kind of looked at him for a moment, frozen in place. I wanted to kill this sucker who had been pointing a live weapon at me. He was just doing his job, but then so was I. From then on, we made even more sure that the rules of engagement were known to everyone who might be involved in an exercise, and the message was passed to all Naval and civilian personnel. Once we called out "Red Cell. Exercise," everyone would know that a scenario had started and not to shoot us!

It was obvious that there had been a miscommunication between the Naval security force and the civilian security contractors. The situation could have ended a lot more seriously, especially for me, but instead we had learned a very significant lesson. Norfolk was a huge facility, made up of a number of smaller Navy bases, and there were just too many people in the chain to be absolutely sure the proper communications went to everyone involved, especially those people carrying weapons.

We had more hazards to face during our Norfolk operations. Pooster and I did one op where we were going after the ships at the piers in close to a classic swimmer attack. Wearing black rubber wet suits, we slipped into the water unseen and swam along the surface, with our faces barely showing as we moved across the sea wall. We planned to place devices on the ships and maybe the gangplanks.

Swimming in that water was like slipping through petroleum. The oil and sludge floating on the surface was rank and even worse under the piers where we slipped in for cover. It was a good thing we hadn't been using Draegers and swimming underwater because that crap would have contaminated our rigs and maybe worse.

Swimming up to this one ship, there wasn't anyplace I could put the IED, it was so covered with crud. The fumes under the pier made our eyes water, and it was more than a little hard to breathe. I started getting sick from the fumes and I don't think Pooster was doing much better. We finally gave up on using the IEDs; there was so much crap around, no one could have seen them anyway.

By the time we finally left the water, the only spots on our faces that were reasonably clean were our eyes and mouths. Everything else was covered in oil. Our wet suits were so oil-soaked we ended up throwing them away. There was no way to get them clean enough to use again.

The water, if you can call it that, was nasty in that area. And we didn't light up any celebratory cigars after that op either. Something about not wanting to go up in a ball of flame. It was weeks before we had all the oil cleaned off ourselves. I was even thinking of shaving off my mustache I was getting so sick of the smell.

CHAPTER 21

THE SUBS OF NEW ENGLAND

The New London submarine base in Connecticut is home to part of the U.S. Navy's nuclear submarine fleet, which makes it a strategically important site and one that should be as secure as possible. To check on that security, Red Cell staged a visit to the New London base in June, soon after we left Norfolk.

The New London sub base is on the Thames River, just a few miles upriver from Long Island Sound. Taking a boat up the river, we were able to penetrate the base by jumping the fence at several locations. We were all making our way to our targets when we were detected in the area. Security was alerted to our presence and the chase was on.

Security was doing a good job of hunting us down. There was some digging going on at the side of the street I was running down just ahead of the security forces. Coming into the street, I could see that the ditch was only about eight feet deep. A new sewer pipe or whatever was being installed, and I saw that as my escape route. At the bottom of the ditch might be a pipe or something I could follow, just kind of crawl into it and see where I turned up. Two of my Teammates split off to one side while my partner kept on going straight ahead. Figuring to break off even further from everyone else and give security multiple targets to chase, I jumped into the ditch.

The ditch was a little deeper than I had thought, though, and the dirt was a whole lot harder. I smacked into the bottom of a square hole feeling like I had broken every bone in my body. Then I scrambled up and started looking for my escape route. Only trouble was, there was no escape route. There wasn't any pipe leading from the hole I had jumped into, it was just a deep square box in the hard earth with me at the bottom of it.

Security pulled up and I was apprehended immediately. The security guys were happy, which is a lot more than I could say about myself. I could hear them saying to each other, "We got a Red Cell guy, we got a Red Cell guy," and I was anything but glad for them. As they put me in the back of their truck, I was thinking, "Oh god, here we go."

An interrogation was coming up for me next, that was one thing I was sure of. The other thing I was sure of was the amount of harassment I was going to receive from my Teammates when I got back to Red Cell. Back at the station, the questions were as I had expected: Who are you? What were you doing? Who are the rest of your people and where are they now?

The only thing I knew about the rest of my team's location was that they weren't with me at the security station. There was no way I was going to tell these guys anything. My capture hadn't been part of the scenario, and I didn't have a false story to tell them. When I was searched, all I had on me was my Red Cell credentials, so I told them, "You know who I am. Yeah, I'm Red Cell. You got a Red Cell guy."

"Okay," the interrogator said. "What were you doing?"

So I started playing the game with them. Giving them some of the answers they could expect from a terrorist. The only other thing I had been sure about proved to be the case later on. When I was released and turned back over to Red Cell to continue the operations, I caught hell from everyone. Messing with the interrogator had been fun, but the other guys never let me hear the end of letting myself get caught.

Chances are my jumping into the pit and getting caught helped the others get away. I had provided a distraction at a critical moment. But the simple fact was I had screwed up and wasn't about to do that again. Plus I had been banged up pretty badly when I hit the rocklike bottom of that pit.

But I wasn't the only one to be embarrassed by the Red Cell operations at New London. One of the ops was against the Submariner's A-School right there on the base. At this school, mostly new recruits into the Navy, fresh out of boot camp, were taught their submariner's rating. We were going to make the school building the site of our hostage/barricade situation.

The classroom we took down was on the second deck of one of the administrative buildings. We penetrated the facility, worked our way to the second-deck classroom, and took the entire room full of students prisoner, as well as effectively taking control of the building. We released the administrative personnel from the building. What we were going to do was use the students as our hostages for the day.

The scenario was only planned to last about six to eight hours, but we had something a little different in mind for the students. Using a modified Mutt and Jeff technique, we were going to try and lure one or more of the students over to our side as part of the exercise. Our side was the aggrieved terrorists from the People's Republic of Whatever, defending the downtrodden of our small country against the overwhelming military might of the Imperialist United States.

The class was all male, so that made some of our actions easy. We talked to the students, and they all behaved well during the first hour or so. They all minded their training and didn't give anything out to us. To increase the pressure on them we had them take their clothes off, leaving them in just their underwear and T-shirts. Then we made them sit in the fetal position by their desks. Their situation was uncomfortable, but that was about all.

In Red Cell, and much of the rest of the military, certain personnel were put through High Risk Survival School. All of us had taken the standard E & E schooling, but the high risk course was different. During that training, you learned how to avoid drawing attention to yourself during interrogation and how to survive that interrogation if you were noticed anyway.

That school also taught us how to avoid the Stockholm syndrome, where people in a very high-stress situation started to side with their captors. This had happened more than once during terrorist incidents. The syndrome could result in the hostages voluntarily shielding the terrorist with their own bodies when the counterterrorist forces made a forced entry. This was something we were going to test out in a small way on our new subjects.

With the students there on the floor, we began talking to them about ourselves, our position, our cause, and why we were operating against the New London base. We went on about how the United States didn't have the right to hold all this nuclear power and certainly not to use it to threaten the rest of the world. The way of life the United States was trying to foist onto the rest of the world by holding the big nuclear stick was alien to most of the Third World to begin with.

We were trying to use the confusion and stress of the moment to get any of the students we could to side with us. Our arguments made some sense, especially if you didn't give the other person time to think about it. Knobber was really persuasive in his arguments. He had this one kid starting to waver, so he pulled him over to the side of the room and kept talking to him in a quiet, earnest tone.

Pretty soon Knobber started really turning it on and subtly pressuring the kid. We had sandwiches with us, so Knobber offered the kid one. He ate and was more comfortable than his classmates on the floor, while Knobber continued talking one-on-one with him. Gradually the kid was moving over to our side. Now he was told he could put his clothes back on.

"Hey, come on down with us and see what's going on," we told him, and took him down to the main administrative office where the rest of the team was conducting negotiations with the security force. The kid relaxed further, and Knobber started asking him about his school and what he thought of the Navy so far, all the usual things that each new recruit had an opinion on or a bitch about.

Because of National security restraints centering on nuclear submarines, we didn't ask the kid anything about what he had been learning or had been taught so far. There was no need for us to ask anything on that level of classification anyway. What we got was the story of the kid's home town, his mom and dad, why he had enlisted in the Navy and volunteered for submarines. We talked about his assignment to classified duty on submarines and what he thought of that.

The kid was opening up to Knobber. That was obvious to all of us. So we kept the kid with us the whole time, and he didn't suffer any more of the indignities we were piling on his classmates.

We had one other person with us besides the student. There had been a civilian female staff member who hadn't wanted to leave with the rest of the staff. She had a Ph.D. and was a psychologist, as I remember. She wanted to have the experience of being in a hostage situation to get some firsthand knowledge of the pressures and stress it put on a prisoner. We agreed to let her remain for the scenario and join in as she could.

When security came up to the outside of the building, we used our female volunteer to help drive them off. Holding the woman very securely by the ankles and with a safety line tied to her waist, we hung her out one of the second-story windows, shaking her a little and threatening to drop her if security didn't back off. The woman was in absolutely no danger at any time during our short standoff, but the situation shook her up a little.

When we pulled her back in, she had gained some of the experience she wanted, and she didn't like it. Her eyes were huge. "Wow" was about the only word she could say for a moment. "I never want to do that again," she finally said. "Don't do that again."

It was obvious that she had gotten good exposure to a hostage's situation. "Just hanging out of that window," she continued, "even though I knew you had me, I didn't like that feeling."

But we had pulled her back in, and security had backed off. They never did do an entry on even the first floor of the building; we simply didn't allow that to happen. But before the problem ceased, we had one other situation to deal with.

We took the kid who had been with us back up to the classroom and started talking to the class as a whole.

"Hey, guys," I said. "First of all, we have to give you a lot of credit. The problem's almost over now. And you should look at yourselves. You're hungry, you're tired, and you're sweaty. You're just sitting there in your underwear. And look at this guy. The whole time, he had food, was dressed, he feels good. But I'm going to tell you guys something. You should know that you did a good job. This guy, he's a fucking traitor!"

And we walked out of the room.

The whole class was stunned for a moment. We went out the

door and stood where we could look through a window at them. Our turncoat was standing alone up in the front of the room with the rest of the class on their feet. We could see several of the students yelling at him, and then they all started to close in on him. That's when we came back into the room and took control. We told the students to get their clothes back on and get ready to leave.

Those students had been just about ready to kill that guy. And all he done was fall victim to the Stockholm syndrome. This had happened in the real world and was a legitimate concern for security forces in working these kinds of scenarios.

After we talked about the problem during the debriefing with the base and security forces, what had happened came out in the open. I don't know if that kid continued on in that highly classified submariner's school, but I believe he moved on to another position in the U.S. Navy fleet. We hadn't planned on being so successful in swinging someone over to our side in what was really such a short time. But we had, and it had made a good point, big time.

What if that guy, or another like him, had talked? And what if he had continued his training to the point where he did have a lot of classified information? He had talked to us a lot. Even in our simple scenario, he had told us a great deal without a lot of coercion. It had been a good example of some of the strange things that can happen to a hostage in a terrorist action.

Not all of our time in New England was taken up with our operations against the sub base at New London. We had proved the vulnerabilities of the base and explained ways it could be made more secure. Some of the guys, including the Skipper, had taken a rented boat up the Thames, flying the Soviet flag, and approached the sub pens. There weren't any procedures in place to stop anyone from doing what they did. So the Skipper's boat continued its little tour, filming the subs at their piers and moving along the river.

Two of the guys from the video crew had family nearby in Massachusetts. They had both been officers in the Teams and wanted to show us a good time while we were in their area. The whole bunch of us went up to a small bay where we could have a lobster feast right there on the water. This was a true frogman's way of having a good time and something we all looked forward to after a hard week chasing around the sub base.

To make things even more interesting, we were going to have a small work boat available to us so that we could spend some time on the water while the food was cooking. The feast was going to be catered; we didn't have any work to do; so we all hit the water in the boat and set out to sea.

There was beer aplenty on board the work boat. Though the sanitary facilities weren't much—a bucket in the pilot house—pissing over the gunwales isn't very hard for Navy men. We all noticed the little rowboat that was being towed along behind us. The conversation turned to SEAL subjects, and it wasn't very long before it was suggested we do cast and recoveries from the boats.

With that suggestion, a couple of us jumped in the water and climbed into the rowboat. As we chugged along, guys would cast off by rolling over the side of the work boat and we would recover them as the rowboat passed. We didn't have a rubber snare, but a strong arm worked well enough. Of course, when I scooped up the Skipper, it may be that my arm slipped around his neck a little. But he was still breathing, and it was all good clean wet fun.

The boat finally took us back in and it was time to eat. The caterers had brought out folding tables and white tablecloths right there on the beach. Lobster, crab, other seafoods, and veggies were all there for the eating. The local families came down and joined in the fun. Though some of what we called fun may not have been what they expected.

We were all sitting around the tables or on the beach, a nice

fire going, eating and enjoying ourselves. Truck had been walking along the beach and found a dead seagull somewhere.
Bringing the carcass back to the party, he tossed it to Sundance,
saying, "Here, I brought something for you."

Sundance grabbed the seagull out of the air and proceeded
to bite the head off it. That guy will eat anything. But not being
satisfied with his seagull head, Sundance tossed it away, and it
landed right on my plate. I was enjoying what I already had and
didn't want any beach kill, so I just picked up the seagull head
and tossed it away.

Whatever the families thought of us, they kept it to them-
selves. But we did get some stares for a while there. I think they
were wondering just what kind of people they had fallen in with.
But it was all right, and the party continued on into the evening.
Besides, no one could find an old whale carcass to feed to
Sundance.

As it came time to go, we loaded the folding chairs into our
van for the trip back. We were taking one of the guy's families
back to their place and then dropping the chairs off. I was driving and Pooster was sitting up front with me. The rest of the
family and some of the guys were sitting in the back of the van
with the chairs stacked on top of the seats all around them. The
road back to the parking lot was a little curvy, and I may have
used some of the driving techniques I had learned back in our
defensive driving course. But no one got hurt when I stopped
and the chairs just slid around.

Later we hooked up with some other old Teammates in the
area and had an impromptu bash with some of their local
friends. As the evening went on, somebody poured Seven-Up on
the linoleum floor in the kitchen, making it nice and slippery.
Then we tried our hand at break dancing, finally diving onto the
floor and sliding into the cupboards. And that wasn't just a few
of us; we all tried our hand at the slip and slide.

The partying went on well into the night, and we all crashed in place sometime in the early morning hours. The next day, one of the local guys was missing. He couldn't be found anywhere, although the vehicle was still where we had left it. Finally someone noticed that the trapdoor to the attic was open. When we looked up there, we found Bobby Mitchell, one of our old Teammates, comfortably curled up in a bunch of pink fiberglass insulation. We were all a little hung over, but Mitchell felt the worst of all of us when he got up and started to itch.

CHAPTER 22

BACK TO THE PHILIPPINES

One of Red Cell's first overseas trips was to Subic Bay in the Philippines and the huge U.S. Navy base there. It was a good trip for us and a major overseas deployment and exercise series. A DC-9 was assigned to us for the duration of the operations and we used it to move the unit and our gear. We flew into Subic with the base already knowing we were coming in to test their security. The Philippines had their own local terrorist threats in the form of the New People's Army (NPA), among other organizations. The NPA had taken credit for killing three Navy officers near Subic Bay back in 1974.

Not everything we did at Subic or in the Philippines was as serious as the real-world terrorists they had on the islands. One of the procedures we had come up with for Red Cell was to check into hotels separately or in very small groups under assumed names. This would help keep local security and law enforcement groups from finding us right away as we conducted our operations. It turned out to have a side benefit.

This one hotel we were staying at had a nice little lounge with a gambling establishment. Purdue managed to really piss off the girl behind the desk at the gambling hall. We never did learn the details of what it was all about, but the girl had the hotel roster and was shouting at Purdue that he wouldn't get away with whatever it was he had done. "That's okay, Mickey," she shouted at Purdue's back as she looked up from the roster. "I have your name, Mickey Mouse." I believe he gave his home town as a place near Anaheim, California, as well.

Before we began our serious operations at Subic Bay, we conducted a tour of the area, going over to the SEAL detachment (det) there and meeting with the guys from the Teams. Cheeks, an old friend of ours, was one of the officers in charge and he gave us a warm welcome. A number of our old Teammates were around, and the det community in general was a good one.

We settled in with the SEAL det for several days while we conducted training with the security forces at and around the base. The security force there had a number of trained dogs that they could even allow into the jungles to track down individuals and groups. Most of these dogs were rottweilers, big, powerful dogs that you really wouldn't want on your case if they weren't happy with you.

One night the security people asked us if we would work with them in a building-clearing exercise. They wanted to see what the dogs would do going into a strange building and tracking down people hidden there. I think Knobber was the only one willing to act as the bait in this little exercise. He put on this heavily padded training suit that the dogs could dig their teeth into without doing any real damage to the person inside.

Knobber went into the building and placed some IEDs, just to test the dogs out fully. The building was a very controlled environment, and handlers would be in there with the dogs, so the situation should be a safe one. But if you've ever seen a fully grown rottweiler with a real mad on, you'd wonder just how good that padded suit was. I wasn't too crazy about putting that suit on, so I just stood and watched.

The exercise went well enough. The dogs found their man, and Knobber found out that a male rottweiler can crush down with something like fifteen hundred pounds of pressure in those jaws. Padding or not, it was still like having your arm clamped in a large, pointy-edged vise. That, and the breed has very strong neck and shoulder muscles, so they can twist you around hard. Afterward, Knobber said the dogs had been a little rough and he didn't care to repeat the experience. So the score came out to something like rottweilers 1, Red Cell 0.

The security people also wanted the dogs to track us through the jungle. My only response to that suggestion was that if I had one of those dogs on my trail, I was taking a live weapon with me. If that dog came near me, I was going to shoot it. The security people thought I was overreacting, but they quit suggesting that exercise.

If I ever planned to go on an operation where I would need to take a dog out, I would carry a suppressed weapon. There was a reason one of the first SEAL suppressed weapons back in the Vietnam days was called a Hush-Puppy. The intent of that pistol was to take out guard dogs silently. For myself, a suppressed Mark II Ruger .22 automatic was the weapon of choice for such actions. If I was unarmed and had to take out a dog, I would try to gut it as it came at me. If I could, I would grab its upper jaw to control its teeth. Of course, with some dogs (and rottweilers come to mind), you'd most likely pull back your hand missing a few fingers.

Now we were ready to start our Red Cell scenarios. Subic Bay was the main Naval Base, and then there was Cubi Point, which was the nearby Naval Air Station (NAS). At Cubi Point were the runways where the planes and helos came in, as well as the support and storage sites to maintain the aircraft.

In effect, there were two separate bases making up the Subic Bay facility. Only a single road connected the two points, the main base and the NAS. Security was starting to set up checkpoints along that road, which was going to make our scenarios more difficult.

For our first hostage rescue scenario, we had to decide who was going to be the target. After going over the requirements of the scenario and who might be available, we decided on snatching the XO of the Cubi Point NAS along with his secretary, a Navy yeoman. The secretary was included after we decided to take the XO right from his office during the day.

To start our mission off, we had to acquire a local vehicle. Cheeks had a nice old car he used to drive around the area. He was offered the option, either loan us the car or we were going to hot-wire it. Cheeks loaned us the car. Handing me the keys, he said, "Just don't wreck it."

"Oh, I won't wreck it," I assured him.

Knobber and I went out the night before the operation, scouting the jungle area near the XO's office. We found a spot to park Cheeks's car where it would be convenient to the office but not easily seen. Duke was going to act as a backup team to Knobber and myself and would bring the car down in the morning.

When we began the scenario the next morning, Duke brought the car and moved it into position. I took the driver's seat, and Duke joined Knobber for the snatch. The two of them came out of the building with the XO and his secretary in tow. The fact that they were holding the officer and the yeoman at gunpoint was a fair clue to everyone that things weren't as they should be.

No one stopped the group when they came out of the building. There wasn't any challenge. People stopped and looked, but that was all we could see. Someone did get to a phone fast and called security, though. Once Knobber, Duke, and the two hostages piled into the car, I took off on our preplanned route.

As soon as I got up on the road and out of the jungle, I turned left and hit the gas. To our right, the O-Club was coming up, and we were on the main road between Cubi and Subic. Down the hill in front of us was a winding road, lined with monkeys up in the trees who could be a greater danger to us than the security forces. To the security guys, we were the enemy but it was an exercise. Those damned monkeys didn't know what an exercise was, and they would attack you if they could.

Not that the security people weren't doing their best to stop us. Near the O-Club, security had blocked the road with a Toyota pickup turned sideways. In the back of our car were the XO and his secretary along with Knobber. Duke was up front with me. Seeing the small pickup trying to block our way caused me to laugh out loud; it couldn't cover the whole road. Duke just told me to go around them.

The left side of the road was pretty well blocked, so all I could do was go over to the right side and ram past. The right side of the road was also where the O-Club had a lot of landscaping in the form of bushes and other foliage. The bushes didn't slow the car down much when I plowed through them, getting around the Toyota in the process, but the shrubbery wasn't quite up to inspection standards after Red Cell had gone by.

Now we were past the roadblock and moving down the hill with a free lane in front of us. There was no oncoming traffic coming up the hill. The security forces had established a checkpoint between Subic and Cubi that left only one lane of traffic open. Going toward Subic like we were doing, our lane would be the one that was open.

Now I saw another security vehicle coming up the road toward us. He turned sideways and blocked the road, but I just kept heading straight for him, his eyes growing larger as I approached. At the last moment, I veered around behind him, just missing his rear bumper.

Reaching the bottom of the hill, I turned right and started toward the checkpoint. Security already had traffic stopped, and the left lane of the road was blocked with some wooden barricades. Not slowing down, I moved into the left lane and started smashing through the barricades.

There was one Marine guard at the checkpoint, and I have to give him a lot of credit. When I came up to the checkpoint, I had slowed down to keep the barricades from flying up and smashing the windshield. That Marine stood directly in my way and refused to move, forcing me to stop. It was either stop or drive right over the man. When the vehicle came to a halt, that Marine leaned forward and put his hands on the hood of my car.

This wasn't going to be enough to stop us, but I wondered just how hard-core this Marine was going to be about the situation. Slowly mouthing the words "One . . . Two . . . Three," I began revving the car's engine. On three, I gunned the engine and the Marine rolled out of the way. With that, we blew through the checkpoint.

A fire station was on the right just half a mile or so down the road. Another unit from Red Cell had taken over the fire station while we had been grabbing the XO and his secretary. The fire station would be the location for the hostage rescue portion of the scenario.

Turning into the parking lot, I stopped the car and we all piled out. Moving quickly into the fire station with our guests, we put up barricades to block the door and waited for security to show up.

The local forces weren't a disappointment. They quickly secured the area and negotiations began. The local Naval Investigation Services (NIS) detachment took control of the negotiations as the security forces got into their long sit and wait posture. Neither security or the NIS office had a team prepped and ready to come in and negotiate or deal with the situation specifically. The negotiations began with NIS establishing communications with us. The security forces had put up their cordon around the area quickly, but not as effectively as they might have thought.

This was only going to be a short problem. At the absolute maximum, we would be at the fire station for three hours. Near Cubi Point, we blindfolded the XO, taped his mouth, and put a pillowcase over his head. In the sleeping quarters of the fire station, we taped the muffled officer into one of the bunks.

The secretary we treated a little differently. We took her into another room, out of earshot of the XO, and talked to her. We told her that we weren't going to handcuff her, secure her, or anything else. What we asked her to do was role-play a position with us. Our goal was to see how well the XO could deal with the situation of being a hostage. Once we explained that to her and asked her if she was willing to go along with us, she readily agreed.

Now it was time to start messing with the XO's head. It can be a lot easier to deal with your own discomfort than with that of a coworker or subordinate. The XO might be able to handle what we were allowed to do to him under the rules of the scenario, but would his imagination run away with him if he thought we were out of control with his secretary? This would be a stress builder for sure.

The woman got into it with us once she saw how we were doing the stunt. We told her what we would do in detail, and she got a big grin on her face. When we asked her if she could scream, she answered, "I think I can do that."

So now it was time for the show. While other members of our team dealt with the negotiators, we tore sheets, making a loud ripping sound, and the woman screamed at us not to tear her clothes off. As we hit lockers and smacked our hands together, she got into her role even further, screaming and sobbing.

The XO went absolutely nuts. He was trying to yell, but the tape kept it pretty muffled and incoherent. I yanked the pillowcase off his head, tore the tape off, and then stuck the pillowcase back on.

"That's it!" he yelled. *"This problem's over! You can't do that! You can't do that!"*

Then we pushed the woman into another room. As this was going on, the XO was struggling and twisting around. Sitting on him, I slipped up his hood and stuck some Copenhagen snuff I had with me into his mouth. He had no idea what I had slipped him, and while he was startled, I lightly tapped him in the face and shouted, "Shut up!"

He just lay there quietly, more than a little stunned. Now that he was shocky, I took the pillowcase off him. Knobber came over to me, having left the woman in the other room, and we both started interrogating the officer. He stood up to the interrogation pretty well, but we could tell he had been badly shaken by the incident and that the reality of this being just an exercise was slipping away from him.

He was looking at us with close to real fear in his eyes. Enough sudden shock and you can forget where you are, and we had this guy pretty well gone. Backing off a little, we gave the guy a breather, then came back on strong. This kept him off balance. We told him that if security tried to come in, he would be the next one. "The same thing that happened to her could happen to you," we told him.

Outside the building, the security forces were trying to figure out a way to breach the building. We saw some of their guys moving around behind the firehouse. Telling the negotiators that we knew what was going on, we said we'd kill some more hostages if they didn't pull back. So whatever the security people had been trying to set up, we derailed their plan and they had to pull back.

One of the first things security had done when they arrived

at the fire station was to control and secure the area. One of the orders that had gone out was not to let any vehicles into the area. So when this huge yellow school bus showed up, no one could figure out how it had gotten onto the site.

Dallas had stolen the bus earlier and just driven it past the checkpoints and up to the firehouse. While security was still wondering how the bus had gotten there, we all piled out of the firehouse and into the bus. The chase was now on.

The plan was for the bus to take us to our DC-9, where we would stage an airport standoff for the balance of the exercise. Once on board the plane, we would let the negotiations continue. But when we left the parking lot, Dallas turned right toward Subic Bay rather than left and back to Cubi and our plane. We were all yelling at Dallas, shouting "Where in the fuck are you going?" along with other choice comments.

Apparently Dallas thought better of his original choice of direction and decided to turn the bus around with a bootleg turn we had learned at driving school. With the bus going forward, Dallas put on the emergency brake and, on two wheels, spun the bus through a smooth 180 degrees. As the back of the bus drifted through the turn, we watched it miss a telephone pole by about six inches. Releasing the parking brake, Dallas stepped on the gas, and now we were headed back toward Cubi Point and our plane.

As we started back the other way, we passed though the checkpoint where I'd had my little face-off with the Marine earlier. Security let us go through the barricades, but now several Toyota trucks were speeding up to us, each with several security personnel in the open back of the truck.

At the Cubi Point NAS, Dallas turned right onto the runway, so we were speeding down the center of this wide concrete runway in a yellow school bus with pickup trucks trying to catch up with us. But we thought we might have a way of dealing with the security trucks. When Dallas stole the bus, he had brought aboard a selection of munitions, mostly smoke grenades, that we had originally planned to use at a barricade if they refused to let us through.

When the security trucks pulled up alongside us, some of the guys pulled the pins on several smoke grenades and lobbed them into the backs of the trucks. Now these guys were choking on thick red, green, and white smoke. Our pursuers lost ground quickly and let us continue on our way.

Getting to our DC-9, we all piled out and climbed up the ladder into the plane. Pulling the ladder up behind us, we moved on to the next stage of the exercise. Now the negotiations were going to begin again. We had our own pilots on board the plane, all of them familiar with the role-playing aspect of being our hostages.

Once on board the plane, our original hostages, the XO and his secretary, were done with their involvement in the exercise. All negotiations between us and the security forces were going to continue using our plane's crew as the hostages. Duke took the XO to a seat near the front of the plane where he could sit and watch the show.

The XO asked if he could smoke, and Duke told him it was all right with us. As the officer lit up a cigarette, his hand shook from all the stress he'd been under. The funny thing was, every time I walked by the tremors stopped and he would stiffen up like a board. We had really bothered this guy by using his secretary. That, and the bus ride to the plane hadn't been the most calming thing in the world.

We continued the negotiations with the security people. At one point we were roughing up our own people to give the security people something to see and keep them off balance. All our guys knew what we would do and how we would do it, so no one got hurt. Besides, we had all gone though a hell of a lot worse just getting though BUD/S and into the Teams.

But this kind of role-playing wasn't something the security

people had ever seen. We were simulating what a real situation could look like and what the results of bad handling of that situation could be. But the negotiators held firm, and finally the exercise came to an end.

Since we never stayed on base if we could help it, we returned to our rooms in the Marriott. The Whiskey River was our hangout for this trip, and we blew off steam there. Back in the rooms, we had our own debrief on the ops and what had gone down.

We celebrated another successful op against the U.S. Navy, which had been useful in showing some of the strengths and weaknesses of the base. Now they could make improvements and increase their security. But our celebrations were never against our own service. They were more a way of breaking free after a number of days of long, weird, mostly sleepless hours.

Other traditions of the Teams continued at Red Cell. For instance, if you weren't being harassed, something had to be wrong. So when we relaxed after this exercise, Dallas wasn't left alone for his spectacular turn in the school bus. Too bad he had to do it 'cause he was going the wrong way. Personally, I was really impressed that he did the turn successfully, and missed the telephone pole too.

Back at the site a few days later, we went to the big theater on base and talked to everyone who had been involved in the exercise. During the big debrief, the Skipper got up behind the podium and told everyone the good and bad aspects of what they had done. The security people had done a great job of trying to contain the situation and reacting quickly to the changes we kept throwing at them. We told them about the lessons they should have learned from the exercise and the areas where they were already very proficient. Then we continued with the way they could improve their actions and prevent what we had done from being repeated. This was something we did on every exercise.

While we were all sitting up there on the stage, Knobber

nudged me and said, "Hey, Denny, don't look, but the XO's sitting off to my left and he's staring at you."

So I continued looking ahead for a while at the audience in general, then turned my head and gave the XO my dead-eyed snake stare. The officer immediately stiffened up again and turned to look straight ahead. This guy was never going to calm down or quit smoking as long as I was around the Philippines.

"Damn," I told Knobber quietly. "We must have really shook that guy up."

This was another of those situations that would probably grow into a story about Red Cell beating up hostages. The people who were actually involved knew what we were doing and how we were doing it. But others, who maybe couldn't see but could only hear the situation, like the XO had, would get the wrong idea. Even later, when they had the chance to see for themselves that no one was hurt, they wouldn't believe it.

This situation kept building up over time, giving Red Cell the reputation of being out of control. The Mutt and Jeff routine, or good cop/bad cop, worked really well on people, more so than they would readily believe. And you could intimidate people by just approaching them and talking to them in the right manner. Physically handling a person could intimidate them without a blow ever being struck. You just have to keep them off balance and everything they experience is magnified, both the good and the bad.

We only had so much time to take control of the situation during an exercise. To make the best use of our time, the people we would secure had to be disturbed as much as possible right from the beginning. The bit with the secretary had really worked with that XO, and we hadn't done anything. He had just filled in the blanks with his own imagination. What was kind of funny at the time was how much the woman had enjoyed the role-playing. She never knew how it had affected her officer until after the scenario was over.

Some time later, during one of our last Red Cell missions, we returned to the Philippines and Subic Bay. This time we weren't there to conduct any scenarios but instead to assess the improvements that had been made in overall security since our last visit.

We did conduct one scenario during that last visit, one we hadn't tried during our first time there. We took one of the local fishing boats, a Bonca boat, sort of a flat open canoe that was common throughout the waters off the Philippines. Using a number of smoke grenades to simulate explosives, we slipped out to where U.S. warships lay at anchor.

The test was to see how long it would take the harbor patrol boats to stop and seize the fishing boat. They responded, but not quite fast enough. Our boat was able to pull alongside a ship at anchor and pop smoke, simulating the detonation of an explosive charge.

It was a good thing we weren't as active on that last trip as we had been earlier. This time the word went around fairly quickly that we were back in town. One name in particular, *A-Has,* "snake" in the local language, made the rounds. The word was out that *A-Has* was back. Later on, I learned that the XO we had dealt with that first time decided to take leave when he heard the rumors of our return.

CHAPTER 23

THE LAND OF THE RISING SUN

The island of Guam in the Pacific, some 2,200 miles southeast of Japan, was one of Red Cell's last stops on its Pacific tour during the summer of 1985.

We had developed a little ritual every time we flew in our DC-9. Sundance took a boom box with him on the flights, and when we were landing or taking off he would play "Live and Die in LA," the theme song from the movie, and just crank it up.

On one flight coming in to Andrews Air Force Base during the winter, the situation got a bit dicey. The airport was closed due to a winter storm, but they turned the lights on for us since we didn't have enough fuel to get anywhere else. With "Live and Die in LA" blasting out, we landed. And we could feel the plane skid and start to slide. We had a female pilot, and that lady really knew her stuff. She fought to keep the plane under control, and we finally came to a stop in one piece.

The only other time we had a hairy landing was when we

were flying in to Guam. There was a big thunderstorm over the Pacific and we were flying right through the middle of it. We had lost our way in the air, and the plane had to be vectored in by the control tower radar on Guam. In spite of the directions, we overshot the field on the first approach. Gunning the engine, we pulled up and around for another try. On the second attempt, we managed to put down safely while getting beaten by wind and rain all the way in.

That landing turned out to be kind of an omen for the rest of the Guam exercise. Personally, I didn't like some of the operations we did on the island due to our own rules of engagement and the local situation.

Though Guam had been a U.S. territory since we liberated it from the Japanese during World War II, and our forefathers in UDT 4 back then had blown open the way, many of the locals didn't like foreigners on their soil. We were not allowed to carry live weapons on our operations, but more than once in the field on Guam, I wished I had a few rounds with me and a pistol that wasn't sealed up tight.

The locals knew we were out there in the brush. In fact a number of them augmented the security force at the U.S. base, and they had been told we were out there. That made us prime targets. A number of U.S. patrols had been jumped by locals in the field and their weapons stolen. Rules of engagement affected a lot more members of the U.S. Military than just Red Cell.

Once, Pooster and I were out on a night patrol doing a recon when we detected someone on our trail. Turning off the trail and curving around back, we were able to watch our own trail, and it wasn't long before we saw three locals tracking us. We decided to abort the operation because there was nothing we could see that justified the risk of our being hit and our weapons being stolen.

On Guam, we were trying some new techniques to breach sensor fields that surrounded sensitive sites. The trouble with sensor fields is that people can get lax when they trust the machines to do their work for them. One of our people was very athletic, even for a SEAL, and he managed to pass a field without setting off any of the alarms. When we penetrated the site, there was a big uproar about how we couldn't have breached the sensor perimeter. Our man simply took the doubters along and showed them how he had done it. Modifications to the system were very soon in place that made that particular type of entry impossible.

In this case, we hadn't beaten the Marines who were on guard, we had simply beaten a sensor system. But that didn't prevent the Marines from quickly doubling the number of guards on duty. The uproar died down before too long and they went back to their standard guard mount, with a considerably upgraded system.

Sometimes we could beat the area, and sometimes the area beat us. Pooster came back to our hotel after an op where he had moved off separately from the rest of us and run into a mud slide while climbing a hill. Back at the hotel, he looked like some very young child's idea of a mud man.

Japan was also on Red Cell's Pacific tour, which included the U.S. Navy facilities at Sasebo on Kyushu, the southernmost of the main Japanese islands. Most of our scenarios involved direct water work, though we did some activity on the base itself. Because of the political arrangements between the Japanese and the U.S. Navy, we had to remain on the base proper to conduct our operations. This limited our flexibility and made operating a bit harder than in other situations. What we did was stay on half the base and keep that area out of play for our scenarios, restricting our active operations to the other half of the base.

Since the half of the base that we considered fair game held the airfield and other facilities, we still had a good set of targets. For one operation against the airfield, Sundance and I acquired a couple of flight suits from an unguarded locker area. Wearing the flight suits, with our hair tucked up under blue caps, we walked into the ready area where the jets were.

The base was supposed to be at a higher than normal state of alert, either THREATCON (terrorist threat condition) RED or YELLOW. Either way, they knew we were in the area and would attack targets of opportunity. Wearing our flight suit camouflage and carrying a sack full of IEDs, we spotted an excellent target in the form of an F-14 fighter parked next to a hanger.

While we walked over to the F-14, we were passed by several security vehicles. Looking over the jet with flashlights, peering into the jet intakes and whatever, we appeared to be maintenance men or pilots performing preflight checks. We made certain that we could have opened the inspection plates over the engine compartment of the F-14, then proceeded to place an IED in plain sight on one of the wings. If we had placed the IED inside the engine compartment, it might not have been discovered before the jet was put into service. So to prevent FOD, or foreign object damage—what the military calls it when you leave tools in the wrong places—we placed our package on the wing of the plane.

As soon as we completed placement of the IED, we went to a nearby pay phone and called in the threat. To be absolutely certain the proper aircraft was searched, we read off the tail number to the security people and remained within sight of the aircraft through their arrival.

When security came around and began their search, it was time for us to go. We just walked away in our flight suits, again looking like we belonged there. No one challenged us or checked our IDs as we left the area. When we returned to our side of the base, the exercise was over and we confirmed that the IED had been found and removed. The object of the scenario had been to see if security was checking people at or near the aircraft or flight line and, if a device could be planted, how long it would take security to arrive on location.

We had to stay on base for our operations, but we did get to go to Sasebo to eat and see the sights. There was one restaurant that we got to like because we could see sumo wrestling there. Most of us got into the sport, and we had our local favorite. An American, a really big Hawaiian, was starting to make a name for himself as a sumo wrestler. Almost every afternoon found us ringside rooting for our favorite. We even got to know the local guy who was running the shop there.

But there was more than sumo wrestling and good eating in our little spot in Sasebo. Acupuncture was also being offered as a treatment for whatever ailed you, although none of us were interested enough to try it. I'd had enough of needle sticks when I got a tattoo on my arm back in my Army days.

Aside from the needles we tried pretty much everything that was offered, soaking up the local culture. Sapporo beer was as good as the food. Kitty was the one who really liked sushi back home, but I got into that too in Sasebo.

We got a good tour of the harbor, mostly just to look at it and make what suggestions we could on security matters. The area was gorgeous, all mountains, green fields, and ocean.

The subject of military attacks came up as part of our mission, and we all had an urge to do a little sightseeing to the spot of one of the world's most well-known attacks, Nagasaki. The excursion turned into a social gathering, with almost the whole crew piling on board a tour bus for the ride to the site of the last A-bomb attack. We were probably too rowdy for the extremely polite Japanese, but we wanted to see the sights and didn't really care what they thought. At Ground Zero Park we went into the museum, where there were two stories of pictures and displays. Walking along and drinking a beer might not have been the most courteous thing we could have done, but we didn't seem to spoil anyone's day at the park.

There was one thing that made an impact on me, and that was the before and after pictures of the city. We all knew something of the history of the Teams and how our forefathers, the World War II UDTs, had expected to lose thousands of their numbers during an invasion of the main islands of Japan. As far as we were concerned, it had been a war and dropping the bombs had been the fastest way to end it with the least overall loss of life.

But the pictures made you pause. In one shot was a living city, showing the ground we were standing on at that moment. In the next picture, taken only a short time later, there was total devastation—all the buildings and structures flattened to the horizon. For myself, it was hard to believe the way the city had been built back up. It also gave me a better feeling for just how important our operations were in keeping weapons of mass destruction from terrorist hands.

Those guard dogs in the Philippines weren't the only critters Red Cell ever had to deal with. For one training exercise, we were asked to conduct a swimmer attack against an anchored Navy ship. Several of us working in pairs would try to attach mines or IEDs to a ship secured a distance from shore. Working against us in the water would be some graduates of the Navy Mammals Program, a number of guard-trained dolphins.

The exercise was a very controlled one. Trainers were in boats nearby, ready to take action if anyone, swimmer or dolphin, was endangered. The trainers had given us a thorough briefing on what to expect and told us not to strike out at the dolphins or otherwise get frisky with them. If we messed with them, the dolphins might get pissed and smack us around a little.

The average adult bottle-nosed dolphin, like the ones the Navy was using, weighs in the neighborhood of four hundred pounds and can swim over twenty-five miles an hour. They can jump twenty feet out of the water and find a golf ball dropped in an Olympic-sized pool faster than you can throw them in. This was not something I particularly wanted to have mad at me.

We weren't worried about hurting the dolphins. Actually, we were pretty sure we could beat them if we were just careful and planned our swims accordingly. Purdue and I worked as a swimmer pair and then on separate attacks, launching from near a bunch of piers. The shafts of the piers gave us some protection, but as soon as we left their cover, we were detected.

It was a weird feeling to see a body suddenly flash by you in the water, looking as big as the shark in *Jaws*. It was nighttime and the waters were dark, but that didn't mean anything to those dolphins. We were in their backyard, they knew all the rules to the game, they owned the bat and ball, and we weren't even going to score.

Right after moving onto the open water I was tagged, if getting poked in the back and pushed ten to twelve feet sideways in about a second is being tagged. I was practically surfing for a moment there. And that wasn't the end of my troubles. The dolphin got its beak tangled in my UDT vest harness and couldn't pull free right away.

The trainers were paddling over to me as I was trying to get the dolphin untangled. My problem was made worse by the fact that Flipper was beating me on the back. It felt like someone smacking me with a boat paddle. Finally the trainer got over to us and told me to leave the dolphin alone!

"I'm trying! I'm trying!" I said as I was being pounded. "Get him off me!"

Finally the trainer got him untangled and free of my harness. I thought I might have provided enough of a distraction for Purdue to continue with the operation and attack the ship. In fact, he got to within ten feet of the hull and was reaching out with his device to plant it when he got hit.

No matter how we tried, as singles, pairs, whatever, these dolphins could nail us. I really didn't like those swims. The dolphins had training harnesses with small green chemlights attached. Occasionally you would see a flash of green as one of them shot past you. That might give you just a bit of warning right before they hit.

None of us made our hits. It was the only time Red Cell was completely beaten by a security force. None of us talked about it later, but we wouldn't volunteer to operate against the dolphins again either. The trainers were some of the most professional people I had ever met. They were a great bunch of guys, and they really knew their animals. That was one experiment by the Navy that looked like it could be a success.

CHAPTER 24

SUNNY CALIFORNIA

By late 1985, we had finally moved our base offices out of the E-ring at the Pentagon. Now Red Cell was staging out of an airport warehouse building right behind Redskin Park at Dulles International Airport. Instead of worrying how much we stood out in the Pentagon, we could finally forget about our clothes and grooming standards and just work on our missions.

Our missions were still taking us all over the country. We were just back from Southern California, where we had hit the Point Mugu Naval Air Station, about forty miles north of Los Angeles, right on the Pacific Ocean. The Point Mugu security people had been sharp. They were an all-volunteer force and had their own reaction team. There was a SEAL we called Postman who had been working with the unit, sharing some of his experience, which was considerable.

From what we knew about Postman, he had been one of the better point men in Vietnam and had also been one of the SEAL dog handlers during that war. The man knew his stuff and eventually came back into the active Teams. After he got out of the Navy the first time, he worked as a postman, delivering the U.S. mail. It was after a dog on his route attacked him, and came out badly for having tried to attack a SEAL, that the name Combat Postman was coined and stuck.

We hit some strategic targets on the Point Mugu base. Some we swam in on, and for others we slipped onto the base using fake IDs. The IDs were ones we had made ourselves. Sometimes we would commandeer an ID if we could pick one up on base or in the local hangouts. A military ID is supposed to be a safeguarded document, so we would always turn in those we had picked up for our missions.

On THREATCON YELLOW, the base is supposed to run random checks of personal IDs. For controlled-access facilities, during the same alert status, security is supposed check all IDs. But just flashing the ID card was often enough to get us into the base. If security checked them closely they would find us, and that was what they were supposed to be doing.

For one of the targets we hit at Point Mugu, we ended up making certain there would be no argument that we had gotten to the site. The high-security target we wanted to hit took some careful planning and observation before we made our move. Late in the afternoon, shortly before nightfall, we moved into our preselected areas. For the observation portion of the mission, we had split up into two teams of two men. Butch Cassidy and I watched the movement of the guard patrols, counting and timing them. There was a roving guard who moved through the area and an occasional vehicle that also moved through on patrol. We marked down the timing of the patrols, roughly every hour for the vehicle and every hour and a half for the guard. It was during that half hour of dead time that we launched our hit.

Our penetration into the general area was a simple one: We

jumped an unguarded gate and patrolled along to our selected site. Between the target and us was a thirty-foot-high cliff. Surrounding the buildings of the compound below us were high chain-link fences topped with barbed tape. But the cliff side of the compound had only a simple little fence, more to keep anyone from approaching the cliff accidentally than to keep people like us out.

So we entered the target compound by rappelling down the cliff. The target building itself was in a high-security area. It was a classified weapons processing building where devices were packed and prepared prior to shipping. This was one of the situations where we were not going to enter the building or bunker directly, just prove we had been there and could have done more.

So we placed some IEDs around the compound, paying close attention to the main building. Once the devices were placed and set, we went back to where our rappelling lines were attached to our ascenders and went back up the lines. Taking a page from the book of some World War II frogmen, we stopped halfway up the cliff and unrolled a banner we had made from a bedsheet. Across the white sheet in big black letters it said RED CELL WAS HERE. That pretty much eliminated any argument from security that we hadn't gotten to the site.

Continuing to the top of the cliff, we wound our lines up and extracted from the area. Despite the tight security, we had been able to enter one of the most valuable targets on the base.

In spite of our successes, the base security team was doing a fairly good job. We even let them do a dynamic entry on us for one exercise, and they conducted it well. We critiqued them during our debrief and discussed how the operation could be made even better. Several of the people were invited by the Skipper to join us on some additional operations we were going to conduct on another Southern California naval facility.

These two men might have been able to handle going against Red Cell on their own territory, but keeping up with us during other exercises could be difficult. We tended not to go in the easy way or slow down much during an op. Duke wanted to be sure the two men the Skipper invited could maintain our killer pace.

Our next mission site was in the Los Angeles area, Seal Beach, a naval facility just south of Long Beach and a couple of miles from the Long Beach Naval Shipyard. For a staging area, we had dropped in on an old Teammate of the Skipper's, Harry Humphries.

Harry had worked with Dick during the Vietnam War and was known as a tough operator. He was living in Huntington Beach with his wife, Katharine. It must have been a bit of a shock to Kath at the start, when all those rental cars pulled up to their condominium and all those guys piled out. Being normal SEALs, we included a wide range of personality types: Some of the guys were very polite, asking after Kath's health and saying how nice it was for them to allow us the use of their home. Other guys said hello and then asked where the food was.

It was a sign of the Humphries' hospitality that they took it all in stride and welcomed us warmly. In the years since, they have become very good friends and I still look forward to seeing them. Their home made an excellent staging area for us, being only a short distance from our target site. Harry also had forty-three-foot sailboat and a good knowledge of the local area. From his boat we were able to launch some swimmer missions and do reconnaissance from the sea side of our target. But before all of that took place, we still had our new volunteers to check out.

Bullet had a pretty good idea of how to test the guys. He pulled me into his plan, and at 4:00 A.M., we woke our volunteers for a little morning PT. We went down to the Bolsa Chica State Beach for our workouts. In good SEAL style, we wanted a little cold Pacific water nearby.

Putting our volunteers in life jackets, we ran them through the surf zone, up and down the beach, and worked out in the sand and the wet. We did this several mornings in a row, not to drain them out but to be sure they had what it took to operate with us. They kept up fairly well, although they weren't terribly happy about it.

We had two major ops planned for Seal Beach, one of which was a hit on a WMD (weapons of mass destruction) storage facility. For the operation, a team of us along with our two volunteers and a cameraman were dropped off at night on the side of Highway 405, which passed by the naval weapons station. We were going to let our two volunteers do the hit itself while the rest of us went along to make sure nothing went wrong and that the rules of engagement weren't violated.

Moving through a soybean field near the site, we were still about half a mile out from our target. We didn't know if the Navy had placed any sensors in the area. Farmers were working the fields around us, so we figured we had a pretty clear path to at least get up to the site. There was a tower overlooking the fields, and we didn't know if the guards had NVDs so we had to remain as stealthy as possible.

We penetrated as closely as we could, intending to let the new guys go into the site. Once they were in, we were going to let them know what it was like to E & E from a secure area. We had our special Red Cell wrist rocket "grenade launchers" with sponge-wrapped M80 firecrackers to start the festivities.

Our volunteers had gotten close enough to the target that we had proved we could penetrate the area. The bang and flash of our taking the facility perimeter under fire was the signal for our new members to begin their E & E. When the fireworks started, things got exciting up on the perimeter quickly. The new guys were able to pull out without incident, and we all regrouped at a spot we had chosen earlier.

Our next operation was going to be a much harder infiltration. Out along the Pacific Coast Highway there was an inlet that ships would move through to load or unload at our target site. Nearby was a large bird sanctuary that was like a huge marshland. We penetrated during low tide, right off the road.

We had to swim our new people part of the way in to the target, but the swim wasn't in water—it was in mud. Every good SEAL and frogman knows it's better to crawl than to try and walk when you get into deep mud. But we walked in.

That was a long, dragging, exhausting walk, which is exactly why we did it, to put the pressure on our new guys. The canal we were going through was only about four feet wide and had some shallow water above all the mud. Our new volunteers were inflating their life jackets before they would get into the canal. Bullet said, "We haven't got time for that," and we both walked through the mud, showing them how it was done. They followed us along on a grueling three-hour penetration to the site. Normally, following that path in would have taken Bullet and me about an hour. But then everyone has to learn what they can and cannot do.

Finally we got to the target, a storage facility near some trap and skeet ranges. Our camera guys, both ex-SEALs, met us at the site. Those guys were very good and we had full confidence that they wouldn't compromise us or give the operation away. The camera crew would patrol right along with us, and they had many of the same skills we had.

One of the cameramen was already at the trap range where he had arranged to meet us. Now we were going to assault the target itself. We let the new guys do a clean hit on the site, setting their IED charges and then returning to where we waited for them. On the way out, one of the new men started complaining that his knee was bothering him.

"Okay," I said. "You go along with the camera guy. He's going to leave another way, but he's waiting until after we've escaped before he moves."

This was good news to the guy with the bad knee and he

readily agreed. As we were moving along, the other new guy started complaining that his ankle was bothering him.

This was a bit much, but I told him to join his partner. The thing was, I said it in something less than complimentary terms. I was pissed and it showed. So the other man joined his partner, and Bullet and I left them behind.

"Come on, Bullet," I said after the other man had left.

"There's a road right here," Bullet said, so we followed a much easier path out. The dirt road led off to a gate in the fence surrounding the site. We jumped the gate and were at our rendezvous point in something like fifteen minutes.

It was about four or five in the morning, right before sunrise. Harry Humphries and the Old Man were waiting for us, complete with a cooler of beer. They knew it was going to be a rough op and were ready to welcome us out in proper form.

The cameraman had seen us start taking the road and he knew what we were doing. The rendezvous point was off the base, at a little pulloff near a bridge. He drove his vehicle to where Harry and Dick were waiting, getting to them well before we showed up. The fact that our new guys were drinking the beer before we had arrived pissed me off. Both Bullet and I told the guys to enjoy the drink and to get ready for our morning PT.

There had been other operations going on with the rest of Red Cell at Seal Beach, not all of which had the same good results we had. On a hostage scenario that I wasn't involved in, Butch and Knobber took the local security chief as their prisoner. By this time we no longer had the lawyer along with us on our operations. That had been one of the cutbacks when the admiral we worked under changed positions.

During the hostage scenario, the security chief, a civilian, was undergoing the same interrogation and stress situation we had put so many others through during our exercises. Knobber was doing the good guy and Butch was the bad guy on the Mutt and Jeff routine. Personally, I didn't particularly care for this security chief. He just struck me as having a bad attitude.

At any rate, he later claimed that Red Cell had abused him severely and that he had suffered long-term difficulties because of the event. Now Red Cell was under scrutiny because we had a civilian complaint. The funny thing was nothing out of the ordinary appeared on the tapes we did of the incident, and this was hardly the only time we had used the Mutt and Jeff routine to induce stress. In addition, later tapes of the debriefing showed this same "abused" guard laughing and joking around with us.

But the damage to our reputation had been done. The Navy settled the suit out of court. Butch Cassidy finally left Red Cell and the Navy, in part because of the pressure brought on the unit by that lawsuit. It severely curtailed our operations for a long time and began a series of investigations that put everything Red Cell did under a microscope.

Before things had hit the fan, we had another change that wouldn't do Red Cell a lot of good in the long run. Admiral Ace Lyons was going through a standard change of command. Since he would no longer hold the 06 position, as OP-06D, we would no longer be under his supervision. Admiral Lyons had been one of the movers and creators of Red Cell who saw its necessity for the betterment of the Navy as a whole. To accomplish that task, he accepted the complaints of other commanders who thought Red Cell was doing nothing more than making them look bad.

Vice Admiral Jones had been an anti–submarine warfare aviator. As the new 06, he didn't have a background that included unconventional operations such as those conducted by Red Cell. He expected to run a tight ship with the commands underneath him. And Red Cell didn't really fit into those plans. But we still had some operations ahead of us.

CHAPTER 25

AND IN THE OTHER DIRECTION

In October we went to Italy to conduct operations against one of our Naval air stations there. Italy had more than its share of terrorist problems. Its home-grown Red Brigade had splintered into several other groups by the time Red Cell arrived in 1985, and just the year before, these groups had declared their opposition to NATO as well as the Italian government.

So our operations had a harder edge than at some other Navy installations. Much like in the Philippines, there had been threats directed at U.S. servicemen in Italy, though not to the same extent as in other countries. The main base Red Cell was going to test was the Sigonella Naval Air Station located on the western side of central Sicily.

Sigonella is both an Italian and an American base in one. The Navy air station rents space from the Italian military. There are two separate naval air stations, Sigonella NAS I and NAS II, separated by about ten miles. While on Sicily, we also took a tour and commented on where the Navy ships come in and moor at the Augusta Bay Port Facility on the eastern shore of the island.

Red Cell was staying at NAS I, north of NAS II, where the personnel support facilities were located. NAS I had been the original base back in the early seventies, but the newer, and much larger, NAS II was where the runways, air terminals, operations, and various commands were located. So we would stage out of NAS I and perform our operations against NAS II.

We spent part of our time in Catania, the nearest Sicilian city to Sigonella. The Skipper had spent some time in Italy on his first hitch in the Navy, when he was an enlisted man, before he joined the Teams. He wanted to show the guys some of the local color, including the food and drink. That was where Red Cell was introduced to grappa, a rough local brandy.

We were all eating supper at a local place with the Skipper ordering for all of us. Pooster and I weren't feeling too adventurous food-wise; we had drunk or eaten something that didn't agree with us. So both of us just had a light pasta dish. The rest of the guys were digging into a local delicacy, the specialty of the house, that the Skipper had ordered.

All the guys were chowing down and enjoying the food. Finally one of them asked the matron of the place just what the dish they were eating was. My pasta looked real good after the answer came back.

What it was called in Italian, I can't remember. What the special translated to in English was "bull's cock."

Knobber had been eating away, chewing at a mouthful of the dish, when the answer came. It was funnier than hell to watch his jaws gradually moving slower and slower. I think just about all of them, including the Skipper, were finished with their meal.

After that memorable dish, the Skipper ordered a round of grappa for everyone. This was one of the roughest drinks I had ever tasted. Back when I was a kid, I had chewed a blade of hay every now and then on the farm; that was the taste of my child-hood that I could compare to grappa. It had an earthy taste, like hay mixed with dirt, only cut with window cleaner. I didn't much care for it, and not a whole hell of a lot stayed down.

But the old Team standby, a good run the next day, helped me get over the local cuisine. The surrounding countryside was beautiful, hilly and covered with vineyards and fields. Protecting their vineyards were the old local Sicilians, carrying their tradi-tional Luparas, what we would call a sawed-off shotgun. In spite of being the rough-tough members of Red Cell, we pretty much stayed on the roads during our runs.

Another local sight we visited was Mount Etna, an active volcano. Every now and then, Etna burps a bit, just to remind everyone nearby who the local landlord really is. Sitting in a local eatery at the foot of Mount Etna, we were having some drinks and food—not the local special this time—and talking to the guys who ran the place. They told us about these Japanese tourists who had come up to see Mount Etna a while earlier.

The tour guides had vehicles that they would take up the sides of Etna, but only so far. You could get good pictures and see the sights, but the locals wouldn't go any closer to the crater than this marked-off safe area. The Japanese tourists had wanted to see more than the guides were willing to show them. So, leaving the locals behind, these tourists walked up to the edge of the crater. They should have listened to the local guides. Etna picked that time to roll over a bit and belch, frying the visi-tors where they stood.

We didn't know if that story was just local folklore to keep the tourists in line or if it had really happened. What we did decide to do was listen to the people who had lived near this active volcano most of their lives. The restaurant was as close as I wanted to get to the open crater of a volcano. Snake had no desire to be cooked in Mother Nature's barbecue.

When we came back from our trip to Etna, our mission had

changed. We ceased operations immediately when we received news that the *Achille Lauro* cruise ship had been hijacked by terrorists in the Mediterranean some twelve hundred miles east of us. The base was on standby alert to support any actions by the United States against the terrorists.

By October 10, the crisis on the ship had ended and the terrorists had boarded an Egyptian Air Boeing 737 for a flight from Egypt to wherever they wanted to go. President Reagan didn't like this situation, especially after it had been confirmed that a U.S. citizen, Leon Klinghoffer, who was in a wheelchair at the time, had been killed by the terrorists. He gave the Sixth Fleet the go order, and U.S. Navy F-16 fighters met the 737 in the air and convinced it to follow their directions to a NATO air base. The 737 landed at Sigonella, taxiing over to the Italian side of the base. The political situation being what it was, the Italians were allowed to take the terrorists into custody, effectively ending the affair for the time being.

A short time later, we ran into a number of our Teammates from SEAL Team Six who were also at Sigonella. We got together with some of the guys, swapped some stories, and had a drink or two. They were doing well, and we congratulated each other on the jobs we were accomplishing. Soon afterward, our Italian missions drew to a close and we returned to the States.

In May I had a big change in my life with Kitty when our first child, my daughter Kacy, was born. Dick Marcinko had a medical technician we called Gundoc, who was also a fully trained diver, EOD man, small arms specialist, and corpsman, who worked with us and helped maintain medical support for Red Cell at the Bethesda medical center. The Skipper's foresight helped a lot when Kitty had trouble with her pregnancy.

Immediately Gundoc got her into Bethesda where she had some of the finest care available. She was sent to the VIP area, where security can be kept tight and the rooms are private and reasonably plush. Things went well enough, and in late May, our package was delivered.

Kacy Chalker was a breech birth, so Kitty was pretty much out of it. I was in the delivery room with her and got to watch the surgery. On May 26, 1986, Snake the warrior went away for a while. In his place was plain old Denny Chalker with a smile on his face as he held his firstborn child. Kacy was a joy, and still is now that she has grown into a graceful, beautiful young woman. She takes after her mother in all the best ways. And makes her dad wonder just which breed of attack dog to get and how many land mines it will take to properly secure the house against young suitors. A big rottweiler and twelve sounds good.

But my job in the Navy and Red Cell took me away from my new family a lot in those days. Kacy grew up occasionally wondering who that big hairy visitor was. A career in the Navy has a price that is paid in time taken from a man's family life. And that price is highest in the Teams.

CHAPTER 26

THOSE ARE BIG LIZARDS

The big Naval reservation on the Cooper River in Charleston, South Carolina, held a large sub base along with a number of other important Naval assets. Swampland bordered much of the base. Nearby, across the river to the north, was the Francis Marion National Forest. This gave a lot of easy access to the base for our Red Cell penetrations, although the base itself was pretty secure.

We did two simultaneous ops during this exercise, one a barricade situation where we took over a building. To do my job, I rented a motorcycle, a Yamaha 400 dirt bike. There were only two ways I was going to be able to get onto the base, and they both involved crossing a large tract of land. The method I chose was to go to a wilderness part of the base and slip through the woods at night, pushing the bike through about fifty yards of thickets. Going up a small hill, I could then cut through the fence, get my bike on the base, and close up the fence behind me.

The other option I considered was to follow the two miles of railroad track that ran out of the base and through some of the surrounding swampland. In spite of having to push the bike through the brush, my entrance choice was the much more comfortable and drier one. My main concern about the railroad track was that I hadn't scouted it out during the day. If I was moving along it in the dark on the dirt bike and a tie was missing, I would be crashing in a hurry. Also, if a train had come along while I was on the track, my only option would have been to jump into the swamp.

Normally, getting wet doesn't mean much to a SEAL, though we are well aware of the value of being warm and dry. But getting into that swamp water didn't just mean getting wet; you could also meet the other security force on the outside of the base. It was gator season when we staged our operations at Charleston, and you could hear those big bull gators bellowing all over that swamp.

Knobber had helped me trailer the bike in to where I wanted to penetrate the site and helped me get the bike through the brush and past the fence. Even pushing along through the woods, we would hit a hole every now and then that was the right size to have been an old gator wallow. After getting through the fence, Knobber took off back to where he left his vehicle. I don't think he felt that meeting a leftover dinosaur was the thing to do either.

Once I was on the base proper, I took the bike past the railroad tracks and through some heavy woods. The area was pine forest, fairly flat, and ended near some ammunition bunkers. Staging from the edge of the forest, I moved to the bunkers to conduct my operation.

Placing IEDs on a few of the bunker doors, I stuck around for a while to see who might come along. About 6:00 A.M. I picked up one of the phones that was on a pole at the bunker complex and called in the threat.

"This is a Red Cell exercise," I told the person who answered the phone. "I'm down here at your bunker area. I have just placed an IED on these bunkers," and I gave him the numbers.

It wasn't too long before a couple of security vehicles showed up. Sitting on the bike, I had been revving it, keeping the motor warm and waiting for the response to my call. With security there, it was time for the chase to begin.

The earth-covered bunkers had sloping sides and were easy to drive the bike up and over. The security vehicles, on the other hand, had to stick to the roads going around the bunkers to keep me in sight. When I finally cut into the woods on my bike, they lost me completely. With no paths wide enough to accept the security vehicles, they would have had to chase me on foot, a losing proposition against a man on a dirt bike.

But then again, maybe they could have caught me if they had kept up the chase. It certainly seemed that Mr. Murphy was on their side. As I rode through the brush, my fuel line broke right where it entered the carburetor and the bike died on me. There was nothing I could jury-rig to repair the fuel line, so I was out of transportation. But while I was having my difficulties, the rest of the guys were holding their barricade operation on another part of the base a couple of miles away. So security was busy that day, and they didn't bother to try chasing me very far.

With my bike dead, I had to pull it along while I worked my way through the woods. Finally getting to a gate in the fence near a local highway, I left the bike in the woods to come back for later. Walking along the inside of the fence line, I decided I would give myself up to the next security force I ran into. My part of the scenario was pretty much over without transportation.

People passed me by without stopping. It wasn't like you couldn't tell I didn't belong there, not with my long hair, civilian clothes, and the pistol I was waving with the red tape on it. But everyone on the base I could surrender to seemed to be involved with our barricade situation.

I wasn't in any kind of personal difficulty. I had a radio with me and could communicate with the rest of my team. I was just bored! There was nothing for me to do but continue walking. Eventually I covered the three miles or so that had separated my bunker op from our barricade situation. Security had set up an outside perimeter around the building that Red Cell had taken over.

Okay, this looked interesting. Since no one wanted to arrest me, I was going to join the party. Getting on the radio, I said, "Hey guys, open up the door. I'm going to make a dash through the perimeter."

Two security men were crouched behind their vehicle, watching the building, so they didn't see me coming out of the woods behind them. They did notice me as I ran past them both, but by then it was a little late. Darting up to the building, I made a grab for the door to join my Teammates inside.

For a simulated weapon during our exercises, we took a number of M80 firecrackers and wrapped them completely with flat dry sponges so that only the fuse was showing. With a wrist rocket slingshot, we could launch these "grenades" a long way with fair accuracy. Before firing, we would wet down the sponges from a squirt bottle of water we carried with us. The wet sponge would contain any blast, and all we would get was a good flash and a loud noise. It wasn't the kind of thing that could be mistaken for a car backfire or other common noise.

The combination of slingshots and firecrackers had worked well for us. The system let us mess with the security forces, placing them under fire in a reasonably safe manner, though we still had to make sure we didn't shoot the "grenades" close to anyone.

During my mad dash though the security forces, one of my Teammates offered his version of covering fire. Yeah, right. I saw him launch one of our sponge-wrapped firecracker grenades at me as I was running up to the building. It went off behind me, but that was probably just because he misjudged my speed when he shot at me.

Things didn't get a whole lot better when I finally made it to the building. Demonstrating that wonderful SEAL sense of humor, some of the guys thought it would be a lot of fun to watch me try to get through a locked door. As I was banging on the door for them to let me in, the rest of the security force started training their weapons on me. It looked like I was finally going to get some attention from security when the guys unlocked the door and let me in.

During the debrief, my adventures with the motorcycle weren't pointed out as a mistake. Instead it was made to look like everything that happened was intentional. Yeah, we planned it that way.

Red Cell had been running exercises for over a year and we had learned a lot, in addition to teaching Navy facilities how to eliminate some of their vulnerabilities. Earlier we had announced to a base or facility when we would be conducting an exercise against them, giving a short time window for when the operations would take place.

What we had learned fast was that bases would immediately go to THREATCON RED when they knew Red Cell was on its way. At RED, the base is all but closed up tight, full examinations are given to all IDs and incoming vehicles, and the watch is often doubled, with twice as many men on duty as normal. This can run twenty-four hours a day, but for how many days before efficiency suffers?

The reaction would be fine, but only if they were willing to remain at that alert level for a year or so. Security wasn't supposed to be beefed up just for the three weeks that Red Cell was threatening a base. It was supposed to run under normal conditions so that we could show any weaknesses in the system.

But that isn't how the average military mind works, especially not the minds of senior commanders who thought we were out to make them look bad. Red Cell had a mission to perform, and that mission was to demonstrate holes in a security system and how to seal them up.

So instead of giving the base a short window of time when they could expect Red Cell to come visiting, we gave them a much broader window. Rather than "Red Cell will be running an exercise against your base sometime during the next three weeks," it would be "the next quarter year," or "the next four months."

If a base could run under THREATCON RED for four months without a degradation in efficiency, there wasn't anything we had to show them. But for the most part, the bases had to run under the normal THREATCON WHITE or YELLOW.

Another problem we saw, but could do little about, was what happened at a base after Red Cell had wrapped operations. If the base had been running under THREATCON RED, it should have dropped back down to YELLOW and remained there for a length of time to ensure that the terrorist threat was over. Instead, bases would drop from RED right down to WHITE when we were finished with our exercises.

Great improvements have been made in the overall security of all American bases in the last fifteen years. They are much more secure now than when Red Cell began its operations. Some of these operational improvements came about because of advances in intelligence gathering and recognition of the terrorist threat. And I like to think that some of the improvements came about because of what we did in Red Cell.

Penetrations of military and other installations are always feasible. The question is: Does the threat have the skills or resources to pull off a penetration? Hardening a site to a possible penetration, turning it from a "soft" to a "hard" target, will help stop an action from taking place. Terrorist groups that see a target that is too hard to attack will move on. Hardening can prevent a situation from ever developing.

CHAPTER 27

BACK IN SUNNY CALIFORNIA

We returned to California and further operations against sites we hadn't hit the first time we were there. On Terminal Island in San Pedro Bay, just a few miles north of Seal Beach, was the Long Beach Naval Shipyard, a huge complex of buildings, docks, and facilities. For Red Cell's operations against the Long Beach facility, we again dropped in on Harry Humphries and staged out of his place in Huntington Beach.

Operations against the shipyard involved our penetrating different parts of the facility, placing IEDs, and otherwise checking the perimeter security. The hostage rescue scenario we had considered was dropped after judging the available time for the ops. My portion of the operation was a more comfortable one than usual, though not for very long.

One of our people got a room at the Navy Lodge, right off the highway and inside the base proper. That night, I jumped the fence surrounding the facility, made my way quickly through a children's playground, and got to the room at the Navy Lodge. The key was there for me, though I didn't use it to get into the room. After my confederate had rented the room, he had unlocked the rear window and left it open just a bit. When I came up to the room, it was a matter of a moment to open the window and slip in.

For the Long Beach operations, I would be running a control point at the room and have it available as a safe house on base. This would give any of our personnel on base a place to run to if they had to E & E during an op. I had also rented a motorcycle and it was registered on the base. This gave me fast transportation and the option of riding around and checking things out prior to an op. Since the bike had a base sticker, it wouldn't draw attention, and with my long hair stuffed underneath a full helmet, I wouldn't stick out too much myself.

One of the scenarios was done to give base security personnel the chance for a little interrogation practice. To do that, they would have to capture one of us. Seems I was volunteered to be the prisoner when someone told base security where our on-base safe house was at the Navy Lodge.

A phone call came in to me at the room one night; "Hey look," the voice said. "They're going to take your room tonight. We're just letting you know."

"Okay," I said. This was new but not that unusual. "What's the drill?"

"They're going to take you prisoner. The check is to see how their interrogation procedures work."

The conversation was short. I was due to have visitors any moment. Sitting there, I was wondering what I could do to make the capture at least a little difficult for them. Looking out one of the windows, I could see their entry team coming up on the outside, getting ready to bust in and grab me.

First thing, I dead-bolted the door so they couldn't come in easily. I had kept the back window of the room open, and since I was on the ground floor, it wouldn't have been any trouble to slip out the back. I could see that the area behind the lodge was clear all the way to the fence. Escape would have been easy. But I was supposed to be captured.

Since I was just wearing shorts, I thought of a fast way to mess with their plans a little bit. Skinning out of my shorts, I jumped into the shower. The entry team burst into the room, immediately secured the area, then moved to the bathroom. Bursting in to the bathroom, they tore open the shower curtain to grab me.

If I had known that was one of the few entry teams to have a woman on it, I probably wouldn't have jumped into the shower. At least I might have kept my shorts on. Okay, good job, Denny!

So I put a towel around myself quickly. Normally an entry team does not burst out laughing when they secure a prisoner, especially not a dangerous terrorist like me. So the joke was on me, and I got dressed quickly.

Securing me with handcuffs, they didn't consider a frisk necessary. After they checked my clothes, the team searched the room. I had left some documents for them to find: the routes I took, a log book, things like that. Some of the materials I had hidden. They found them during their sweep, so that part of the exercise went well. Taking me to the security building, they started the interrogation.

First thing they wanted to know was my full name. "You've already got my ID," I said. "You already know." With that, I started not fully cooperating with them. If I was asked a question, I would answer it with the least possible information. I wasn't going to jeopardize any of Red Cell's ongoing operations on the site, but I did keep them moving forward on the interrogation.

My little grilling went on for about three hours. Then the word came in that the problem was over. I was released with the understanding that I had to go out through the gate. Almost all the problems were over; there was only one man still on base continuing his exercise. So I was allowed to leave and rejoin my group.

We had our debriefing the next day. Everything had gone pretty well at the base, security had done a good job, and there hadn't been any major incidents. We had a meal with the security people during a relaxed get-together. My little shower-room scene was the punchline of a joke or two during that particular social session.

CHAPTER 28

GHOSTS

As part of our Pacific trip, we went to Hawaii to conduct operations at Pearl Harbor and the Navy bases surrounding it. For the Hawaiian exercises, we had specific dates when we would start and stop our operations. The exercises began with a briefing for the base commanders and security forces. Everyone got to know everyone else, what we were there for, and what we expected to accomplish. As usual, we received a less than delighted welcome.

Red Cell wasn't operating like any other kind of inspection team the Navy had. We didn't go in to look at how secure a base was; we tried to breach its security though direct action. In other words, we operated in a real-world situation, and all the higher command officers wanted us to operate under artificial rules of engagement. They didn't want a terrorist exercise; they wanted a stilted, think-tank type of war game where the chances of winning were much more in their favor. That, and we often disrupted the smooth flow of base operations that commanders are so fond of.

The Pearl Harbor facilities were laid out quite differently than the other Naval bases we had operated against. Working sugarcane fields butted right up against base borders. And there were recreational shore facilities and beaches that were Navy property but were separated from the base proper. The other Hawaiian installations were surrounded by civilian tourist and vacation sites that we couldn't disturb. But there were a number of recreation sites set up just for the military families. These sites we looked at as legitimate terrorist targets.

For my first operation at Pearl we targeted one of the recreational beaches the Navy maintained. The beach was six miles up the coast from the base with sugarcane fields growing between it and the main base. The beach was surrounded by a fence with a gate and some security next to the parking area. Our job was simply to penetrate the beach, plant an explosive device, get away, and then call it in.

The start of our operations had already been announced, and the whole base and all of its surrounding facilities should have been on THREATCON RED. But the beach hadn't been closed, and we couldn't see anything more than ID checks going on at the gate. Since they were checking the IDs, we decided against trying to slip through the gate.

We rented a jeep and went cross-country a bit to approach the fence line at the beach. I was glad we knew a little about where we were because some of the locals might not have taken kindly to our passing through their fields. Since we were on an exercise, none of us were carrying weapons.

Taking the jeep as close as we could to the beach, we parked it and started to walk in. Passing a small junkyard, we saw three local Hawaiians who didn't look any too friendly. The locals kept their eyes on us, but there wasn't any incident as we worked our way past. The hardtop jeep we had left behind wasn't a big worry; it was insured and we had locked it up before leaving.

After walking about another half a mile, we could see the ocean. Now it was a simple matter of following the ocean until we hit the fence. Coming up to the fence, we just rolled our pants up and walked into the water and around the fence. If we had been spotted and caught, that was part of the game. We weren't doing anything fancy, just a straightforward penetration.

But no one stopped us. Once at the shore, we blended in with the people there. Taking our pants off (we had worn swim suits under them), we went to the center of the beach and sat down. There was a fair crowd of people on the beach and we just sat around for half an hour or so, making conversation and keeping an eye out for security.

Our long hair and mustaches didn't blend in very well, but we were tanned and fit, and no one seemed to take much notice of us. In a backpack was our IED. Leaving the pack where it was, we got up and started walking up to where the gate and security guard were, just checking out the area. Finally, we put our pants back on, slipped back out the way we had come in, and made our way to a phone.

Calling in the IED, we caused a reaction from the security staff. They came out and secured the beach, clearing it of all people before calling up EOD to deal with our little package. Forcing the people from the beach was an inconvenience for them, but nothing compared to what a real bomb would have been if it had detonated. The security staff did what they had to and conducted their part of the exercise correctly.

Another major target was the big Naval facility on Ford Island in Pearl Harbor itself. Doc Holliday and I had planned to take a kayak from a civilian park on one side of the harbor over to Ford Island for our operation. We would paddle across the water right over the USS *Arizona* National Monument on the most direct approach to our target. In spite of Red Cell running fast and loose with the rules when we were on an exercise, chances are the National Park Service would have had us for lunch if they caught us going over the USS *Arizona* in a kayak.

Before we did our operation, we had to do a reconnaissance of the shoreline of Ford Island, preferably one where we wouldn't be easily noticed. That same USS *Arizona* National Monument and the guided tours that were given there less than a few hundred yards from our target were going to provide our recon.

The tour was conducted from a ferryboat run by the Park Service. The USS *Arizona* had been declared a national cemetery after the Pearl Harbor attack. In her rusting steel hull were the bodies of hundreds of U.S. sailors, which had never been recovered during the war. We conducted our recon of Ford Island, but we also made note of just where we were.

The USS *Arizona* memorial is a moving one to most of its visitors, even more so to a member of the Navy. You couldn't help but think of those thousand sailors entombed in the steel hulk below. One of the guys got pretty emotional during the visit. Being a SEAL and a member of Red Cell, he was not particularly soft-spoken or used to keeping his feelings to himself. Basically, he growled at all the Japanese tourists who were visiting the memorial along with us. We quickly left before anything could happen, with our snarling Teammate firmly in tow.

In spite of the distractions, the recon showed us what we wanted to know, and the kayak insertion looked like a good one. That night Doc Holliday and I got into the kayak and moved out toward Ford Island. There were Navy patrol boats in the harbor running searches, but we were never detected. When we passed over the USS *Arizona*, though, things turned a little weird.

It was a warm, humid night, like so many on Oahu. But over the hulk of the sunken battleship, it felt as if the temperature dropped to just above freezing. It seemed like a lot more than just cold chills running down your back; more like a wind chill factor that passed right through you. It was not just water and steel that we were passing over. The battleship *Arizona* was a piece of history, and it seemed that she didn't like being disturbed.

After passing the memorial, we were easily able to get ashore, pull up, and camouflage the kayak. Our primary target area was on the other side of Ford Island, so we had to trot across the width of the island, crossing a golf course and another open area. Security vehicles came into sight, but we concealed ourselves in the grass until they had passed, and then continued on.

One of our targets was a warehouse where we did a quick in-and-out, leaving an IED in our wake. Penetrating one of the administration buildings, we placed several IEDs and returned to the kayak. There hadn't been many personnel on the island when we hit it, more of a skeleton crew than a full alert staff, and the operation went without a hitch.

For a hostage rescue scenario, we took over a barracks, which was on the main base, close to a gate and the main civilian highway beyond. We simply climbed over the fence at the gate to gain access to the base and our planned target. Securing the building, we gathered up anyone inside and made them our hostages for the duration of the exercise.

The security force of the base had incorporated the SWAT team from Honolulu into their overall plan of reaction. The SWAT cops were also staged on base for our exercises. We received word that they were setting up to do a dynamic entry on the barracks.

To set up our escape, we called Sluggo and told him to meet us at the back gate by the highway at a preset time. Once he was at the gate, we would abandon the barracks, climb over the gate, and get the hell out of there.

The word came in that the SWAT forces were on their way,

and we quickly left the barracks, slipping out the back windows and running for the fence. Once we had cleared the fence and were off the military base, we figured we were good. We were in a civilian area, and Sluggo was on his way to get us. The only problem was, no Sluggo.

Walking down the road a little, we kept our eyes open for our missing transportation. Duke, Doc Holliday, Bullet, myself, and a couple of other guys were in our little mob. After about half a mile, we just sat on the guardrail, waiting for our next action. The next move wasn't made by us. It showed up in the form of blue flashing lights on top of a bunch of SWAT police cars.

The police stopped all the civilian traffic with their three police cars set sideways across the road. A bunch of the biggest law enforcement guys I have ever seen got out of the cars and stood there behind them. Funny thing was, all these cops were wearing mouth guards, like they were getting ready for a full-contact football game. Which may have been what they had on their minds, only we were the visiting team.

They shouted, "Freeze! Nobody move!" We shouted back, "Exercise!" Neither one of our groups had much impact on the other. Ronnie had one of our red-taped pistols, and he pulled it out, shouting "Bang! Bang!"

That wasn't quite as bad as his follow-up yell of "Hey, I got you."

Our exercise was quickly deteriorating to a game of cops and robbers. Only in our case they were real cops and had real guns, though they hadn't pulled them yet. And we thought it would be nice to regain control of the situation before they did.

"Hey, Ronnie," we said, "relax man, just relax." The cops looked like they meant business and weren't in the mood for any lighthearted games. So, of course, that was when Sluggo finally showed up with our getaway vehicle.

Slewing the car sideways and stopping right in the center of our little standoff, Sluggo leaned out with his red-sealed weapon, also shouting "Bang, bang, bang, bang! You're all dead!"

This was starting to get a bit silly. Duke shouted out to Sluggo, "Sluggo, get the fuck out of here. You're late! We'll talk later."

The cops took us back to their headquarters on base and the exercise ended there. They were a really good bunch of guys, and I was glad we hadn't had to meet up with them on a serious occasion. In person, they were very professional, as well as being some of the biggest cops I've ever met.

For the most part, the exercises at Pearl Harbor went well. One of the senior commanders gave the Skipper a bit of an argument during the debriefing. The senior officer insisted that a kayak attack by Red Cell had been thwarted by one of the security people under his command.

Apparently a female security officer claimed to have taken out one of our boats with a Stinger missile launcher she had available at her station. The Stinger is a shoulder-fired heat-seeking antiaircraft missile, not the most proper weapon to fire at a small unpowered boat floating on the water. Our camera-man had been filming the incident and spoke to the security officer after the exercise.

Red Cell insisted that our exercise had gone forward legitimately. What the Skipper finally used to seal his argument with the senior officer was a bit of the videotape where the female said she didn't even know how to fire or operate the Stinger, just how to pick it up and which end to point at a target. She hadn't known how to work the weapon she "saved" her ship with.

CHAPTER 29

ANOTHER MOVE, ANOTHER COMMANDER, AND THE END OF AN IDEA

Around the time Dick started Red Cell, investigations were just beginning to get under way back at SEAL Team Six. The investigations involved the starting up of the unit and how materials had been obtained and suppliers decided on—all things that were well above my position in the unit. I didn't know what was going on, if anything. Most of what was being investigated didn't involve my specific work, and there was enough of that to keep me busy.

Dick's style of leadership centered on trusting the men under him. And he may have trusted people more than he should have. But in the Navy, the commanding officer of a unit or a ship is given a great deal of responsibility and power. That responsibility wasn't something Dick had ever ignored before and he wasn't going to start now.

When the investigation was building up, Dick had to leave Red Cell. He wasn't relieved of command. It was just that he had to go up to the Washington Navy Yard to be available to the Naval Investigative Service based there.

While all this was going on, Duke, who had been second in command at the unit, took over running Red Cell in Dick's absence. We didn't see any problem with Duke running things. Things had to be kept going, and that's why Duke took over. We still had missions to complete. Taskings were sent in from various commands for us to test different facilities. Red Cell still had a mission to perform, and we got on with what we had to do.

Admiral Lemoyne had taken over the position that had been held by Admiral Lyons earlier. Now we had an overall commander who wanted things run tighter, especially while the investigation was going on. At Admiral Lemoyne's direction, all Red Cell operations were suspended for six months pending the results of Dick's investigation. We couldn't stay at home, and we couldn't operate in the field. What we did do was go in every day to the warehouse at Dulles and work out to keep up our general training and fitness levels. There was little else we could do.

When the investigation reached the point that a trial was going to be conducted and Dick had to defend himself legally, he had to relinquish command of Red Cell. This wasn't something any of us could do anything about directly. It was a loss for us, but the best thing we could do for Dick was move forward with the unit he had created and do the very best job we could. All of us at Red Cell had been questioned about how things had been done years before at Six, but most of what they were looking for was so far above our positions that we couldn't tell them anything.

The only good that came out of the end of the investigation for us was that we finally went operational again. Now under Duke's leadership, we conducted exercises again.

Command now made the decision that we should be closer to a military installation for our support and training rather than in a converted warehouse at Dulles. Following our directives, Red Cell moved its base of operations to the Indian Head Naval Ordnance Facility in Maryland, on the Potomac River south of Washington. Another warehouse, this one just outside the base, became our new home base.

Kitty and I were living in Herndon at that time and Ho Ho was living nearby. Just about every day Ho Ho and I would drive some fifty miles to Indian Head. Pooster had moved to another place when Kitty and I moved to Herndon. So the penthouse was closed, and he commuted from the D.C. area down to Indian Head every day on his own. On rare occasions during the week I would spend the night at the warehouse, but I wanted to spend time with my family, so I made the drive.

Duke had been running things fine after Dick left, but when we arrived at Indian Head we had a change of command to go along with our new location. Captain Rick Woolard took over running Red Cell. He had been a Teammate of Dick Marcinko's in Vietnam and had also been the CO of SEAL Team Two from June 1982 to June 1984.

In spite of any feelings we may have had as individuals about what had happened to Dick, nothing had changed for the unit. We still had our mission statement and tasking at hand. The feelings toward Rick Woolard were no different than they would have been toward any other new CO stepping aboard a Navy command. He was new to me and a number of others, but some of the guys in the unit had served under him before.

The new captain had a reputation as an operator and knew how to get together with his men, SEAL style. After the change of command, we had a get-together at the local VFW hall. The "meeting" went on into the wee hours of the morning. Unit business wasn't the topic of the night; it was more the wetting down of a new commander and a chance for us to get to know him as an individual.

To save time the next morning, we slept right there in the hall. The next day we were introduced to Mrs. Woolard when the new commander's lovely wife came down to the hall. Something about looking for her car, which Rick had taken the night before.

His wife may not have been too happy with the immediate situation, but then she had probably seen her husband being broken in to a new command more than once. Our socialization techniques tended to follow the old Team school of thought, in which a proper wetting down was considered necessary.

We spent a lot of the time immediately after Captain Woolard's arrival getting our Indian Head compound squared away and ready for operations. Red Cell was more than two years old, and officer and personnel rotations were coming up. A bunch of new meat came in and we started breaking them in to what we had been doing.

Most of the original crew at Red Cell started rotating back to the Teams. Some of the guys went with Duke over to SEAL Team Four Commissioned in 1983; others went back to Six. By late summer 1987, Bullet, Sundance, and I were the last of the old crew left at Red Cell. I was the ordnance chief at the time, so my turnover to a new man took the longest. When it came time for me finally to leave Red Cell, I decided to take up the offer Bob Gormly had made to me earlier and went back to SEAL Team Six.

Red Cell continued on for a number of years but never returned to its original charter and method of operating. Gradually the rules of engagement became more and more restrictive. Soon the unit came to be just an advisory one. Red Cell would go to a Navy base, observe their methods of operation and their procedures, and comment on where they could be improved. The unit was finally dissolved in the early 1990s.

CHAPTER 30

RETURN, OPERATE, AND FINALLY LEAVE

I returned to SEAL Team Six from Red Cell to find a few changes in the Team. We had become larger, with an additional technical group to aid the other groups in operating their small boats. Training continued to be hard and long, but with the larger Team came a little more time for a home life. Active missions were still relatively few and far between, but there was enough happening to keep your blood circulating.

MISSION: Search of [Classified]
LOCATION: [Classified]
DATE:[Classifed]

During one of our hot missions, we were operating as a quick reaction force, almost a SWAT team really, with a breacher team assigned to us for dynamic entries. With the breachers opening the door, the rest of the squad would be able to concentrate on getting in and conducting the mission, and we would be at full strength right from the get-go.

We were operating in a semipermissive environment on this op. Most of the population was glad we were there, but we still had to stay alert for unfriendlies who could pop up from almost anywhere. That forced us to keep our wits about us constantly, with no time for any kind of break.

We had been given an intel dump on a building we were going to search for intel and other possible targets. No pictures of the place were available to us and we were working under a fast timetable, so we pored over what information we had, to fix the place firmly in our minds.

We decided to break the platoon into two units and do a simultaneous entry. My unit would come in from the top, working our way down from the roof of the large house, while the second unit went in through the front door and came up from the bottom.

We would get to the roof from a Blackhawk helicopter, fast-roping down as the other unit went into position at the front. The house looked out on a beach, so there was plenty of room for the other unit to fast-rope down from their bird. My unit was in the second bird.

The first helicopter pulled up at the front of the house and blasted sand across the front of the building as the first unit exited. When they went in, we came in fast and low, kicking the rope out and sliding down as the helicopter did a fast flare and stopped right above the flat roof. Over twenty-five armed men had been dropped from the hovering helicopters in seconds.

As we fast-roped down, the semipermissive aspect of our environment became obvious as a figure some distance away started taking potshots at us. It didn't seem to be a dedicated sniper; more like a farmer in a field some two to three hundred meters away. The *crack, crack* of the bullets snapping by was familiar enough to me. The weapon sounded like an AK-47, something that had been pointed my way before.

We quickly scrambled to the balcony and lined up for the breach. As we huddled against the wall of the building, one of the guys called out, "Hey, what's that?"

"Hey, we're being shot at," he was told. It was certainly a lot different from my first combat insertion back on Grenada. Then everything concerned us, and eyeballs grew wide as the bullets went by. Now we just kind of chuckled. Someone was shooting at us, but we weren't the new guys in combat anymore.

Then something very new happened to me, something I hadn't experienced before in a combat situation. We had planned to go in a side window of the house, a more unexpected point of entry than a door. But when we came up to our planned entry point, it was heavily barred. A sliding glass door was farther down the balcony, and that looked like the next best point to go through.

As we moved into our new position, I saw an armed guard running in the yard below us with what looked like a guard dog. We couldn't let this guy get away and possibly bring in reinforcements. So I snapped up my M4 carbine, lining up the sights as the buttstock hit my shoulder. Sighting in on the man, I squeezed back on the trigger, and . . . *click*.

Click? What's this *click* shit? The guard had run out of my line of sight as I yanked back on the charging handle to my M4. As the round popped from the chamber, I caught it in the air and slipped it into my pocket. The immediate action of clearing and reloading my weapon had been almost instinctive and the matter of a second or two at most. But I had never had my weapon fail to fire on me while in combat. That Murphy character who messes things up according to his own rules is a real bastard.

Now the breacher team was in position prepping the front door for entry, and they ran into another aspect of the building's security. The double oak door had a heavy iron security gate reinforcing it. That made the entrance a lot stronger than our sketchy intelligence reports had led us to believe. They told us about their situation over the radio as they prepared to go through the front door anyway.

There's an old frogman rule for demolitions: When in doubt, overload your target. That rule was now brought into play. To make sure the door went in on the first blast, the breachers used more explosive than they normally would have. It would be better to put up with a larger explosion and get through the door on the first try than to have to reload after warning everyone inside exactly where you were.

As the breachers and front squad made ready to go in the front, my team and I moved to the sliding glass door. When the front door went, we would rake the glass door with a shotgun, throw in a crash, and then enter and start our room-to-room search.

As the squad leader, I wanted to make sure I had the most control of the room we were going into, so I was the third man in line rather than right up front. The sliding door opened into a bedroom with the far door open, and we could look down into a small part of the house. The center of the house was one of those living rooms with an open ceiling, and we could just see into it as the entry went forward.

The countdown went out over our radios: Three . . . Two . . . One . . . Go, go, go! Our breacher fired on the sliding door as the front crew blew their breaching charge. That old frogman rule may have a drawback when applied to door breaching: the boom of the front breaching charge shook the whole building.

Through the open door of the bedroom, I could see the heavy front door come blasting in, knocked clean off its hinges by the explosive. The door blew through the living room and out the back of the house, along with a large selection of the living room furnishings. It all ended up in and around a swimming pool at the rear of the building.

"Holy shit!" I thought. But there was no time to reflect on flying doors. The training we had been doing for years makes many of the reactions to a breach automatic. I was through the door and covering my sector while the front door was still in the air and the echoes of our crashes were ringing through the building.

We cleared the bedroom we had entered in seconds. Shattered glass had been driven across the room from the blasts of the shotgun clearing out the door. With the door smashed open, another member of the breacher unit threw in a crash before the glass had even stopped falling. With the noise and flash of the crash detonating, we piled in through the door and fanned out, covering all points of the room. No one was there.

To the side of the bedroom was another door. My shooting partner went up to the door, and I stepped up behind him. He opened the door and threw the crash in and before I could stop him, he went in through the door before the crash had fired. Grabbing at him and shouting, "No!" I had to follow him into the room, which turned out to be an unoccupied bathroom. The crash went off right in front of us, the thundering noise and brilliant flash of light bouncing off the walls of the small room.

Dazzled by the flash of light, all I could see were multicolored dots dancing in front of my eyes. My partner wasn't in any better shape than I was. Neither of us were seriously hurt but we were out of the running for a moment.

Ducking back into the bedroom, I told Tee, my leading petty officer, that I was blinded and to take over the mission. He could see that I was blinking to clear my eyes. He took the unit and went deeper into the house.

Within a minute, at least the dancing lights were going away. Going out the bedroom door to catch up with the rest of the crew, we came out on a balcony overlooking the living room. Or what was left of the living room.

We blasted through that house room by room and floor by floor. But the quarry we were chasing weren't there, and our search for intelligence information came up with very little. We did find some nice cigars, though.

The helos came in and picked us up in front of the house. Our friendly farmer with the AK-47 didn't put in another appearance, and that armed guard was really having a lucky day as none of us saw him later.

Downstaging from the op, I had the opportunity to take that misfired round from my pocket and get a good look at it. The very slight dimple on the silver primer in the base of the brass case told me the story. I had gotten a light primer hit when I pulled the trigger on that running guard. The firing pin hadn't struck the round with enough force to fire it—I hate Murphy. It was something that happened, thankfully very rarely. It just hadn't been that guard's day to go.

MISSION: Area Search
LOCATION: [Classified]
DATE: [Classified]

During an overseas deployment of U.S. troops, a report came into our headquarters about an island that was being used as a relay station or possible listening post to gather and transmit information regarding U.S. troop movements. As the closest available Special Operations unit, we were given the task of going in and searching out the clandestine transmitting station. Since the target was a small island just off shore, it was in the environment we felt most at home in, the sea.

To give us more maneuverability around the island, we were going to make a two-pronged insertion. One squad would go in on a Blackhawk helicopter and quickly take control of the land and beach. A second helicopter, a much larger CH-47

Chinook, would come in with a second squad and an inflated rubber boat.

The CH-47 would do what we called a "soft duck" drop. A soft duck was where the helicopter came down to the surface of the water with its rear cargo ramp fully lowered. With the ramp awash, inflated Zodiac F-470 rubber boats would be pushed out of the cargo bay and into the water. Our fellow SEALs would use the rubber boats to circle the island, both covering the shore and giving us a quick way off the island without having to bring in a bird for an emergency extraction. Given the small size of the island and its unknown ground conditions, using the boats was the most prudent course of action.

When the CH-47 had completed its soft duck insertion, it would move back to the mainland and land on the beach there. That kept the bird close by. If we found any communications gear or other valuable intelligence material, the CH-47 would be able to take us in once we were on shore and fly us back to base.

The insertion went forward without a hitch and the bird flew off to the beach. On board the Blackhawk, my squad moved up to the island without taking any fire or seeing any movement. The ground was covered in heavy grass, and with an unopposed landing zone, we decided to jump in from the hovering bird. When the Blackhawk's landing wheels were just above the waving grass, the squad and I jumped off and the bird pulled away.

Landing a helicopter on an unknown surface could be dangerous, so simply jumping off into the grass seemed the simplest way to get in fast and minimize the exposure of the bird. We were right about the unknown surface, and we were wrong about jumping off the bird.

That was pretty tall grass. In Vietnam, they called the stuff elephant grass. Not because elephants liked eating that kind of grass but because elephants could hide in that kind of grass.

Jumping from the bird, we fell into the grass and kept on falling until the grass was over our heads. The ground level wasn't the five feet down we thought it was. That was just how far down the grass bent in the downwash of the helicopter blades. The ground was ten feet beyond that.

So we fell fifteen feet and smacked into the ground. Untangling ourselves, we straightened up, took a heading, and moved out. On the island was a small, broken-down hooch that was the only standing structure in sight. Clearing out of the grass, we could see the hooch but still without seeing any other activity at all.

With one man of a shooting pair moving forward while his partner covered him, we approached the hooch. It was a native building made of bamboo and straw matting. Without speaking a word, we moved into the building and searched it completely and quickly. We had trained and worked with each other so long, no words were needed, just the occasional hand or arm signal.

It was obvious to us that the building had been used as living quarters by someone. Food scraps, utensils, and other scattered material told us that whoever had been there had left in a hurry. But that leaving was for another reason than our arrival. It was plain to see that the place had been abandoned days before. There was no sign of any signaling or intelligence-gathering equipment.

Moving out, we searched the entire little island, which was only some fifty yards across but had some fairly high ground for such a small place. Down on the beach we found the mouth of a small cave, partially submerged in the water at the edge of the shore.

One of the guys quickly stripped down and moved into the water to search the cave. Swimming into the mouth of the opening, he was never out of earshot of the rest of us. The opening turned out to be the mouth of a small washhole in the shore, cut by the action of the water and not deep at all.

With our Teammate once more dressed and on shore with

the squad, we could see that the search of the island was coming up dry. Calling in the other squad offshore in the F-470 boats, we climbed aboard and moved back to the mainland.

The tide was starting to come in, so taking the boats back to the mainland went easily. But when we got to the bird, it wouldn't crank over. For some reason the engines were dead, and we couldn't take off. Now the incoming tide was a problem. The bird was specially equipped for our missions, with a large quantity of secure communications gear on board. There was no way we could leave it with all that gear on board.

All of us who were able lent a hand to the crew of the stricken bird, while our radioman called for another helo to come out with an APU (auxiliary power unit) that would supply enough juice to get the bird's engines started. But with the tide coming in, the helo was going to get washed pretty deeply, and that specialized equipment on board was expensive, so as the message was going out, so was the gear on board the bird. As the crew disconnected what they could, we humped it into our boats and up the beach. Putting the gear well above the high tide line, we could at least keep it from getting wet or otherwise damaged.

Then one of the guys noticed a number of helos moving in and out of an area a short distance inland that we couldn't see clearly. Since our aircraft were the only things flying through the area, we knew the birds had to be friendly. With no answers coming in over the radio, getting help from friendly forces seemed to be the next best choice.

The helicopters were overflying an area only half a mile or so from where we were. There was a good road leading up to where they were that passed close to the shore. The whole area was like a ghost town. There was no civilian movement whatsoever. Aside from the helicopters in the distance, we were apparently alone.

Darkness would be falling soon and we had to make some move to change our situation. My squad's officer told me to take one of the men with me and head to where the other helos were. That looked to be the only way to get another helo or an APU to our downed CH-47 before full dark settled in on us.

My partner and I moved out at a brisk pace, but we didn't move so fast that we would make a target of ourselves. With our weapons at the ready, we moved to the road and continued up it.

Everything we passed—every building, hut, and shed—was empty and abandoned. The earlier feeling of moving through a ghost town was even stronger. We were moving at a fair clip but maintaining a watch on our flanks. It was getting cold as the sun went down, but the chill wasn't just from that. Vehicles were abandoned along the road. Houses stood open and mute. No one was around. All we saw that had been living was the occasional dead dog. It was like we were jogging along in one of those last-man-on-earth science fiction movies. Weird was the only way to describe it.

When we reached a hilltop near the helos, we waved one down. The bird was a CH-46 and the crew recognized us as U.S. forces and came down to land nearby. Going up to the pilot, I told him about the situation down on the beach. The situation had to be getting worse there, because the water had been up to the CH-47 when we both left.

The pilot agreed to get us an APU to start up our bird, so we headed back to the beach. The water was starting to come into the CH-47 now. Finally a helicopter came in with an APU and we were able to crank over and start the CH-47's engines.

We lifted the bird off and left the APU sitting there on the ground for the moment. It was a lot more important to gather up all the gear we had pulled out of the bird. Once we had all the gear gathered up, we piled it, our boats, and our squads into the bird that had brought in the APU. Lifting off, we met up with our original transportation back at the airport. Now we had to truck everything back into the first bird and let the technicians get on with the job of hooking it all back up and testing it.

For a mission that turned out to be a dry hole, we had come very close to losing a very expensive chunk of gear. It had been an experience.

At the end of the 1980s, President Bush finally called an end to the terrorism conducted against the United States and her citizens by a drug-running dictator, Manual Noriega of Panama. In December 1989, I was part of a combined Special Operations unit that joined with the rest of our military in the operation Just Cause.

We eliminated Noriega as a threat to our own country and to Panama. Democratic elections were held, giving the people a real chance of controlling their own destiny after we pulled out. When Desert Shield and then Desert Storm took place in 1990 and 1991, my brothers in the Teams conducted their operations well. They even impressed General Norman Schwartzkopf, who had earlier said he did not see a use for Special Operations Forces in any of the services.

My family life had changed as well. We now had two daughters in the Chalker household. Tess Maria Chalker came to us on February 18, 1991. Kitty had an easier childbirth this time, at least in one sense. She didn't need major surgery to deliver Tess. I was able to attend the delivery and of course with Kitty awake and feeling every part of the delivery, she voiced her opinions about me personally and all men in general as she brought our daughter into the world. After having been with me and my Teammates for a number of years, she had an excellent command of the saltier ways of voicing her displeasure.

It was kind of funny, but within a few years of being born, Tess was involved in my career in a very direct and unusual way. Things had changed in the world to make everyone's lives a little different. After the breakup of the Soviet Union, our great enemy for so long, the world had become anything but a more stable place. Terrorists still had plenty of countries willing to sponsor them as a means of covert warfare. A lot of the old players in the terrorist game had disappeared, but there were still enough to go around, and new groups were cropping up like fungus. Smaller countries had plenty of up-and-coming dictators to keep the local pots boiling. The United States had interests abroad in all the corners of the globe. And the SEALs, along with the rest of the Special Operations Forces, never knew which arena we would be ordered to next.

We always seemed to have our nose in something as the world's last superpower. Having to act as the world's policeman is a two-edged sword, kind of a damned-if-we-do-and-damned-if-we-don't situation. If we here in the United States don't act on a situation where civilians or a general population is suffering, we're looked on as heartless and cruel. But when we do go in and wave that big stick, trying to keep the worst of the violence away from those who can't defend themselves, we're called the aggressors. It's a classic catch twenty-two.

At least with the SEALs and the rest of the SOCOM (Special Operations Command) forces, the politicians have a sharp scalpel to attack the problem with rather than a sledgehammer. The problem with smacking the wrong target with a sledgehammer is that the hammer can sink in and get stuck. Then you have a hell of a time pulling it back out.

With all the possible actions and different places where we might have to operate, the Teams have always had to keep on top of things and be ready for anything. Once we were on standby and had to prep for two different crises. One of the hot areas was in Africa and the other practically in another hemisphere. To cover both these spots, we had to split our assault group into two operational teams.

Part of my job was helping to decide which platoon would cover which area. The African spot was running hotter than the other and looked to be the best for action coming up soon. Neither platoon could decide where they wanted to go. Opportunities for active operations were few, and all the guys wanted their chance for a hot op. Finally we decided to let chance take a hand.

We put the names of the squads in a hat and let the most junior guy in the unit draw a slip out. The name drawn got the first pick. The other boat crew won. They chose Africa, so we took the other by default. Just like much of the rest of the world, we would watch CNN and see that the African situation looked like it was heating up fast. There was no animosity over which unit took what mission; we were all part of the same Team. It was just that some players might manage to get on the field first for this one.

While we were both on standby, a couple of workups on possible missions came up for Africa. Within a two-week period, the other crew had been recalled to base twice. Coming in, they would get their brief and prep for an op.

The mission always comes first, and we helped load out our Teammates for their op. And as things have gone before, the ops were downstaged and canceled. The rule held true: Don't get your hopes up for an op until you're doing your insert.

One night while I was at home, my beeper went off. A recall had gone out, and I headed in to the Team area. Our site had heated up suddenly and now we had an op. The task was to go into a hot area and recover an American citizen who was in danger. The "citizen" was an eighteen-month-old baby.

While prepping for this operation, some mild animosity built up in the Team. The right-time-right-place rule had come into effect. When I helped the other unit prep for their possible operations, I felt a strong desire to go with them. Strong desire? Hell, I would have given my left testicle to be going with them.

The others had worked up their ops for Africa and were disappointed when they were canceled. But that was the area they had chosen. Now it was our turn to get ready. There was some grumbling from the ranks, from the guys who weren't going to go. But that sort of thing should be expected from a bunch of highly trained hard chargers who wanted the chance to prove themselves and just saw one chance slip away.

And it wasn't just the crews that had prepped for Africa who were losing their chance to go. I was going since I was the chief of squad two, as well as the senior chief of the platoon at the time. Our assault group chief, and the group leader himself, were going on the op. But not everyone from our crews would be accompanying us.

What I had to do was choose the men who would be going with me on the pickup itself. The other squad crew chief also had to pick a limited number of men to go with him. It was not an easy decision to make, even though we both made the mission tasking our guide. Both of us picked three men to accompany us. These would be in addition to other support SEALs who were assigned to the op for different reasons.

Picking the guys who would go was one of the hardest decisions I ever had to make as a SEAL senior chief. These were my Teammates and I had trained hard with each one of them. I knew their capabilities, skills, and attitudes as well as I knew myself. And just as I would have been, some of them would be disappointed at being left behind.

Personal friendships had to be put aside. Length of time in the unit couldn't be a factor. The choice had to center on who had to do what and which person was the best qualified for the job. A secondary factor was to try and keep shooting partners together. Partners knew each other best, and a hot op was where that knowledge would prove the most valuable.

We were going in to pull people out. The child was the primary target—she was a U.S. citizen and had been born in this country—but her parents were also coming out with us. To make sure any possible protests from the locals wouldn't be a problem, I wanted heavy guns to go in with us. In the SEALs this meant M60 gunners. Rat was one of my 60 gunners, and for that reason he was one of the first men chosen to go.

Providing security at the landing site had to be addressed, so two men were picked who filled that slot the best. Lastly, we needed communicators, so a pair of radio operators were picked. Mato was the most senior guy in my crew. He was not only good at comms, he was a great point man and general operator. These six men would go along with the two of us and the boat teams from the technical group, who were also fully qualified SEALs we had all trained with extensively.

The technical group worked with their boats constantly. They could do over-the-horizon operations and hit the target in some of the worst conditions imaginable, all without being detected. They could handle any of our specialized boats, from running the engines to piloting the craft to supplying close-in fire support with a boat's weapons. They would get us there and back. The final insertion, recovery, and extraction would be up to us.

On this op, we would be taking four boats into the target. The boats would be our low-profile Zodiac F-470 inflatables, now called CRRCs, for combat rubber raiding craft. The plan was fairly simple. We would go in from a Navy ship, launching our 470s while still over the horizon, move in to the beach, pick up the cargo, and move back out to our parent ship.

Simple, yeah. But there were still a thousand things that could go wrong. Staying flexible and being able to meet the situation, that's what the Teams do.

Our very small unit went into isolation and received further briefings. We put together our plan of action based on the intelligence we had on the target and the situation. What was different in the Teams from the rest of the Navy, and the military as a whole, was that the enlisted men could put together an operational plan and the officers would listen to our experience. The assault group leader took the plan we had worked up and moved it forward through the headshed, command headquarters, and higher command.

During our discussions about the op, the question of maybe having to swim the kid out to the boats came up. This was something we all became concerned about. Moving through the water while protecting such a small child was a problem, and I had the solution sitting at home.

"I tell you what," I told the assault group leader, "I've got an eighteen-month-old baby of my own at home. I've got a carrier for her that you wear on your chest. What if I go home and get that. We could mount a couple of LPUs (life preserver units) on it. If we had to swim out, at least we would have that to hold the kid securely."

That made sense to everyone there. Problem was, I had to break isolation in order to go home and get the carrier. Permission was given for me to run home. Rushing off base, I got to my house as quickly as I could.

Kitty knew I had been recalled, and she knew that I couldn't answer any questions, so she never bothered to ask much. But when I asked her for our brand-new baby carrier, she wanted to know why.

This was not one of the times it's a whole lot of fun being a SEAL. "Well, we just need it for a gag. I'll bring it back."

"Well, don't destroy it, Chalker."

"I won't destroy it," I promised. "I'll bring it back, and nothing will happen to it." And with that, the very specialized equipment needed for our operation was secured.

Getting back to the base, I headed to the rigger's shop in the air loft to work on the carrier. With the help of the riggers, who maintained and sewed up our parachutes when they needed it, several LPUs were attached to the carrier. Any one of the inflatable LPUs would have been enough to support the baby easily.

The original colors of the carrier were fluorescent orange

and yellow, not the best camouflage for a combat environment. Black spray paint changed the colors easily enough. The rigger also helped me put some PT-mat foam padding on the inside of the carrier to be sure the baby would be well protected in case I had to move fast.

Another specialized piece of gear I couldn't have easily gotten through regular channels now had to be prepared. Taking the pacifier I had grabbed up from home, I sterilized it and sealed it in a plastic bag. Tying the bag to the carrier with a length of 550 parachute cord, my rig was pretty much set. Putting on all my normal equipment, the carrier sat right up high on my chest without any problem. The baby would be secure for a swim.

Loading out for the trip to the airfield, we finished up our preparations in the Team area. Intel had come in on the operation, and it still looked like it might be a simple one. There was a timeline that was pretty tight and had little room for mistakes. A rendezvous on a hostile beach had been set up, not a long way from a city. We had to hit that beach at exactly the right time and place. There wouldn't be a chance for a second attempt.

With our pallets of gear on the trucks, we headed out to the airfield. Confidence was high, but we each concentrated on our job. It's when you lose that concentration and take things for granted that problems come up. My Teammates and I had been training far too long to make that particular mistake. Boarding the planes, we flew to a forward Navy base to hook up with a ship.

Waiting for us at the forward base was a fast frigate that would act as our transportation platform for the operation. For the first time, I would be going on an active op aboard a regular U.S. Navy ship. Last-minute intelligence and the final time schedule came down to us at the base. Loading onto the ship, we were on our way.

Things were moving fast, and we kept right up with the situation. During transit we went over our plan, polishing the last-minute details. Our Team skipper was along with us doing liaison between our units and the Army officer from SOCOM who was overseeing our op at that time.

In spite of all the heavy hitters we had in the loop, the planning and execution of the op were still very much a team effort. It wasn't one guy's idea or plan. Our assault group leader made certain that his senior enlisted men had their input on the op, and he listened to each man in the unit. He trusted the senior enlisted, myself included, with assigning operational responsibilities to the men. During the briefings, we passed out the details for insertion, extraction, E & E if something went wrong, radio frequencies, call signs, and all the other facets of a modern special operation.

The beef of the plan—the actions on the objective—the assault group leader, the other squad chief, and I ironed out among ourselves. Squad Two, my selected guys, would go in and maintain outside security for the meeting site. They would immediately spread out and establish a perimeter after our landing. I would go in with the rest of the unit, including the assault group leader, and we would meet with the target people. My job was to take care of the baby. I would have what we called the "precious cargo," and my whole world would revolve around getting that kid out safely.

Riding the ship down to the target area was an experience. The crew offered us berthing, but we turned it down, preferring to get what little sleep we might back in the hangar area where our gear was. We did eat in the chief's mess, which was great. The ship took good care of us, and my hat's off to that chief's mess to this day.

Our Team master chief had showed up at the forward Navy base along with our CO and boarded with us for the op. He told me that he wished he was going on the mission just as badly as I would have if the positions were reversed. But the bottom line was that we had proposed a plan for the operation and it had moved smoothly up the ladder in getting approved. This was something our CO was very good at.

"You guys have been doing this business," he said. "You've been in the trenches just doing it. When you say something is going to work, I trust you. If you say it's not going to work, it's not going to work. Now, is this operation going to work?"

"We can make it work," we said.

That was all he needed to know. He brought us the final go-ahead, and we were on.

While we were under way to the target area, we practiced getting our boats and gear into the water. Our dry runs consisted of getting the gear secured on the boats and the boats smoothly into the water, located and spaced properly so that we could quickly board in the dark. The practice showed the teamwork of the SEALs in action. Each of the coxswains knew where his boat would be and how to get to it. Each boat crew could get to its assigned place. This was important because we would have to do the real operation in the dark to minimize the possibility of detection.

In addition, we conducted talk-through drills, practiced our actions once on target, and confirmed that everyone knew where he would have to be and what was expected of him. The coxswains set to work making sure each of their boats was as prepared as the rest of us were. This action lasted through the night and the next day as the frigate continued on its course.

The ship's crew jumped in to help. Boatswain's mates, cargo handlers, everyone on the ship turned to. If we needed help, sometimes even before we could ask, one of the crew would show up and things would get done the best way possible.

This made me think of the frogmen of World War II, the UDT operators who are the SEALs' grandfathers, and all the other amphibious forces who worked from the sea. Was this what it had been like for them? This was the first time I had seen an integrated U.S. Navy ship and crew gear up and focus on a single goal. Each man had his job to do and worked smoothly with the ship and the rest of the crew. They were at battle stations and remained on alert the entire operation. The crew and their ship were like a single entity, like something alive. It was an impressive sight.

In the chief's mess, we were having our last hot meal before the launch. While we were eating, a silence fell across the ship as the ship's chaplain came on the MC overhead (shipboard P.A. system) and made an announcement: "We have some people on board who are going into harm's way. I would like to say a little prayer for them and wish them the best. Until they come back and link up with us, may they be in God's hands."

The meal over, the chiefs, including the master chief of the ship, stood to shake our hands. "We'll be back," I said. "Have a cold beer waiting."

"We'll have cold beer," the master chief said.

It was good to see the Navy swing into operation with all the chiefs integrating into a smooth machine. We did our last prep and staged for insertion. It was great to watch the guys cammie up and get ready for the op. For the younger guys, this would be their first mission in a combat zone. As they smeared the dark cosmetic on their faces, I could see questions in their eyes, the same questions I had asked myself when heading in to Grenada: Would I be all right? Would I do my job? What would happen if the bullets started flying? And, the strongest of all, would I let my Teammates down?

Hell, I knew those questions, as did every SEAL and frogman who had gone into combat before us. But this was my chance to see it in their eyes. "Hey, look," I said to the group. "Everyone's coming back. Everyone does what they're supposed to do and everything will work out fine. Hopefully, there won't be a shot fired. We'll pick the people up and be on our way. But if something does go wrong, well, we covered the what-ifs in your training and in the briefing. If there's a firefight, we break up into teams and head for the water. There's other combat vets here. If you get into trouble, just follow their lead."

In general, that was exactly what we would do. The difference would be if I had the kid on my person and the shit hit the fan. In that case, I had the precious cargo and my whole being would be concentrated on getting into the water and away from that beach. The rest of my Teammates would be putting out a field of covering fire to give me and what I carried the best chance they could. Then they too would head for the water. And as they pulled out, fire would come from the boats to cover their withdrawal.

You don't dwell on the possibility of failure. You cover the problems and establish the procedures to deal with them. We would remain flexible and face whatever came.

The operation was short, and a success. It was around 0200 to 0300 hours in the morning, after things had finally wrapped up, that getting some sleep became my new mission. Helicopters would be coming in to take the family to another destination. After being up a day and a half, I was in the hangar on the fantail with the rest of my team sleeping soundly when our CO came into the room.

In a situation where you haven't had much sleep and have come in off an operation, you sometimes don't react as you normally would when you finally crash. When the captain shook my shoulder to wake me up, I don't think he expected me to jerk up and grab him. Coming out of a deep sleep, my hand was up before I knew it and the captain was slapping it out of the way.

"Denny, Denny!" he called out. "It's me!"

"Oh," I said. "Sorry, Skipper."

"I want you to get up," he continued. "The mother would like to thank you and get a picture with you."

So I got up, half asleep, and followed the captain up to the deck. The family was there, all with their helmets and flight jackets on, the baby all bundled up, waiting to board the helo. I had been so deeply asleep that I never heard the bird come in. But the mother wanted to extend her thanks to me again. Standing with them for a photo, I still hadn't washed all the camo off yet. We said our good-byes. I watched them board the bird and never saw them again.

When the ship returned to the forward base, we downstaged off the ship and thanked the crew warmly for the cooperation we had received. It would have been a much harder op if we hadn't had that ship and her professional crew to back us up. Everyone lent a hand getting our gear off, and off we went.

At the base we had a big debriefing. Like so many SEAL operations, this one had never happened. But we knew what we had done, and it was something to be proud of. We went out for some pizzas and beers to celebrate after the debrief, but before we went, I had some real startling news dropped into my lap.

In a small office he had available, the Army general in overall command gathered a few of us from the mission. He had a little more to say than the "Well done" we had received from him. And what he had to say shocked me more than a little. Seems there was a bit more riding on our operation than a family's freedom.

In that office, the Army officer told us, "Good job done. Because if you guys hadn't pulled it off, your command would be gone and you'd all be reassigned."

"Pardon me, sir," I said, stunned. "Off the record, just what are you talking about?"

"Just that. There wouldn't be a specialized SEAL command if you had failed. But both I and your captain had confidence that the operation would come off."

Apparently the op had been considered such a hot one, sensitive and absolutely necessary, that if we had been unsuccessful, our whole command would have been disbanded. What the logic behind this was, I don't know. Maybe the politicians who control the purse strings thought that if we couldn't do the op, we weren't worth paying for. But such are the politics of the higher commands. I suppose that if we had been disbanded, our future missions would have gone to another SpecOps unit.

After absorbing this news for a second, I asked, "Why weren't we told?"

"That was your captain's decision."

Well, that was certainly a kick in the ass. After thinking about it for a while, I could sort of see why he hadn't told us. The weight of the future of our whole command would have been a very heavy load to carry on a hot op. Thoughts about a possible failure might be just what it took to cause a failure.

But the consequence of a failure didn't matter. What did matter was that we had accomplished our mission successfully. Loading our gear on an airplane, we left the Navy base for southeastern Virginia and home.

We were still on standby when we got back. And there was still a little friction with the guys who couldn't go. But they remained professional about the situation in spite of their disappointment. I know I probably would have felt the same way. It had been a good op, and for some of these hard-trained SEALs, it may have been the last opportunity to get some real-world action before they finally left the service. But the mission came first.

The mission happened so fast that many of the guys at our command never even knew it had happened. The word was put out during a debriefing later, which was the first many of the guys knew about it.

This kind of op, a fast-moving water-oriented mission, was exactly what the SEALs were intended for. For us, the mission resulted in little exposure. The friendlies on land had a much harder time of it, having to move the targets to the pickup site and maintain a watch against being compromised. Once the mission was completed, their relief was probably much greater than ours.

Of course, when I got home, I couldn't tell Kitty anything about what had happened. The earlier excuse about using the baby carrier for a gag didn't hold up very well when she saw the painted, cut-up remainder. The first thing she said after my return was, "Who's paying for it?"

"The Navy will," I told her.

The funds for a baby carrier expended during a mission never did come through. But I couldn't have picked a better operation to be my last combat op.

CHAPTER 31

TO GIVE SOMETHING BACK

After my last operation, it was time to make some decisions about my career. I was selected for promotion to master chief, but that meant I would have to leave the command where I had spent so much of my SEAL career. I was made a big offer: the position of command master chief, the highest-ranking NCO of a unit, at the Special Warfare Training Command. My career in the Teams had come full circle. I would be returning to the place where it had begun over a dozen years earlier.

I had started as an individual who was eager to learn and to excel. Like so many others, I had stepped forward to undergo the greatest challenge offered by the U.S. military, to become a Navy SEAL. The challenges never stopped coming, and I welcomed each one of them so that I could become a better operator, have a better chance of surviving the rigors of a career that's unlike any other on the planet, and remain one of the elite, one of the best.

There hadn't been a challenge or a task that came along that I didn't eventually feel comfortable with in the Teams. As the command master chief of the training command, I was giving something back to the community that had given me such a good run during my Navy career.

I almost had to give them everything I had even before I got there. On our driving trip from the East to the West Coast, Kitty and I took our new baby daughter, Tess, with us. Kacy we left with her grandparents in Ohio. As we approached California, Kitty became very ill. By the time we got to San Diego, she had a full-blown case of pneumonia, two different types at the same time. Immediate hospitalization saved her. It was a near thing for several weeks, but she pulled through. Now we had a chance for a somewhat more normal family life in Southern California.

Even though I was now in charge of the staff at BUD/S, the students and the instructors still had a lot to teach me. Some of the lessons were good and some bad. Others were just funny. But my experience in the Teams meant a lot. The students looked up to me, and I could motivate them because of that. The instructors knew where I was coming from and what I wanted to do.

It was the Team credo that I most wanted to make these young students understand: Teamwork makes the Teams. Some of them grasped it right away. Even lower-ranked enlisted men could find it in themselves to speak up; improve their partner, boat crew member, or even class; help them put out that extra amount that most of them never knew they had. Others never did understand the Team ideal.

In one class, I had one hell of a time with a few of the leaders. In the Teams, our officers work alongside the men, getting right down and dirty with the lowliest enlisted man. This is important. SEAL officers have to lead, not just tell you what to do. My commanding officers hadn't always operated with me in the field; that wasn't their job. But they could have. Each man coming into Six had to go through our Green training. They had to be fully qualified to operate. If not, how could they be certain of what we could do?

In this class I had several officers who had been in the Army before coming into the Navy and BUD/S. They had the attitude that the officers were better than the enlisted men—an attitude I had seen more than once in my lifetime. But that wasn't how the Teams worked.

I took these two young leaders into my office and spoke to them in reasonable privacy. Without mincing words, I told them that they were both maggots, if not lower than maggots. At least maggots helped clean up garbage; these two *were* garbage.

As nobodies, didn't they understand the meaning of the word *Team*? There was no *I* in the words *SEAL Team*. And who the hell were they to think they were above our traditions, which had served us well for fifty years? Far better men than they had gone though our training and proved its worth on a hundred battlefields.

In my opinion, it was the enlisted community that could make or break an officer. If the enlisted men didn't have respect for you, if they didn't think you could do the job—not just order it done—they wouldn't follow you. That could make OER (Officer's Efficiency Report) look very bad, and his career prospects look even worse.

They may have gotten the message. They graduated from BUD/S and became Teammates.

But there were other classes with leaders I could work with well. To help with the motivation of a class, I would try to inject some humor where I could. There was one class where I had a lot of help getting the humor passed along.

There was an ensign, or enswine as we would say, named Pease. Today I understand he's a good officer and a credit to the Teams. But the thing I liked about him then centered on a personal quirk.

While I was running his class through PT, I would look over

at Ensign Pease and he would be smiling. No matter how hard I worked the class, he would be smiling. The son of a bitch just kept smiling. Finally I put the class through flutter kicks, where they were flat on their backs and kicking their straight legs up and down. Having them stop kicking and hold their legs six inches off the ground, a very strained position, I walked over to Ensign Pease.

As the class held the position, barely, I jumped in Pease's face. "Enswine," I shouted, "what in the fuck are you smiling at? Are you smiling at me?"

"Hoo, yah, Master Chief!"

"Do you think I'm pretty?"

"Oh no, Master Chief."

"Oh, so you're saying I'm ugly?"

"Oh no, Master Chief."

"Then you're telling me I'm cute? What are you, Enswine? Are you gay?"

By this time the instructors are in the back of the class biting their lips to keep from laughing. Even the class, in its uncomfortable position, is chuckling a bit. And Ensign Pease is trying to keep up his end of the conversation without saying the wrong thing. Which was an impossible task right then. But he was still smiling.

"Wipe that god-damned smirk off your face," I told him.

And he couldn't. It was like his little smile was a permanent part of his expression. During runs, I would go right up to him and get in his face: "Pease, I see you're still smiling. What are you smiling at?"

Even during Hell Week, Ensign Pease was smiling. Late in the week the smile was a little lopsided, but it was still there. Even when he was dingy, and going through the chow line trying to motivate his people, Pease had his smile on. And that grin got the biggest when he graduated with his class.

There was always an interesting day at the training command. Days could easily be the most interesting during Hell Week. Students and instructors never ceased to amaze me. The students could come up with the most ingenious ways of trying to outwit the instructors, and the instructors worked just as hard to nail the students.

Joe Hawes was one of my first phase instructors, and we became very good friends. Joe is a very noticeable man, being large even for a SEAL. Shoulders roughly the size of bowling balls, huge arms, and an even larger chest to support all this are topped with an intelligent mind, quick wit, and a ready grin. Fear of Instructor Hawes's wrath could reduce a trainee to a puddle on the ground. But Hawes was never one to let the chance for a good joke go by. And you could hear his laugh all through the compound.

If a student wanted to DOR (drop on request), he had a set chain of command to go through. The situation had changed a bit from the earlier days at DUD/S. Students now had a chance to change their minds and go back to training when they DORed for the first time. This was both a cost-saving measure for the Navy (it cost us a lot to put a student through BUD/S, even just the first few months) and a way to keep a possibly good SEALs from making a mistake. Sometimes students just had what we called a "brain fart" and DORed. After a little reflection, they wanted to continue with the program.

To DOR, a student first went to the instructor, then to the phase chief above him, and several others along the line including a number of officers. There was also a short chain, where the student would be brought to the master chief for a fast talk. It sometimes just took a bit of a shaking up or a motivational word to get these kids back on the trail. But there were exceptions.

Joe had to send this one student down to me. There was no question in his mind that I needed to speak to this man, and he wanted to be in attendance. With Instructor Hawes behind him, the young man walked up to where I was sitting back in my chair, drinking a good cup of Navy coffee.

"What's the problem?" I asked the student in a fairly gruff tone.

"I want to DOR, Master Chief Chalker."

"Why do you want to DOR?" I asked as I took a sip of my coffee.

"I'm just not a morning person, Master Chief."

Joe wasn't in the way as my mouthful of coffee sprayed across the room. He was leaning against the wall laughing.

"*What?*" I shouted at the kid.

"I'm not a morning person."

"You're not a morning person? Then why in the fuck did you volunteer for this program?"

"Well," he said kind of abashedly, "I didn't know you got up at four and five in the morning."

"And what do you think is going to happen to you out in the fleet?"

"Well, I think I'll get to sleep in a little bit. I won't have to work so hard out there."

"Well, let me tell you something. You'll probably be getting up at four and five o'clock in the morning to swab the deck on a ship. You're going to be haze gray and under way. Now what do you want to do?"

"I'm just not a morning person. . . ."

"*What do you want to do?*"

"I want to DOR."

"Fine. Instructor Hawes, take charge of this man."

Joe has this great little-boy bit he does when he's going to mess with someone. "Come on, come on," he told the student as he waved him out of my office. And with a big grin on his face, he walked that student through the chain for a DOR, enjoying every moment of it. Just about everyone had the same reaction I did. Although they may not have been drinking coffee at the time.

Looking back on it, I suppose it could be considered a logical reason for quitting BUD/S. But it had to be the weirdest excuse I had ever heard.

CHAPTER 32

MEET THE KIDS AND MEET THE MAN

The command had asked me to be the master chief in part because of my career. The students could see me as a SEAL who had "been there and done that." There weren't as many combat veterans in the Teams then as there had been when I went through training. When you had a man who had seen what the training did in the real world, that could give some of the students the extra push that would help them over the hump. Sometimes, though, any reputation I had wasn't what the students remembered.

When one class managed to piss me off a bit, I told them to be on the grinder standing on the fins (painted swim fins spaced out on the ground) at 0700 hours on Saturday morning. They were to be in starched uniforms and their green helmets, ready for an inspection.

I had screwed up a little bit too, though. I had promised my two girls I would take them to Sea World that Saturday. They are very important to me, so I was going to combine the two trips, stopping off for my students first.

My five-year-old, Tess, was growing up into a bright young girl, intelligent, precocious, and not afraid of anything. Kacy was eleven and a little more reserved. But both of them were looking forward to the Sea World trip and to seeing what Daddy did at work.

I had told the watch what would be happening that morning. When I showed up with my girls in tow, it was 0745 hours. The students had been standing on the grinder for forty-five minutes when I walked in wearing civilian clothes.

The class snapped to attention when I entered the grinder. While I slowly walked to the podium against the wall opposite the doors, I barked "Drop!" With that command, the students would immediately drop to the ground and assume the starting push-up position, what was also called the "front leaning rest."

The drop command could be followed with "Push them out!" That meant the students did a set of twenty push-ups, counting their cadence loudly. With the push-ups completed, the students would shout a "Hoo yah!" for whoever had ordered them to drop. In my case, they shouted, "Hoo yah, Master Chief Chalker!"

With a snapped "Recover" command from me, they had to scramble to their feet and quickly resume the attitude of attention. They cannot move after completing the push-ups or being ordered to drop until they are told to recover. As I made the students rise and fall rapidly a number of times, my girls were walking along behind me watching the situation with wide-eyed wonder.

Approaching the podium, I brought the girls up with me. To warm up the class a bit, I had them drop and then recover rapidly about twelve times in a row as I walked that short distance. That exercise can get your blood flowing.

Just as I approached the podium, I had them drop. They

froze in position. Once on the podium, I put Kacy to my right and Tess to my left. "Get your god-damned heads up when I'm talking!" I growled.

Tilting their heads back, the class strained to look at me as I started to chew on them a bit.

"I want you guys to know one thing," I called out. "Today is Saturday. I was supposed to take my two daughters to Sea World today. But since you guys messed up, I had to bring them in here. So here's what I want you guys to do.

"First of all, you took liberty from my wife. So I want you to punch them out for Miss Kitty."

So they quickly knocked out twenty push-ups, shouting out "Hoo yah, Miss Kitty!" when they finished.

Then I gave them the Recover command. When they were back on their feet, I made them drop again. "Now I want you to knock them out for my eldest daughter here, Miss Kacy."

Push-ups again, then a "Hoo yah, Miss Kacy."

"Recover! Drop! Now you will push them out for my youngest daughter, Miss Tess."

Push-ups and a loud, "Hoo yah, Miss Tess!"

"Recover."

Now I started to talk to them about what they had done and what was happening to them. As I went into why they had been standing there since 0700, a small voice to my side spoke up. "Drop," Tess said.

And the class immediately dropped into the position.

Then Kacy went, "Recover."

And the class snapped to their feet.

This went on about three times while I stood there with my mouth hanging open. But woe betide the student who didn't snap to when the order was spoken. In spite of their work, some of the students were beginning to grin a little bit. They were enjoying the situation. But they weren't going to be allowed to show it very much.

"Woah, woah, girls, stop," I said as they completed another set of commands. Now I was having to work hard not to burst out laughing. I made the students hit the surf zone and then return. With an order to clean up the grinder, I told them they would then be on liberty. And I took my family to Sea World for the day.

After that morning, when Kitty came by to pick me up after work, the girls were often with her. Tess always wanted to come in and get her daddy. The watch knew who she was and pushed the button to unlock the door. Tess got a charge out of that. Then she would run down to my office, looking for me.

"Dad, Dad, Mom's here!"

"Okay, just a moment, Tess."

Then while I was finishing up, Tess would go to the door and peer out at the compound. "What are you doing, Tess?" I asked.

"I want to play with the green helmets again."

A couple of instructors who knew the story thought the situation was funny. If any students had screwed up right about then, I'm sure they would have been gathered up for Tess to play with.

Politics were never something that particularly interested me. I paid attention to what was going on with the leadership of the country, but I had a job to do that kept me busy, so I couldn't be bothered with what went on in Washington unless it looked like the Teams were going to be sent somewhere again.

The majority of my SEAL career was spent under the Reagan administration. With his desire to build up the U.S. military during the 1980s, and his recognition of the importance of Special Operations Forces, Ronald Reagan probably affected my professional life more than any other U.S. president. I liked the man. He got the job done. He didn't sit back and play games.

If you were going to do something against the United States, he was coming after you.

President Bush had served in the Military himself and knew what it meant to be on the sharp end. As a Navy pilot in World War II, he had been shot down over the Pacific. He didn't seem to be one who would use the U.S. Military frivolously. I had met President Bush both when he was president and when he was vice president. Both times I was reasonably impressed.

But I didn't have any direct involvement with a sitting U.S. president until the Clinton administration. Every time a U.S. president came down to the San Diego/Coronado area, they liked to go on a run with Navy SEALs in attendance. This happened about every year or so, and each U.S. president had done the run. President Clinton wasn't any different. In fact, he was probably more than usually gung-ho about having SEALs around him during his jog.

For President Reagan, there had been competitions among the Teams and then the SEALs to see who would get to run with him. With President Bush, it was much the same—more volunteers than there were slots available. Whole platoons wanted to go on these runs. Names had to be drawn out of a hat like a lottery, or you gave the assignments as a reward. When President Clinton came to Coronado late in my tenure as command master chief of the training center, things were a little different.

A call from the force master chief up at WarCom came in for me requesting the names of two SEAL volunteers from each command to run with the president when he came to the area in a few weeks. I didn't think there would be any problem with this; I didn't particularly like the man, but he was our commander in chief. Apparently, though, a whole lot of the rest of the community also didn't particularly care for the leader of the present administration.

When I put out the call for volunteers at Morning Quarters, it was several weeks before the president would arrive in the area. There were no immediate volunteers to run with our commander in chief. I didn't give this a lot of thought, but it soon became more of a problem.

Every day at Morning Quarters, I would put out the request for volunteers to the instructors and the SEALs under my command. And every morning the only answer that came back was seagull cries and some pounding surf noises. This soon became the big joke of Morning Quarters. I would put out the request for volunteers and then listen to the ocean for a few minutes.

Time was going by and I didn't have any names to send up to WarCom. There wasn't any way I was going to assign one of my men to do what was just some publicity work if they didn't want to. Eventually it was only a few days before the names had to be turned in. This couldn't be a last-minute thing; names had to be given to the Secret Service well in advance of the president's arrival.

The WarCom master chief called down to me and told me he needed two people. "Look," I said, "I can't force anybody. I just can't do that. If I can't get any volunteers, I will be one of the runners, and I'm sure I can get one of the officers or another chief to volunteer to go with me."

Finally it was the day of the deadline when I had to turn in two names, and it looked like I was going to be one of them. Then another part of my job as command master chief came up. There were two young second phase instructors who had messed up pretty badly. They had been late to arrive at work and an evolution had to start without them. When I heard about this situation, I told the chief in charge of that phase not to deal with it himself but to bring these two men down to my office.

"Look," I told the two instructors once they were in front of me. "You two messed up. So I'm going to give you a choice. You can run with the president, or you can come in Friday and Saturday this weekend, and Friday and Saturday next weekend, and have the duty."

Having the duty meant they would both be up most of the night and be responsible for securing the area and making sure everything went right during the weekend. Not the most fun job in the Navy but one that gets done every day. The weekend was only a few days away, though, and these two young SEALs probably already had liberty plans put together.

"The run with President Clinton is this Saturday," I continued, like they didn't know this already. "If you go on that run, it will clear the record and you will not have to pull any additional duty for your little infraction."

I figured I was covered, only things didn't go the way I wanted them to, at least not right away. Both instructors just answered, "Forget about it!" and left my office.

It wasn't long before one of the pair thought about what he had to do and came back to talk with me.

"Master Chief," he asked, "both weekends with the duty?"

"Yes, this weekend and next weekend. Or you can do one Saturday on a run."

Looking around a little, like he was trying to see if anyone was looking, the instructor decided that running with the president was the lesser of the two punishments.

"Okay, I'll run," he said.

And I had my first volunteer. It was much later in the day when the second instructor showed up at my office.

"Master Chief," he asked, "if I run I won't have to stand the duty?"

"That's right," I answered him.

"And the duty is for both Fridays and Saturdays?"

"Yes."

"Okay, but I have one request."

"What's that?" I asked a little puzzled.

"I don't want to be running next to him, because I don't want my picture in any papers."

Personally, I understood this and thought it was pretty

funny, but I didn't let the instructor know that. "I have no control over that. But seriously, I doubt it."

So I called up to WarCom. "Hey Jim, I have my two volunteers for the run."

Laughing, the master chief asked me how I had come up with them. I said, "Let's just say I made them an offer they couldn't refuse."

So the two SEALs ran with President Clinton on that Saturday and that was the end of the story. I retired from the community before that particular situation came up again. Stories were coming out of Washington on a weekly basis about another "personal situation" of the president's, and he didn't command a lot of respect in the military community—at least not around the Teams, in this command master chief's opinion.

CHAPTER 33

THE LONG WALK AND THE LONGER PARTY

had arrived at the training command when Class 192 or 193 was just getting started. By my second year there, I had a pretty good handle on how to deal with some of the problems a class could have. Motivation of the students was one of my primary jobs. Each man had to pull himself through the training. But I was given the chance to talk to each class. This was an important part of my assignment as the command master chief and one I took very seriously.

Near the end of my first year at the command, my centennial class, Class 201, was set to begin Hell Week. One hundred BUD/S classes had trained and graduated since my class, Class 101, had left the grinder back in September 1978.

Tom Rewierts was the warrant officer in charge of first phase training then; Joe Hawes was one of the instructors; and Joe Gowart was the senior chief of the phase. Right before Hell Week, the fifth week of training, most classes were well motivated. Normally, I would talk to the class, tell them a little about what they might expect and what would be waiting for them on the other side. Just kind of pump them up a little bit more and maybe give some of the students the extra push that might get them past a bad spot.

The trouble was, my centennial class wasn't doing very well. Bluntly, it was acting like a piece of shit. The student leadership wasn't clicking into place and doing its job. And the class didn't have much time left to get its act together.

"We've really got problems with this class," Tom Rewierts said to me. "Man, I hate to tell you. They just seem not to have any motivation at all."

This was a new situation for me, and I decided to come up with a new strategy to address the problem. It was an entirely different approach than my normal motivation speech.

There was just a week to go before Class 201 would face Hell Week. Before facing the students in the classroom, I made a few arrangements with the first phase instructors. After I went into the room and onto the stage, I wanted all the staff to gradually fill in behind me. The students would have no way of knowing that this setup was any different from the usual one.

When I entered the room, the class stood to attention and the class leader called out "Master Chief Chalker!" The students followed quickly with a loud "Hoo yah, Master Chief Chalker!" This had been an established procedure all during training whenever a group of students first saw an instructor. But there seemed to be just the slightest lack of enthusiasm in their class "Hoo yah."

I was wearing my khaki uniform that day, complete with all my ribbons and decorations. I had always been proud of my uniform, and as a master chief I always tried to set an example for how to look and act at all times. What these students didn't know yet was that a set of ribbons can cost a lot of money, and I had just put a brand-new set on my khakis. Now I was going to play a different game with their heads.

"Just sit the fuck down!" I snarled suddenly. Then I started to unbutton my shirt. "Look," I said to the crowded room, "I've tried talking to you as a command master chief here. But things just don't seem to be working."

As I walked back and forth on the stage, I took my shirt off and started crumpling it up in my hands. "Now I'm going to talk to you as a Team guy." And with that, I threw my uniform shirt, with my brand-new set of decorations, across the room and into a wall, just beating the hell out of it.

I started laying into the class about Teamwork and just what it meant to be a SEAL and a member of the Teams. I pointed out just what a piece of shit they were, how they weren't pulling together. I told them they couldn't make it individually through the week they would be facing soon, let alone through the whole training course. They had to work as a Team. Each man had to give everything he had and then give even more for the Teammates standing next to him.

Going flat out, I listed each of their faults as future members of the Teams. Finally I challenged them personally: "I don't care if one of you, two of you, five of you, or all of you come up here on the stage and get it on with me if you don't like what I'm saying."

Starting at the top with the class leader, I moved down through the ranks, giving each one of them a fair share of grief. This wasn't what they had expected, and I had the rock solid attention of everyone in the room, including the instructors.

When I finished giving them my motivational lecture, telling them just what it took to be in the Teams and what we were looking for in men, I told them that none of them really deserved to be there. I snarled about how they didn't have the Teamwork, they didn't have the leadership, and if they didn't start pulling together now, they weren't going to make it much further as a class.

Some of the instructors were just staring at me by this time. You don't normally motivate men by telling them what a bunch of shits they are. The class as a whole was staring at me intently, and a few of the instructors were looking at me with a more stunned expression, their mouths wide open.

I wrapped up and prepared to leave the room. When they got up to Hoo yah me, I told them to sit the fuck back down, that they didn't deserve to Hoo yah anyone, they hadn't earned that right yet. And I stormed off the stage, leaving a room full of stares and silence behind me.

Back in the first phase office, most of the instructors filtered in behind me. They thought I was really pissed. I had practically peeled the paint off the classroom walls during my tirade. As they looked at me, I turned around with a big grin on and said, "Well, do you think I got the point across?"

"Damn, Denny," Dod Coots said, "I heard a couple of those guys whispering how they would sure hate to meet the master chief in a back alley in that kind of a mood."

"Why do you think I had all of you up on stage with me?" I asked. "If they took me up on that challenge, I figure I could have handled maybe five of them. The rest of you guys would have had to back me up."

That was the one and only time I pulled something like that on a class. But it was my centennial class, and I felt they needed an extra push. Within a week they had gotten their act together and did a 180-degree turnaround. They were motivated, and off they went.

One of the students had jumped up after I left the classroom and bellowed out, "The master chief's right!" and then he started berating his classmates. It wasn't long before they were all pretty pissed off themselves, and it was that anger that helped get them to pull together. It just took a hard shove to get them moving on their own.

I had left my uniform shirt crumpled where it had fallen. While we were in the office, one of the instructors asked me if they should go back and get it. I told him to wait until the students had left. Finally one of the instructors went in and brought my shirt down to my office. As I had suspected, my enthusiasm had gotten the better of me, and I had to replace some of the ribbons. At fifty to sixty bucks a set, I didn't want to play that particular game with a lot of classes.

It wasn't too long after that class went through that it was time for me to retire from the service. My last class "Hoo yah" was going to ring out across the grinder. If I had pushed it, I could have stayed active several more years. But my twenty years in the Navy were up, and if I left now I could look forward to a new career on the outside.

A lot of my earlier commanding officers had already retired and were doing well on the outside. Dick Marcinko was the man I had always considered the Skipper. He was the one who had chosen me to join SEAL Team Six and then Red Cell. As the man responsible for the greater part of my career, he was someone I wanted to have standing at my side when I was piped ashore for the last time.

It was an honor to have the Skipper beside me at my retirement ceremony. He had gone through a lot from the Navy and the officer community in the Teams when he left. Outside of reunions, he hadn't been on a military installation in any kind of official capacity in years. But he was the man I wanted to help see me off, and I wasn't going to allow the politics of the higher ranks in the Navy to keep that from happening.

The Skipper had ruffled a lot of feathers when he ran SEAL Team Six and then Red Cell. He had been hounded out of the service by higher ranking leaders who had a greater interest in the politics of the moment and their own appearance than in accomplishing the mission. His successes in the civilian world after his Navy career really rankled some. He was without question the man I wanted at my retirement in an official capacity. If my request had been turned down, it would have hurt. But there were a lot of other places I could go to be with my shipmates.

Jim Gerarden, Captain McGuire, and especially my commander at the time, Captain Joe Yarborough, knew what I wanted to do at my retirement and helped me get it done. Admiral Tom Richards understood my loyalty and approved my retirement ceremony plans. There were some last-minute arguments, but with Captain Yarborough at my side, they were cleared away. It was a very proud moment when I stood on that stage set up in the grinder at the Special Warfare Training Command, the American flag hanging down as our backdrop, and Commander Richard Marcinko, USN (Ret.) was piped aboard with all proper courtesies.

The retirement of a career SEAL isn't just for him. It's a time-honored Naval tradition that is also for his family and his command. Standing with your friends and Teammates, you feel a great honor, and more than a little sadness. Sometimes I wonder if all the ceremony, traditions, specific actions, and responses aren't to keep you from thinking too much about what is actually going on. You're retiring from the Navy, and even more, you're leaving the active Teams.

That last walk, when you are piped ashore for the last time, led by your family, in front of your friends and Teammates, is a long one. Flanked by sideboys, you walk off the stage in what seems like slow motion. The boatswain's pipes are sounded to signal your leaving, and then you're done. This was it. I would no longer be wearing an active uniform or operating beside these individuals, my Teammates, my brothers. An old life was over and a new one was to begin—as soon as the retirement party was over.

My conversations and handshakes after the retirement ceremony were a pleasure, but it still had an unreal feeling about it. Pictures were taken with my friends, and I had almost an entire police SWAT team there that I had been working with and helping to train as the director of operations of GSGI (Global Studies Group International) along with Harry Humphries. Good close friends such as Ernie and Mary Emerson, Brian Bush, Harry and Katharine Humphries, Bill and Elizabeth Adkins, Bruce and Margaret Sheldon, and others were there. Military uniforms, police uniforms, civilian suits, dresses, and street clothes all mixed together, swirling around the grinder. Then it was on to McP's Pub for the real party.

Greg McPartlin was a corpsman and a Teammate who operated with SEAL Team One in Vietnam. He's since opened up McP's Irish Pub in Coronado, up the road from the SEAL compound. It's a second home to a number of past and present Teammates, and we took the place over for my retirement. My parents were there, along with my sisters and other relatives. Two of my old family friends, Mark and Tim Robinson, were there. I wish Don, their older brother, could have been there that day as he had been an inspiration to me as I was growing up.

My former skipper Bob Gormly was there along with a number of folks I never expected to make the trip to Southern California just for my retirement. Gifts for Kitty and myself showed up in large numbers, and I began to feel overwhelmed. Doug Kingery and Tim McGee from the Bell Gardens SWAT team, my partners at Metro Tactical Products, were there in uniform, as was Bill Murphy, also in his dress blue Huntington Beach police uniform. We had more cops at my party than the entire Coronado Police Department had on their rolls. Members of the U.S. Border Patrol and other agencies enjoyed the good times on McP's patio that afternoon and well into the evening. Weapons were given to me as gifts but they were sent home in a van prior to the drinks coming out in volume.

Greg McPartlin and his manager, Scotty, said later that we went through more kegs at that party than any other retirement they had ever hosted. My dad had a great time, along with everyone else. It's like a little family there at McP's, one I enjoy a lot. My mug up there on the rack is number 55A; Kitty has 55B.

Everything has to end sometime. And my retirement was a great way to end my time in the service. I still stay active with my friends in the SEAL community and elsewhere. Dennis "Snake" Chalker, Inc., is doing training all over the world, and the adventures haven't stopped. They've just changed sponsors. I even have a website now at www.snake-chalker.com. I guess everyone has to be dragged into the modern world eventually.

EPILOGUE

I was motivated to become a SEAL when I first met two of them in jump school while I was in the Army. My desire centered on the challenge. Challenges are something I've always liked, and I love it when someone says it cannot be done.

Bull. There's always a way, especially if you're flexible. The Teams have not only taught me the importance and strength of teamwork but also the value of being positive about accomplishing the task. I maintain this philosophy in my present career.

The day I retired from the Teams was the hardest day of my life. I will never hang the holster up, but I did have to hang up the chance to come in every morning and gather with the rest of the Special Warfare family. I miss that dearly. I know now what my former Teammates went through and what the Teammates behind me will be going through. It's tough, real tough. You have to learn not to look back. You go ahead and do what makes you happy, but you never forget where you came from.

This book consists of the times I had and experiences I lived through with a number of my Teammates. Some names, places, dates, and all operational procedures were omitted to protect my Teammates and the Special Warfare community. This book has allowed the reader share the good and the rough times I experienced while in the Teams. A life in the Teams can be very beneficial if you so desire, and it can be very hard on you and your loved ones, even when the game is over and the final goal has been scored.

For those who are thinking about becoming SEALs, I want you to understand that it is not all glory. It is a very tough, exacting job. Many want it, but few are willing to pay the price. I feel lucky that I was offered the opportunity to do a job that most can't ever try.

Those who desire to volunteer should understand that it is a mental job even more than a physical one. Physically, ignoring discomfort becomes second nature to you. Mentally, you have to look inside yourself and submerge what you want for the betterment of the Team. There is no *I* in the Team's vocabulary. You must think positively and never say "No, I can't do it."

Today I look forward to the East and West Coast reunions as well as the muster held at Fort Pierce, Florida, every year. This is an opportunity to see how the community is keeping up with the latest technology and to meet Teammates of the past and present. Once a Teammate always a Teammate.

My company today, DSC Inc., is a takeoff from my Naval career. I put my college degree to work offering training in the tactical arena for law enforcement and government agencies. It keeps me active in the field I enjoy most. It feels good to pass on the experience that brought me home safe so that others may come home safe.

No one can successfully imitate or impersonate a real frogman or SEAL. That fact is glaringly obvious to any individual who has completed training and served with the elite of the elite. I do not consider myself the best, but I have been fortunate enough to serve with them. My life has been given to my God, my country, the Teams, and my family.

The Trident, that physical symbol of a Teammate, was best described by a Navy Cross holder, Barry Enoch. The eagle surrounds an anchor, the symbol of the service from which we come. It is grasping Neptune's spear for the guarding of the seashores. The pistol shows that we are always ready to bear arms in defense of others. Above it all the eagle stands with its wings spread against the sky in which we move.

Barry Enoch states that the Trident is the only military emblem on which the eagle holds its head down; it is lowered in remembrance and respect for all those who served, were wounded, or gave their lives in the Teams.

To end this first saga, here's a short Team toast: "Here's to it. Bees do it, dogs do it, if you can't do it, fuck you, call us and we'll do it."

GLOSSARY

Boot (bootlegger) turn—A 180-degree turn done in a vehicle while it is moving forward. The parking or emergency brake is used in conjunction with the wheel to execute the turn. Called a bootleg because of its earliest use by moonshiners and bootleg liquor runners.

CCT (combat control team)—A team of Air Force personnel organized, trained, and equipped to locate, identify, and mark drop/landing zones, provide limited weather observations, install and operate navigational aids and air traffic control communications necessary to guide aircraft to drop/landing zones, and control air traffic at these zones.

CinC (pronounced "sink")—The commander in chief of a Navy unit or the president of the United States. A Navy CinC is usually of flag rank (admiral) and is in charge of a large area, command, or fleet.

Crash (short for flash-crash)—A stun grenade or other distraction device. Throwing in a crash before entering an enclosed area can distract or stun the occupants for several seconds, giving the advantage of the first shot to those entering the room.

ENVIRONMENTS
- *Permissive*—A situation where all the locals are backing your actions. This includes the local law enforcement and the public. You are able to travel reasonably freely. When you are going to take down a target, the only concern is what is within the structure or target itself. Example—a terrorist action.
- *Semipermissive*—A situation where some of the locals are not hostile to your presence. Local law enforcement, government, or militias may be actively against your actions. You have to maintain a secure perimeter around the target area. Example—Grenada.
- *Nonpermissive*—An open combat zone. This is not the same as a free-fire area where you are allowed to shoot first, but all locals and other forces are considered hostile unless proven otherwise. Example—Vietnam.

Escape and evasion (E & E)—The procedures and operations by which military personnel and other selected individuals can leave an enemy-held or hostile territory and return to friendly hands.

HUMINT (HUman INTelligence)—Information gathered on a subject by people on the ground, either trained intelligence specialists or locals.

J turn—A 180-degree turn done while a vehicle is moving backward. The turn is primarily accomplished by using the steering wheel.

Loadout—The equipment, munitions, and materials for an operation or exercise. A loadout can include all the weapons, ammunition, and equipment used by a single man or by an entire unit.

Navy platforms—Ships and other assets of the U.S. Navy used to launch from or go to during an operation.

NVDs (night vision devices); also *NVGs (night vision goggles)*—Electro-optical devices that are handheld, weapon mounted, or worn over the eyes to magnify or convert available light and allow vision at night.

THREATCON (TERRORIST THREAT CONDITION)
- *WHITE*—Nonspecific threat of terrorism against U.S. military personnel or facilities in a general geographical area. This threat may be based on information that terrorist elements in an area have general plans concerning military facilities.
- *YELLOW*—Specific threat of terrorism against U.S. military personnel or facilities within a particular geographical area. This threat may be based on information that terrorist elements are actively preparing for operations in a particular area.
- *RED*—Imminent threat of terrorist acts against specific U.S. military personnel or facilities. This threat may be based on information regarding plans or preparations for terrorist attack against specific persons or facilities.

Trident—The common name for the Naval special warfare insignia. It is a large, gold, uniform device made up of four parts: the anchor, which symbolizes the Navy; Neptune's three-pronged trident, which symbolizes the underwater world; a cocked flintlock pistol that shows the Team's constant preparedness for war; and behind it all is the bald eagle, symbol of the United States of America.

WarCom; also *SpecWarCom* and *NavSpecWarCom*—The Navy Special Warfare Command, the overall command structure for the Navy SEAL Teams and all their attached units.

WMD (weapons of mass destruction)—Nuclear, chemical, or biological weapons that will affect an area or population far out of proportion to the physical size of the weapon.